Mac® OS X
FOR
DUMMIES®
2ND EDITION

by Bob LeVitus

WILEY

Wiley Publishing, Inc.

Mac® OS X For Dummies®, 2nd Edition

Published by
Wiley Publishing, Inc.
909 Third Avenue
New York, NY 10022

www.wiley.com

Ⓦ Wiley Publishing, Inc. is a trademark of Wiley Publishing, Inc.

About the Author

Bob LeVitus, often referred to as "Dr. Mac," has written more than 40 popular computer books, including *Dr. Mac: The OS X Files* and *Mac OS 9 For Dummies* for Wiley, Inc.; *Mac Answers: 2nd Edition* for Osborne/McGraw Hill (with Shelly Brisbin); *Stupid Mac Tricks* and *Dr. Macintosh,* both for Addison-Wesley; as well as recent titles, such as *The Little iTunes Book* and *The Little iDVD Book* for Peachpit Press. His books have sold more than a million copies worldwide.

He has penned the popular Dr. Mac column for the *Houston Chronicle* for more than 5 years and has been published in dozens of computer magazines over the past 15 years. A tireless publicity hound, Bob's achievements have been documented in major media around the world. (Yes, that was him juggling a keyboard in *USA Today* last year!) He's known for his expertise, trademark humorous style, and ability to translate techie jargon into usable and fun advice for regular folks.

Always a popular speaker at computer user groups and trade shows, Bob has spoken at more than 200 seminars here and abroad, presented keynote addresses in three countries, and produced a series of training seminars in five cities. (He also won the Macworld Expo MacJeopardy World Championship three times before retiring his crown.)

Bob is considered one of the world's leading authorities on Mac OS. From 1989 to 1997, he was a contributing editor/columnist for *MacUser* magazine, writing the Help Folder, Beating the System, Personal Best, and Game Room columns at various times.

Prior to giving his life over to computers, he spent almost seven years at Kresser/Craig/D.I.K., a Los Angeles advertising agency and marketing consultancy and its subsidiary, L & J Research. He holds a B.S. in Marketing from California State University.

Bob LeVitus lives in Austin, Texas with his wife Lisa, children Allison and Jacob, and a small pack of semi-domesticated animals.

Dedication

This book is dedicated to my wife, Lisa, who taught me almost everything I know about almost everything except computers.

Author's Acknowledgments

Special thanks to everyone at Apple who helped me turn this book around in record time: Keri Walker, Nathalie Welch, Ken Bereskin, Alicia Awbrey, Bill Evans, Reena Spektor, Tim Holmes, Greg (Joz) Joswiak, Tom Boger, and all the rest. I couldn't have done it without you.

Thanks also to super-agent Carole "Lobster" McClendon, for more deal-making far beyond the call of duty. You've been my agent since I started in the business 15 years ago, and I want you to know that you're a treasure.

Big-time thanks to the gang at Wiley: Mike "Let's-make-a-deal!" Roney, Tom "The Whipcracker" Heine, Linda "The latest in a long line of whipcrackers" Morris, Teresa "Can you rewrite this?" Artman, Bob "Is the damn thing done yet?" Woerner, Andy "Boss Man" Cummings, Barry "No humorous nickname yet" Pruett, technical editor Brian Hubbard, who did a rocking job, and all the others.

Extra special thanks to Dennis R. Cohen, for technical support as well as for updating several of the chapters for me. It's been an honor and a privilege to work with the only guy I know who's been using OS X longer than me. You rock, dude!

Thanks for my family and friends for putting up with me during my all-too-lengthy absences during this book's gestation.

Special thanks to Saccone's Pizza, Lucky Dog Chicago-style hot dogs, Iron Works authentic Texas BBQ, Taco Cabana, Bass Ale, Sam Adams, and ShortStop for providing sustenance as I worked.

And finally, thanks to you, gentle reader, for buying this book.

Publisher's Acknowledgments

We're proud of this book; please send us your comments through our online registration form located at www.dummies.com/register/.

Some of the people who helped bring this book to market include the following:

Acquisitions, Editorial, and Media Development

Project Editor: Linda Morris

Acquisitions Editor: Bob Woerner

Sr. Copy Editor: Teresa Artman

Technical Editor: Brian Hubbard

Editorial Manager: Kevin Kirschner

Media Development Manager: Laura VanWinkle

Media Development Supervisor:
Richard Graves

Editorial Assistant: Amanda Foxworth

Cartoons: Rich Tennant
(www.the5thwave.com)

Production

Project Coordinator: Kristie Rees

Layout and Graphics: Joyce Haughey, Jackie Nicholas, Jeremey Unger

Proofreader: John Tyler Connoley

Indexer: TECHBOOKS Production Services

Special Help
Rebekah Mancilla

Publishing and Editorial for Technology Dummies

Richard Swadley, Vice President and Executive Group Publisher

Andy Cummings, Vice President and Publisher

Mary C. Corder, Editorial Director

Publishing for Consumer Dummies

Diane Graves Steele, Vice President and Publisher

Joyce Pepple, Acquisitions Director

Composition Services

Gerry Fahey, Vice President of Production Services

Debbie Stailey, Director of Composition Services

Contents at a Glance

Table of Contents

Introduction

● ●

*Y*ou made the right choice twice: Mac OS X and this book.

Take a deep breath and get ready to have a rollicking good time. That's right. This is a computer book, but even so, it's going to be fun. What a concept! Whether you're brand spanking new to the Mac or a grizzled old Mac-vet, I guarantee that discovering the ins and outs of Mac OS X will be fun and easy. Wiley Publishing, Inc. (the publisher of this book) couldn't say it on the cover if it weren't true!

About This Book

This book's roots lie with my international bestseller *Macintosh System 7.5 For Dummies,* an award-winning book so good that it was offered by now-deceased Mac cloner Power Computing in lieu of a system software manual. Now I'm back with *Mac OS X For Dummies,* 2nd Edition, and updated for OS X version 10.2 Jaguar. This book combines all the old, familiar features of the previous books (*Mac OS 8 For Dummies, Mac OS 8.5 For Dummies,* and *Mac OS 9 For Dummies,* and both previous versions of this book) with updated information about the latest, greatest offering from Apple.

Why write a *For Dummies* book about Mac OS X? Well, Mac OS X is a big, complicated personal computer operating system. So I made *Mac OS X For Dummies,* 2nd Edition a not-so-big, not-very-complicated book that shows you what Mac OS X is all about without boring you, confusing you, or poking you with sharp objects.

In fact, you'll be so darned comfortable that I wanted to call this book *Mac OS X without the Discomfort,* but the publishers wouldn't let me. Apparently we *For Dummies* authors have to follow some rules, and using the word *Dummies* in the title is one of them (maybe the biggest one).

And speaking of dummies, remember that it's just a word. I don't think that you're dumb. Quite the opposite! (If you're reading this in a bookstore, approach the cashier with your wallet in your hand, buy the book, and I'll know you're even smarter!) I also wanted to call this book *Mac OS X For People Smart Enough to Know They Need Help,* but you can just imagine what Wiley thought of that.

This book is chock-full of information and advice, explaining everything that you need to know about Mac OS X in language you can understand. I also supplemented it with tips, tricks, techniques, and steps, all served up in generous quantities.

Conventions Used in This Book

To get the most out of this book, you need to know how I do things and why. Here are a few conventions used in this book to make your life easier:

- ✔ When I want you to open an item in a menu, I write something like "Choose File⇨Open," which means, "Pull down the File menu and choose the Open command."

- ✔ Stuff you're supposed to type appears in bold type, **like this.**

- ✔ **Sometimes an entire a sentence is in bold,** as you'll see when I present a numbered list of steps. **In those cases, I** debold **what you're supposed to type,** like this.

- ✔ Web addresses, programming code (not much in this book), and things that appear onscreen are shown in a special monofont typeface, `like this`.

- ✔ When I refer to the menu, I'm referring to the menu in the upper-left corner of the Finder menu bar that looks like a blue Apple (called the *Apple menu*). For example, I may say, "From the menu, choose File⇨Open." I do *not* use the symbol to refer to the key on your Mac keyboard that may or may not have both the ⌘ and symbols on it. I refer to that key (called the *Command key*) with the equally funky ⌘ symbol and write something like, "Press the ⌘ key." So, when you see , think Apple menu.

- ✔ For keyboard shortcuts, I write something like ⌘+A, which means to hold down the ⌘ key (the one with the little pretzel and/or symbol on it) and then press the letter A on the keyboard. If you see something like ⌘+Shift+A, that means to hold down the ⌘ and Shift keys while pressing the A key. Again, for absolute clarity, I will never refer to the ⌘ key with the symbol. I reserve that symbol for the menu *(Apple menu)*. For the Command key, I use only the ⌘ symbol.

What You're Not to Read

The first few chapters of this book are where I describe the basic everyday things that you need to understand in order to operate your Mac effectively.

Even though OS X is way different from previous Mac operating systems, this first part is so basic that if you've been using a Mac for long, you may think you know it all. But hey! — not-so-old-timers need a solid foundation. So here's my advice: Skip through stuff that you know to get to the better stuff faster.

Other stuff that you can skip over if you're so inclined are sidebars and any section marked with a Technical Stuff icon, which I talk about in a moment.

Foolish Assumptions

Although I know what happens when you make assumptions, I've made a few anyway. First, I assume that you, gentle reader, know nothing about using Mac OS X. What I do assume is that you know what a Mac is, that you want to use OS X, that you want to understand OS X without digesting an incomprehensible technical manual, and that you made an excellent choice by selecting this particular book.

In any case, I do my best to explain each new concept in full and loving detail. Maybe that's foolish, but . . . oh well.

Oh, and I also assume that you can read.

How This Book Is Organized

Mac OS X For Dummies, 2nd Edition is divided into six logical parts, numbered (surprisingly enough) Parts 38 through 43. Just kidding; they're actually numbered Parts I through VI, except that they're numbered using those stuffy old Roman numerals instead of Arabic numerals.

It's better if you read them in order, but if you already know a lot — or think you know a lot — feel free to skip around and read the parts that interest you most.

Part I: Desktop Madness: Navigating Mac OS X

This first part is very, very basic training. From the mouse to the Desktop, from menus, windows, and icons to the snazzy new Dock, it's all here. A lot of what you need to know to navigate the depths of Mac OS X safely and sanely is in this section. And although old-timers may just want to skim through it, you newbies should probably read every word. Twice.

Part II: Rounding Out Your Basic Training

In this part, I build on the basics of Part I and really get you revving with your Mac. Here I cover additional topics that every Mac user needs to know, coupled with some hands-on, step-by-step training. I start with a look at each and every OS X Finder menu in full and loving detail; then I move on to talk about the all-important Finder in depth. Next up is a chapter about how to open and save files (a skill you're sure to find handy), and finally I take a look at removable media (which means *ejectable disks*) and how to manage it.

Part III: Doing Stuff with Your Mac

This part is chock full of ways to do cool stuff with your Mac. In this section, you'll discover the Internet first — how to get it working on your Mac, and what to do with it after you do. Next, I show you the ins and outs of printing under OS X. You also read about many of the applications that come with OS X, plus how to make your copy of OS X look and feel just as you like it. That's all followed by the lowdown on the Classic Environment, and possibly the most useful chapter in the whole book, Chapter 15, which details each and every gosh-darned System Preference.

Part IV: U 2 Can B a Guru

Here I get into the nitty-gritty underbelly of Mac OS X, where I cover more advanced topics, such as file sharing, backing up your files, and the all-important troubleshooting chapter, Chapter 18.

Part V: The Part of Tens

Last, but not least, it's The Part of Tens, which is mostly a Letterman rip-off, although it does include heaping helpings of tips, optional software, great Mac Web sites, and hardware ideas.

Part VI: Appendix

Last, but certainly not least, I cover installing Mac OS X in the Appendix. The whole process has become quite easy with this version of the system software, but if you have to install OS X yourself, it would behoove you to read this helpful Appendix first.

Icons Used in This Book

You'll see little round pictures (icons) off to the left side of the text throughout this book. Consider these icons as miniature road signs, telling you a little something extra about the topic at hand. Here's what the different icons look like and what they all mean.

Look for Tip icons to find the juiciest morsels: shortcuts, tips, and undocumented secrets about OS X. Try them all; impress your friends!

When you see this icon, it means that this particular morsel is something that I think you should memorize (or at least write on your shirt cuff).

Put on your propeller beanie hat and pocket protector; these parts include the truly nerdy stuff. It's certainly not required reading, but it must be interesting or informative or I wouldn't have wasted the space.

Read these notes very, very, very carefully. Did I say *ver*-y? Warning icons flag important information. The author and publisher won't be responsible if your Mac explodes or spews flaming parts because you ignored a Warning icon. Just kidding. Macs don't explode or spew (with the exception of a few choice PowerBook 5300s, which won't run OS X anyway). But I got your attention, didn't I? It's a good idea to read Warning notes carefully.

These icons represent my ranting or raving about something that just bugs me. Imagine foam coming from my mouth. Rants are required to be irreverent, irrelevant, or both. I also try to keep them short, more for your sake than mine.

Well, now, what could this icon possibly be about? Named by famous editorial consultant Mr. Obvious, this icon highlights all things new and different in Mac OS X version 10.2 Jaguar.

Where to Go from Here

Go to a comfortable spot (preferably not far from a Mac) and read the book.

I didn't write this book for myself. I wrote it for you and would love to hear how it worked for you. So please drop me a line or register your comments through the Wiley Online Registration Form located at www.dummies.com.

Did this book work for you? What did you like? What didn't you like? What questions were unanswered? Did you want to know more about something? Did you want to find out less about something? Tell me! I have received more than 100 suggestions about previous editions, most of which are incorporated here. So keep up the good work!

You can send snail mail care of Wiley Publishing, Inc. (the mailroom there will see that I receive it), or send e-mail to me directly at macosxfordummies@boblevitus.com. I appreciate your feedback, and I will _try_ to respond to all e-mail within a few days.

So what are you waiting for? Go — enjoy the book!

Part I
Desktop Madness: Navigating Mac OS X

The 5th Wave   By Rich Tennant

"It's been two days, Larry. It's time to stop enjoying the new-computer smell and take the iMac out of the box."

In this part . . .

Mac OS X sports tons of new goodies and features. I'll get to the hot new goodies soon enough, but you have to crawl before you walk.

In this part, you discover the most basic of basics, such as how to turn your Mac on. Next, I acquaint you with the Mac OS X Desktop: windows, icons, the Dock, the Finder — the whole shmear.

So get comfortable, roll up your sleeves, fire up your Mac if you like, and settle down with Part I, a delightful little section I like to think of as "The Hassle-Free Way to Get Started with Mac OS X."

Chapter 1

Mac OS X 101 (Prerequisites: None)

· ·

In This Chapter

▶ Defining Mac OS X

▶ Finding help if you're a beginner

▶ Turning on your Mac

▶ Shutting down your Mac without getting chewed out by it

▶ Knowing what you should see when you turn on your Mac

▶ Taking a refresher course on using a mouse

· ·

Congratulate yourself on choosing Mac OS X, which stands for Macintosh Operating System X — that's the Roman numeral *ten*, not the letter *X* (pronounced *ten,* not *ex)*. You made a smart move because you scored more than just an operating system upgrade. Mac OS X version 10.2 Jaguar includes dozens of new or improved features to make using your Mac easier as well as dozens more that help you do more work in less time. Now you can use these new features to be more productive, have fewer headaches, reduce your cholesterol level, and fall in love with your Mac all over again.

In this chapter, I start at the very beginning and talk about Mac OS X in mostly abstract terms. You can turn your Mac on if you like, but most of this chapter has no hands-on material. What you will find, however, is a bunch of important stuff that you need to know in order to proceed. If you're a total beginner to the Mac experience, you should probably read every word in this chapter. Even if you're past the beginner stage, you may want to skim these sections anyway to refresh your memory.

Those of you who are upgrading from an earlier version of Mac OS to Mac OS X should read the Appendix right about now for installation information.

Gnawing to the Core of OS X

Along with the code in its read-only memory (ROM), the operating system (that is, the *OS* in *Mac OS X*) is what makes a Mac a Mac. Without it, your Mac is a pile of silicon and circuits — no smarter than a toaster.

"So what does an operating system do?" you ask. Good question. The short answer is that an *operating system* controls the basic and most important operations of your computer. In the case of Mac OS X and your Mac, the operating system

- Manages memory.
- Controls how windows, icons, and menus work.
- Keeps track of files.
- Manages networking.
- Does housekeeping. (No kidding!)

Other forms of software, such as word processors and Web browsers, rely on the operating system to create and maintain the environment in which that software works its magic. When you create a memo, for example, the word processor provides the tools for you to type and format the information. In the background, the operating system is the muscle for the word processor, performing crucial functions like the following:

- Providing the mechanism for drawing and moving the window in which you write the memo
- Keeping track of a file when you save it
- Helping the word processor create drop-down menus and dialogs for you to interact with
- Communicating with other programs
- And much, much more (stuff that only geeks could care about)

So now that you have a little background in operating systems, take a gander at the next section before you do anything else with your Mac.

Don't let that UNIX stuff scare you. It's there if you want it, but if you don't want it or don't care, you'll rarely even know it's there. All you'll know is that your Mac just runs and runs and runs without crashing and crashing and crashing.

The Mac advantage

Most of the world's PCs use Windows. You're among the lucky few to have a computer with an operating system that's intuitive, easy to use, and, dare I say, fun. If you don't believe me, try using Windows for a day or two. Go ahead. You probably won't suffer any permanent damage. In fact, you'll really begin to appreciate how good you have it. Feel free to hug your Mac. Or give it a peck on the CD-ROM drive slot — just try not to get your tongue caught.

As someone once told me, "Claiming that the Macintosh is inferior to Windows because most people use Windows is like saying that all other restaurants serve food that's inferior to McDonald's."

We may be a minority, but we have the best, most stable, most modern all-purpose operating system in the world. Here's why: UNIX — on which Mac OS X is based — is widely regarded as the best industrial-strength operating system. For now, just know that being based on UNIX means that a Mac running OS X will crash less often than an older Mac or a Windows machine, which means less downtime. But perhaps the biggest advantage OS X has is that when an application crashes, it doesn't crash your entire computer, and you don't have to restart to continue working.

A Safety Net for the Absolute Beginner (Or Any User)

In this section, I deal with the stuff that the manual that came with your Mac doesn't cover — or doesn't cover in nearly enough detail. If you're a first-time Macintosh user, please, *please* read this section of the book carefully — it could save your life. Okay, okay, perhaps I'm being overly dramatic. What I mean to say is that reading this section could save your *Mac*. Even if you're an experienced Mac user, you may want to read this section anyway. Chances are that you need a few reminders.

Turning the dang thing on

Okay. This is the big moment — turning on your Mac! Gaze at it longingly first and say something cheesy, such as "You're the most awesome computer I've ever known." If that doesn't turn your Mac on (it probably won't), keep reading.

If you actually thought that flattery would turn on your Mac, you should probably read *Self-Psychotherapy For Dummies* before you continue with this book. (And if you think that book exists, maybe you should check out *Gullibility For Dummies*.)

If you don't know how to turn your Mac on, don't feel bad — just look in the manual that came with your Mac. Apple, in its infinite wisdom, has manufactured Macs with power switches and buttons on every conceivable surface: on the front, side, and back of the CPU, and even on the keyboard or monitor. Some Macs (including most older PowerBooks) even hide the power button behind a little plastic door. Because of the vast number of different configurations, I can't tell you where the switch is without devoting a whole chapter just to that topic. (Can you say booooo-ring?)

What you should see on startup

When you finally do turn on your Macintosh, you set in motion a sophisticated and complex series of events that culminates in the loading of Mac OS X and the appearance of the Mac OS X Desktop. After a small bit of whirring, buzzing, and flashing (meaning that the operating system is loading), OS X first tests all your hardware — slots, ports, disks, random access memory (RAM) — and so on. If everything passes, you hear a pleasing musical chord and see the tasteful gray Apple logo in the middle of your screen and a small wheel cursor (the startup version of the spinning pinwheel "wait" cursor that appears in Technicolor when your Mac is very busy) somewhere on the screen. Both are new in Jaguar and both are shown in Figure 1-1.

Figure 1-1:
No more smiley Mac or multicolored beach ball cursor at startup. These are their Jaguar replacements.

✔ **Everything is fine and dandy:** Next, you see the soothing blue Mac OS logo, the words *Mac OS X,* and a status indicator with messages that tell you that the Mac is going through its normal startup motions. Makes you feel kind of warm and fuzzy, doesn't it? If all this fanfare shows up on your screen, Mac OS X is loading properly. In the unlikely event that you don't see the gray Apple logo, the soothing messages, and the familiar Desktop, see Chapter 18 where I show you how to troubleshoot your system.

Then, you may or may not see the Mac OS X login screen, where you enter your name and password. If you do (you'll only see it if your Mac is set up for multiple users; don't worry, I tell you all about this in Chapter 16), press the Enter key and away you go.

If you don't want to have to type your name and password every time you start or restart your Mac (or even if you do), check out Chapter 16 for the scoop on how to turn the login screen on or off.

Either way, the Desktop soon materializes before your eyes. If you haven't customized, configured, or tinkered with your Desktop, it should look something like Figure 1-2. Now is a good time to take a moment for positive thoughts about the person who convinced you that you wanted a Mac. That person was right!

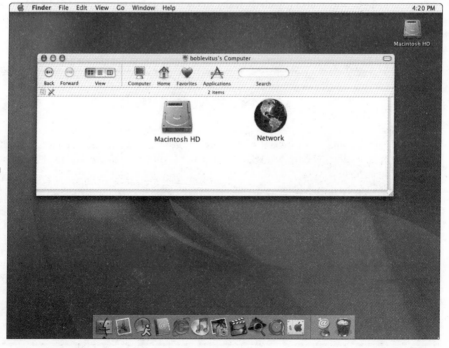

Figure 1-2:
The
Mac OS X
Desktop
after a
brand,
spanking
new
installation
of OS X.

✔ **Sad Mac:** If any of your hardware fails when it's tested, you could see a black or gray screen that may or may not display the dreaded sad Mac icon (shown in the left margin) and/or hear a far less pleasing musical chord known by Mac aficionados as the *Chimes of Doom.*

Some older Macs played the sound of a horrible car wreck instead of the chimes, complete with crying tires and busting glass. It was exceptionally unnerving, which may be why Apple doesn't use it anymore.

The fact that something went wrong is no reflection on your prowess as a Macintosh user. Something inside your Mac is broken, and it probably needs to go in for repairs (usually to an Apple dealer). If any of that's already happened to you, check out Chapter 18 to try to get your Mac well again.

If your computer is under warranty, dial 1-800-SOS-APPL, and a customer service person can tell you what to do. Before you do anything, though, skip ahead to Chapter 18. It's entirely possible that one of the suggestions there can get you back on track without you having to spend even a moment on hold.

✔ **Flashing question mark disk:** Although it's unlikely that you'll ever see the sad Mac, most users eventually encounter the flashing question-mark-on-a-disk icon (shown in the left margin) or a flashing folder icon in place of the usual happy Mac. These icons mean that your Mac can't find a startup disk, hard drive, network server, or CD-ROM containing a valid Macintosh operating system. See Chapter 18 to try to ease your Mac's ills.

The legend of the boot

Boot this. *Boot* that. "I *booted* my Mac and. . . ." or "Did it *boot?*" and so on. Talking about computers for long without hearing the *boot* word is nearly impossible.

But why *boot?* Why not *shoe* or *shirt* or even *shazam?*

Back in the very olden days — maybe the 1970s or a little earlier — starting up a computer required you to toggle little manual switches on the front panel, which began an internal process that loaded the operating system. The process became known as *bootstrapping* because if you toggled the right switches, the computer would "pull itself up by its bootstraps." This phrase didn't take long to transmogrify into *booting* and finally to *boot.*

Over the years, *booting* has come to mean turning on almost any computer or even a peripheral device, such as a printer. Some people also use it to refer to launching an application: "I booted Excel."

So the next time one of your gearhead friends says the *b*-word, ask whether he knows where the term comes from. Then dazzle him with the depth and breadth of your (not quite useful) knowledge!

How do you know which version of the Mac OS your computer has? Simple. Just choose About This Mac from the menu (that's the menu with the symbol in the upper-left corner of the Finder menu bar). The About This Mac window pops up in the middle of your screen, as shown in Figure 1-3. The version that you're running appears just below *Mac OS X* in the center of the window. Click the More Info button to launch Apple System Profiler, which has much more information, including processor speed, bus speed, number of processors, caches, installed memory, networking, storage devices, and much more. Discover more about this program in Chapter 13.

Figure 1-3:
See which
version of
Mac OS X
you're
running.

Shutting down properly

Turning off the power without shutting your Mac down properly is one of the worst things you can do to your poor Mac. Shutting down your Mac improperly can really screw up your hard drive, scramble the contents of your most important files, or both.

If a thunderstorm is rumbling nearby or if you're unfortunate enough to have rolling blackouts where you live, you may *really* want to shut your Mac down. (See the next section where I briefly discuss lightning and your Mac.)

To turn off your Mac, always use the Shut Down command on the menu (which I discuss in Chapter 6), or you can press the Power key once and then click the Shut Down button. On new Apple Pro keyboards, which don't have a Power key, press Ctrl+Eject instead and then click the Shut Down button that appears (or press the Return key, which does the same thing).

Eternally yours . . . *now*

Mac OS X is designed so that you never have to shut it down. You can configure it to sleep after a specified period of inactivity. (See Chapter 15 for more info on the Energy Saver features of OS X.) If you do so, your Mac will consume very little electricity when it's sleeping and will be ready to use just a few seconds after you awaken it (by pressing any key or clicking the mouse). On the other hand, if you're not going to be using it for a few days, you may want to shut it down anyway.

Note: If you leave your Mac on constantly and you're gone when a lightning storm or rolling blackout hits, your Mac may likely get wasted. So be sure that you have adequate protection if you decide to leave your Mac on and unattended for long periods. See the section "A few things you should definitely NOT do with your Mac" elsewhere in this chapter for more info on lightning and your Mac. If I plan to be away from mine for more than a few hours, I usually shut it down, just in case. I also shut it down before I go to sleep each night.

Of course, most of us have broken this rule several times without anything horrible happening. Don't be lulled into a false sense of security, however. Break the rules one time too many or under the wrong circumstances, and your most important file *will* be toast. The only times when you should turn off your Mac without shutting down properly is if your screen is frozen or if you crash and you've already tried everything else. (See Chapter 18 for what those "everything elses" are.) This doesn't happen often — and less often under OS X than ever before — but when it does, turning your Mac off and then back on may be the only solution. Sometimes even that doesn't work, and you may have to unplug the computer from the power outlet to get it to reboot.

A few things you should definitely NOT do with your Mac

In this section, I deal with the bad stuff that can happen to your computer if you do the wrong things with it. If something bad has already happened to you — I know . . . I'm beginning to sound like a broken record — see Chapter 18.

✔ **Don't unplug your Mac when it's turned on.** Very bad things can happen, such as having your operating system break. See the preceding section where I discuss shutting your system down properly.

✔ **Don't use your Mac when lightning is near.** Here's a simple life equation for you: Mac + lightning = dead Mac. 'Nuff said. Oh, and don't place much faith in inexpensive surge protectors. A good jolt of lightning will fry the surge protector right along with your computer as well as possibly frying your modem, printer, and anything else plugged into it. Some surge protectors can withstand most lightning strikes, but these warriors aren't the cheapies that you buy at your local computer emporium. Unplugging your Mac from the wall during electrical storms is safer and less expensive. (Don't forget to unplug your external modem, network hubs, or other hardware that plugs into the wall as well — lightning can fry them, too.)

✔ **Don't jostle, bump, shake, kick, throw, dribble, or punt your Mac, especially while it's running.** Your Mac contains a hard drive that spins at 5,400+ revolutions per minute (rpm). A jolt to a hard drive while it's reading or writing a file can cause the head to crash into the disk, which can render many or all the files on it unrecoverable. Ouch!

✔ **Don't forget to back up your data!** I beg you: Please read Chapter 17 now before something horrible happens to your valuable data! If the stuff on your hard drive means anything to you, you must back it up. Not maybe. You must. Even if your most important file is your last saved game of Tony Hawk Pro Skater 2, you still need to realize how important it is to back up your files.

In Chapter 17, I discuss how to back up your files, and I *strongly* recommend that you read Chapter 17 sooner rather than later — preferably before you do any significant work on your Mac. Dr. Macintosh sez: "There are only two kinds of Mac users: those who have never lost data and those who will." Which kind will you be?

✔ **Don't kiss your monitor while wearing stuff on your lips.** For obvious reasons!

Point-and-click boot camp

Are you new to the Mac? Just learning how to move the mouse around? Now is a good time to go over some fundamental stuff that you need to know for just about everything you'll be doing on the Mac. Spend a few minutes reading this section, and soon you'll be clicking, double-clicking, pressing, and pointing all over the place. If you think you've got the whole mousing thing pretty much figured out, feel free to skip this section. I'll catch you on the other side.

Still with me? Good. Now for some basic terminology.

- **Point:** Before you can click or press anything, you have to *point* to it. Place your hand on your mouse and move it so that the cursor arrow is over the object that you want — like on top of an icon or a button. Then click the mouse to select the object or double-click it to run it (if it's an application or an icon that starts up an application). You point and then you click — *point-and-click,* in computer lingo.

- **Click:** (Also called *single-click.*) Use your index finger to push the mouse button all the way down and then let go so that it produces a satisfying clicking sound. (If you have one of the new optical Apple Pro mice, you push down the whole thing to click.) Use a single-click to highlight an icon, press a button, or activate a check box or window.

- **Double-click:** *Click twice* in rapid succession. With a little practice, you can perfect this technique in no time. Use a double-click to open a folder or to launch a file or application.

- **Control-click:** Hold down the Control key while single-clicking. Control-clicking is the same as right-clicking on a Windows system and displays a menu (called a *contextual menu*) where you Control-clicked. In fact, if you are blessed with a two- (or more) button mouse (I personally use the four-button Kensington Turbo Mouse Pro Wireless and recommend it highly), you can right-click and avoid having to hold down the Control key.

- **Drag:** *Dragging* something usually accompanies clicking it first. With the mouse button held down, move the mouse on your desk or mouse pad so that the cursor — and whatever you select — moves across the screen. The combination of pressing the mouse and dragging it is usually referred to as *click-and-drag.*

- **Press:** A *press* is half a click. Instead of letting go of the mouse button to finish the click, keep holding it down. In most cases, your next step is to drag the mouse somewhere — down a menu to choose a command or across the screen to move an object, for example.

- **Choosing an item from a menu:** To get to Mac OS menu commands, you must first open a menu and then pick the option that you want. Point at the name of the menu that you want with your mouse cursor, press your mouse button down, and then drag your mouse downward until you select the command that you want. When the command is highlighted, finish selecting by letting go of the mouse button.

If you're a long-time Mac user, you probably hold down the mouse button the whole time between clicking the name of the menu and selecting the command that you want. You can still do it that way, but you can also click once on the menu name to open it, release the mouse button, and then drag down to the item that you want to select *and then click again.* In other words, OS X menus stay open for a few seconds after you click them, even if you're not holding down the mouse button. Go ahead and give it a try . . . I'll wait.

A pop quiz on mousing

For those of you who need to hone your mousing skills, here's a little quiz:

1. How do you select an icon?

A. Stare at it intently for five seconds.

B. Point to it with your finger, slap the side of your monitor, and say "That one, stupid!"

C. Move the mouse pointer on top of the icon and click once.

2. When do you need to double-click?

A. Whenever you find yourself saying, "There's no place like home."

B. When you're using both hands to control the mouse.

C. When you want to open a file or folder.

3. How do you select multiple items or blocks of text?

A. Get several people to stare intently at the items that you want to select.

B. Attach multiple mice to your Mac.

C. Slide the mouse on your desk, moving the onscreen pointer to the location where you want to begin selecting. Press and hold down the mouse button. Drag the pointer across the items or text that you want to select. Then let go of the mouse button.

4. How do you move a selected item?

A. Call U-Haul.

B. Pick up and tilt your monitor until the item slides to the proper location.

C. Point to the item and hold (press) down the mouse button. With the mouse button still held down, drag the pointer to the new location and let go of the mouse button.

If you haven't figured it out by now, the correct answer to each of these questions is C. If any other answer sounded remotely plausible, sit down with your Mac and just play with it for a while. If you have kids at your disposal, watch them play with your Mac. They'll show you how to use it in no time.

Chapter 2

Meet the Desktop

• •

• •

*T*his chapter is where I get down to the nitty-gritty about the nifty new Mac OS X Desktop — the place where you start doing stuff with your Mac.

Those of you who've been using Mac OS for a while may find some of the information in this chapter repetitive; some features that I describe haven't changed from earlier versions of the Mac OS. But in Mac OS X, much more is new than the version number. Although you still use the Desktop for many of the same tasks, it looks very different, with lots of new tools and features and terminology that you need to know before you can call yourself truly Mac OS X savvy. Besides, if you decide to skip this chapter — just because you think you have all the new stuff figured out — I assure you that you'll miss out on sarcasm, clever wordplay, shortcuts, awesome techniques, a bad pun or two, and lots of good advice on making the Desktop an easier place to be. If that's not enough to convince you, I also provide a bunch of stuff that Apple didn't bother to tell you (as if you read the manual anyway!).

Tantalized? Let's rock.

Clearing Off the Desktop

Just about everything that you do on your Mac begins and ends with the Desktop. This is where you manage files, store documents, launch programs, adjust the way your Mac works, and much more. If you ever expect to master your Mac, the first step is to master the Desktop.

Some folks use the terms *Desktop* and *Finder* interchangeably to refer to the total Macintosh environment that you see — icons, windows, menus, and all that other cool stuff. Just to make things confusing, the background that you see on your screen — the backdrop behind your hard drive icon and open windows — is also called the Desktop. In this book, I refer to the *Finder* as the Finder, which I discuss in Chapters 7 and 8. When I say *Desktop,* I'm talking about the background behind your windows and Dock, where your hard drive icon appears.

Got it? The Desktop is convenient and fast. Put stuff there.

Check out the default Mac Desktop for OS X in Figure 2-1.

Touring the Desktop

The Desktop is the center of your Mac OS experience, so before I go any further, I need to quickly describe its most prominent features:

- **Desktop:** The *Desktop* is the area behind the windows and the Dock, where your hard drive icon (ordinarily) lives. The Desktop isn't a window, yet it acts like one. Like a folder window or drive window, the Desktop can contain icons. But unlike most windows, which require a bit of navigation to get to, the Desktop is a great place for things that you use a lot, such as folders, applications, or particular documents. The next section discusses the default icons that you see on the Desktop when you first load up OS X.

- **Dock:** The *Dock* is the Finder's main navigation shortcut tool. It makes getting to frequently used icons easy, even when you have a screen full of windows. Like the Desktop, the Dock is a great place for things you use a lot, such as folders, applications, or particular documents. Besides putting your frequently used icons at your fingertips, it's almost infinitely customizable, too; read more about it in Chapter 3.

If you used an earlier version of Mac OS, think of the Dock as the OS X version of the Apple menu in Mac OS versions of the past. Yes, the OS X Finder *does* have an Apple menu, but it doesn't work at all like the Apple menu in earlier versions of Mac OS. See Chapter 6 for more info on the Apple menu.

- **Icons:** *Icons* are the little pictures that you see in your windows and even on your Desktop. All icons are containers that hold things that you work with on your Mac, such as programs and documents. In Chapter 4, I cover icons in detail, and the next section discusses the icons that you see on the OS X Desktop when you first boot up your Mac.

- **Windows:** Opening most icons (by double-clicking them) makes a window appear. Windows in the Finder show you the contents of hard drive and folder icons, and windows in applications usually show you the contents of your documents. For the full scoop on windows, check out Chapter 5.

- ✔ **Menus:** *Menus* let you choose to do things, such as create new folders; duplicate files; cut, copy, or paste text; and so on. Find out all about them in Chapter 6.

- ✔ **Aliases:** Use *aliases* of things that you use often so that you can keep the originals tucked away in one of your perfectly organized folders. Check out aliases in Chapter 4.

  If all these new terms such as *alias, Dock,* and so on seem strange to you, don't worry — I explain all of them in detail in the rest of the chapters in Part I.

Sniffing out the default Desktop icons

Icons on the Desktop behave the same as icons in a window. You move them and copy them just like you would an icon in a window. The only difference is that Desktop items aren't in a window: They're on the Desktop, which makes them more convenient to use.

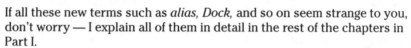

Figure 2-1:
The default
Mac OS X
Finder and
Desktop.

Actually, if you look at your Home directory (click the Home button on any Finder window toolbar or use the shortcut ⌘+Shift+H to open a window displaying Home), you see a folder named *Desktop* that contains the same icons that you place on the Desktop (but not the hard drive icons). The reason for this folder is that each user has an individual Desktop. But I'm getting ahead of myself. You find out much more about Home, users, and all that jazz in upcoming chapters.

To move an item to the Desktop, simply click its icon in a window and then drag it onto the Desktop.

✔ **Hard drive icons:** The first icon that you should become familiar with is the icon for your hard drive (refer to Figure 2-1). You can usually find it on the upper-right side of your Finder window when you first start the Mac. Look for the name Macintosh HD, iMac HD, or something like that (upper-right corner of Figure 2-2), unless you've renamed it. (I usually do rename my hard drive, but I haven't done so yet in Figure 2-2. To rename your hard drive, just double-click its name and type a new one.)

✔ **Disk icons:** Disk icons appear on the Desktop by default. When you insert a CD or DVD, its icon appears on the Desktop just below your hard drive icon (space permitting), as shown in Figure 2-2.

If you don't see a disk icon on your Desktop, skip ahead to Chapter 6, where I discuss Finder Preferences. That's where you can choose whether to see disks on your Desktop. In Figure 2-2, you can see the icon for *The Rising*, Bruce Springsteen's latest CD, which I'm listening to as I type this.

✔ **All and sundry:** In Figure 2-2, you see two additional icons: A Picture document, which is a picture I've been working on; and Grab, which is the Apple screen capture utility included with OS X.

I actually use Ambrosia Software's wonderful Mac OS X screen capture utility, SnapzPro X (www.ambrosiasw.com), for almost all the screen shots in this book. If you have a need for capturing what's on your screen, it's a zillion times better than Grab and was Jaguar-savvy before Jaguar even shipped!

Picture this: A picture on your Desktop

I'd be remiss if I didn't mention that you can change the background picture of your Desktop. If you're sick of the default Desktop picture, here's how to change your Desktop picture:

1. **From the Desktop, choose ⌘System Preferences or click the System Preferences icon in the Dock.**

   The System Preferences window appears.

2. **Click the Desktop icon.**

   The Desktop Preferences window appears.

3. **Either drag a picture icon to the well or click the Collection pop-up and choose Choose Folder to select a new picture for your Desktop.**

   The picture *well* is the little rectangle right under the words Current Desktop Picture. The name of the current picture appears to the right of the well.

   If you don't know how to choose a picture by using the Open File dialog, look in Chapter 8. And for more info on using System Preferences, check out Chapter 15.

In Figure 2-3, you can see my Desktop with a background picture I made to celebrate the release of Jaguar. (If you want a reminder of what the default Desktop background looks like, refer to Figure 2-1.)

Figure 2-2:
The
Desktop
is a good
place to
keep oft-
needed
icons.

Figure 2-3:
My
beautified
Desktop.

Chapter 3

"What's Up, Dock?"

*I*n this chapter, I take a look at the Dock, which is the section of the Desktop that gives you quick access to frequently used applications. The Dock is also a quick way to pull a file or application that's already open to the front so that you can work with it. Read on to discover how to use the Dock and how to customize it so that it works and looks just the way you want.

Running Down the Dock

Take a minute to look at the row of pictures at the bottom of the your Mac OS X Finder screen. That row, ladies and gentlemen, is the *Dock* (shown in Figure 3-1), and those individual pictures are *icons* (which I discuss in Chapter 4). When you click a Dock icon, you either

🖝 Open an application, file, or folder

🖝 Bring an open application, file, or folder to the front of all others

When you press (click but don't let go) most Dock icons, a menu appears.

Figure 3-1:
The Dock
and all its
default
icons.

By default, the Dock contains a number of commonly used Mac OS X applications, and you can also store your own applications, files, or folders there. I show you how to do that in the "Adding icons to the Dock" section, located later in this chapter.

Most items that you find on the Dock when you first use Mac OS X are probably familiar to you already. If they aren't, they certainly will be in time. In the following sections, I give you a brief description of each, moving from left to right; I also point you to the parts of this book where I cover the item in more detail.

The Dock is a great place to store your favorite icons and have quick access to them, but don't confuse the Dock with *Favorites* — you know, those files, folders, or URLs that you see when you click the Favorites button in the toolbar at the top of Finder windows. Adding to Favorites doesn't affect the Dock's inventory; likewise, putting an item on the Dock doesn't add it to your list of Favorites.

Finder

The Finder application (which I discuss at length in Chapter 7) is always open. Click the Finder icon (shown in the left margin) to open a Finder window. You can open as many Finder windows as you want by choosing File⇨New Finder Window or by using the keyboard shortcut ⌘+N. (Hold down the ⌘ key and then press the N key.)

Mail

Click this icon to launch Apple's OS X e-mail application, appropriately named *Mail,* with which you can send and receive e-mail. I describe Mail in glorious detail in Chapter 11.

iChat

Click this icon to launch Apple's OS X instant messaging application, *iChat,* with which you can send and receive instant messages (IMs). I describe iChat in loving detail in Chapter 11.

Address Book

Click this icon to launch Apple OS X's eponymously named address book application, Address Book, where you store information about people (contacts). I describe Address Book in more detail in Chapter 13.

Internet Explorer

 Microsoft's Internet Explorer is the Web browser included with Mac OS X. Click this Dock icon to launch Internet Explorer, which I discuss in detail in Chapter 11. You might have seen its lowercase *e* icon before — especially on Windows machines.

iTunes

 iTunes is a major part of Apple's digital hub. With iTunes, you can listen to MP3 files that you download from the Internet, audio CDs, and Internet radio stations, and you can also build your own library of MP3 files from CDs that you already own. I talk more about iTunes in Chapter 13.

iPhoto

 Use iPhoto, another major part of Apple's digital hub, to download photos from your digital camera, organize them, print them, make slide shows and Web pages from them, and much more. I talk more about iPhoto in Chapter 13.

iMovie

 iMovie is yet another major part of Apple's digital hub. Use iMovie to make high-quality movies complete with transitions and titles. I talk more about iMovie in Chapter 13.

 If you like this sort of digital stuff, check out *The Digital Hub Bible*, written by Dennis Cohen (with a little help from yours truly), published by Wiley Publishing, Inc. This epic tome dedicates hundreds of pages to each of the digital hub applications, making it a great all-in-one reference for the Apple i-apps (iChat, iDVD, iMovie, iPod, iPhoto, iSay, iKnow, iWill . . . the list is endless).

Even if I do say so myi-self.

Sherlock

 Use the Sherlock 3 application to grab and display information gathered from the Internet, including stock news; general headlines; movie previews, locations, and show times; Yellow Pages listings; eBay auction activity; and much, much more. Track down more info on Sherlock in Chapter 11.

Sherlock is no longer the program that you use to search for things on your local disks. And it's not the program that you're used to: Sherlock 3 is a whole new ball of sleuth. If you didn't like Sherlock before, try it now. This edition is definitely not the Sherlock that you used to know.

QuickTime Player

QuickTime, Apple's multimedia application, is yet another part of its digital hub. It provides you with a format for playing movies, audio programs, and streaming audio and video. Read more about QuickTime in Chapter 13.

System Preferences

Click the System Preferences icon on the Dock to open the System Preferences application. System Preferences, as I describe in Chapter 15, gives you access to all sorts of settings that you use to configure your Mac just the way you like it. Clicking the Dock icon is the same as choosing System Preferences from the Apple menu; both open the System Preferences program.

Apple — Mac OS X

The Apple — Mac OS X icon launches your Web browser (Internet Explorer) and takes you to the Mac OS X section of Apple's Web site.

Trash

The Trash icon is unique among Dock items: It's not a file or application that you open. Instead, you drag things to this icon to get rid of them.

Don't want it? Trash it

The *Trash* is a special container where you put the icons that you no longer want on your hard drive or removable media storage device (such as Zip). Got four copies of TextEdit on your hard drive? Drag three of them to the Trash. Tired of tripping over old letters that you don't want to keep? Drag them to the Trash, too. To put something in the Trash, just drag its icon on top of the Trash icon and watch it disappear.

Like other icons, you know that you've connected with the Trash while dragging when the icon is highlighted. And like other Dock icons, the Trash icon's name appears when you move the cursor over the icon.

Taking out the trash

You know how the garbage in the can in your garage sits there until the sanitation engineers come by and pick it up each Thursday? The Mac OS X Trash works the same. When you put something in the Trash, it sits there until you choose the Finder⇨Empty Trash command or use the keyboard shortcut ⌘+Shift+Delete.

 While items sit in the Trash waiting for you to empty it, the Trash basket shows you that it has files waiting for you there . . . just like in real life, your unemptied Trash is full of crumpled papers.

 You can also empty the Trash from the Dock by pressing the mouse button and holding it down on the Trash icon for a second or two. The Empty Trash menu pops up like magic. Move your mouse over it to select it and then release the mouse button. Control-clicking will pop up the menu immediately.

 Think twice before you invoke the Empty Trash command. After you empty the Trash, the files that it contained are (usually) gone forever. My advice: Before you get too bold, read Chapter 17 and back up your hard drive several times. After you get proficient at backups, even though the files are technically gone forever from your hard drive, you can get them back if you like (at least in theory).

Digging stuff out of the Trash (yech!)

As with all icons, you can open the Trash to see what's in there — just click its icon in the Dock. If you decide that you don't want to get rid of an item that's already in the Trash, just drag it back out, either onto the Finder or back into the folder where it belongs.

iDVD

One last thing: If your Mac has a *SuperDrive* — Apple's DVD-RW burner — you may see an icon for iDVD in your Dock. *iDVD* is another digital hub application, used to create beautiful DVDs that can be played on OS X's own DVD Player or any standalone DVD player.

Workin' the Dock

The Dock is a convenient way to get at oft-used icons. By default, the Dock comes pre-stocked with icons that Apple thinks you'll need most frequently, but you can customize it to contain any icons that you choose. In this section, I tell you all about the Dock — how to use it, how to customize it, how to resize it, and more.

Using Dock icons

Dock icons work just like other icons except that instead of double-clicking them, you only single-click them. (I further discuss icons in Chapter 4.) Note that when you single-click a Dock icon, it doesn't become highlighted. Instead, any chosen Dock icon moves up and out of its place on the Dock for a moment, letting you know that you've activated it. Check out Figure 3-2 to see an animated Dock icon — it's still on the Dock, but it's raised higher than the inactive ones.

Figure 3-2:
A raised
Dock icon:
selected
and
opening.

Many Dock icons also do a little bouncy dance when that program isn't active (its menu bar isn't showing and it's not the front-most program) to inform you that it desires your attention. If you notice that the icon for an open application is dancing, give it a click to find out what the program wants or needs.

When an application on the Dock is open, an up-arrow (which looks like a small black pyramid) appears below its Dock icon, as shown in Figure 3-2.

To discover the name of a Dock icon, just move your cursor over any item on the Dock, and the item's name appears above it (as shown in Figure 3-3). This feature is quite handy because you can't view Dock items as a list in the same the way that you can with icons that are stored in windows. And, as you can read in the section "Resizing the Dock" later in this chapter, you can resize the Dock to make the icons smaller (which does make them more difficult to see). Hovering your mouse cursor to discover the name of a teeny icon makes this feature even more useful.

Figure 3-3:
Move your
cursor over
a Dock icon
to display
its name.

Adding icons to the Dock

You can customize your Dock with favorite applications, a document you update daily, or maybe a folder containing your favorite recipes — whatever you need quick access to. The following sections tell you what kind of stuff to put on the Dock and how to add an icon to the Dock.

Knowing what to put on the Dock

Put things on the Dock that you need quick access to and that you use often, or add items that aren't quickly available from menus or the toolbar. If you like using the Dock better than the Go menu or the Finder window toolbar, for example, add your Documents folder to the Dock.

I suggest adding these items to your Dock:

- **A word processing application:** Most people use word processing software more than any other application.

- **A project folder:** Suppose that you follow my advice and store all the files that you create in the Documents folder or subfolders thereof. One of those subfolders contains all the documents for your thesis, or the biggest project you have at work, or your massive recipe collection . . . whatever. Add that folder to the Dock and then you can access it much quicker than if you have to open your Documents folder first.

  When you *press* (click but don't let go) on a folder icon, a handy hierarchical menu of its contents appears. Give it a try — it's great.

- **A special utility or application:** StuffIt Expander is an essential part of my work because I receive a lot of stuffed and zipped files. You may prefer to have handy a *File Transfer Protocol* (FTP) application (used to download files from the Internet), a graphics application such as Photoshop, or a calendar program.

- **Your favorite URL:** Save a link to a site that you visit every day — one that you use in your job, or a favorite news site, or your personalized page from an Internet service provider (ISP). Sure, you can make one of these pages your browser's start page, but the Dock lets you add one or more additional URLs.

  Here's how to quickly add a URL to the Dock. Open Internet Explorer (IE) and go to the page with a URL that you want to save on the Dock. Click and drag the small icon that you find at the left of the URL in the Address bar (see Figure 3-4) to the right side of the Dock and then release the mouse button. Your URL is now in place. When you click the URL icon that you move to your Dock, IE opens to that page.

You can add several URL icons to the Dock, but bear in mind that the Dock and its icons shrink to accommodate added icons, thus making them harder to see. Perhaps the best idea — if you want easy access to several URLs — is to create a folder full of URLs and put that folder on the Dock. Then you can just press and hold your mouse on the folder (or Control-click the folder) to pop up a menu with all your URLs.

Figure 3-4:
To save a
URL to your
Dock, drag
its icon from
the Address
bar.

Even though you can make the Dock smaller, you're still limited to one row of icons. The smaller that you make the Dock, the larger the crowd of icons that you can amass. You have to determine for yourself what's best for you: having lots of icons available on the Dock (even though they may be difficult to see because they're so tiny) or having less clutter but fewer icons on your Dock.

Putting an icon on the Dock

Adding an application, file, or folder to the Dock is as simple as dragging it there. Follow these steps to add an icon to the Dock:

1. **Open a Finder window containing an application, file, or folder that you use frequently.**

   As shown in Figure 3-5, I chose the StuffIt Expander application (it's highlighted). I use StuffIt Expander constantly to decompress archives of files received in e-mail or downloaded from newsgroups on the Internet. (Find the StuffIt Expander application, if you're interested, in the Utilities folder inside your Applications folder.)

2. **Click the item that you want to add to the Dock and drag it out of the Finder window and onto the Dock.**

   An icon for this item now appears on the Dock.

You can add several items at the same time to the Dock by selecting them all and dragging the group to the Dock. However, you can delete only one icon at a time from the Dock.

Figure 3-5:
Drag an
icon onto
the Dock
to add it.

Removing an icon from the Dock

To remove an item from the Dock, just drag its icon onto the Desktop. It disappears with a cool *poof* animation. By moving an icon out of the Dock, you aren't moving or copying the item itself — you're just removing its icon from the Dock. Think of it like a library catalog card: Just because you remove the card from the card catalog doesn't mean that the book is gone from the library.

When you open an application with an icon that doesn't ordinarily appear on the Dock, its icon magically appears on the Dock until you quit that application. And when you quit, its icon magically disappears from the Dock. In other words, you see a temporary Dock icon for every program that's currently open; these temporary icons disappear when you quit the program. If you want to keep an icon in the Dock permanently, you have two ways to tell it to stay around after you quit the program. You can Control-click (or click-and-hold) and then choose Keep in Dock from the menu that pops up, or you can drag the icon (for an application that's currently open) off and then back onto the Dock without letting go.

Setting Dock preferences

You can change a few things about the Dock to make it look and behave just the way you want it to. To do so, just choose Dock⇨Dock Preferences from the menu (or the *Apple menu,* meaning the menu beneath that symbol in the upper-left corner of the Finder menu bar). In the Dock dialog that opens (see Figure 3-6), you can adjust your Dock with the following preferences:

Figure 3-6:
The Dock
Preferences
window.

- ✔ **Dock Size:** Note the slider bar here. Move this slider to the right (larger) or left (smaller) to adjust the size of the Dock on your Finder. As you move the slider, watch the Dock change size. Now *there's* a fun way to spend a Saturday afternoon!

  As you add items to the Dock, each icon — and the Dock itself — shrinks to accommodate the new ones.

- ✔ **Magnification:** This slider controls how big icons grow when you pass the arrow cursor over them. Or you can deselect this check box to turn off magnification entirely.

- ✔ **Position on Screen:** Choose from these three radio buttons to attach the Dock to the left side, the right side, or the bottom of your screen (the default). Personally, I prefer it on the right side of the screen.

- ✔ **Minimize Using:** Select from this handy drop-down list to choose the visual effect (animation) that you see when you click a window's Minimize button. The Genie Effect is the default, but the Scale Effect seems a bit faster to me.

- ✔ **Animate Opening Applications:** Mac OS X animates (bounces) Dock icons when you click them to open an item. If you don't like the animation, deselect this check box, and the bouncing will cease evermore.

✔ **Automatically Hide and Show the Dock:** Don't like the Dock? Maybe you want to free up the screen real estate at the bottom of your monitor? Then select the Automatically Hide and Show the Dock check box; after that, the Dock displays itself only when you move the cursor (mouse) to the bottom of the screen where the dock would ordinarily appear. It's like magic! (Okay, it's like Windows, but I hate to admit it.)

If the Dock isn't visible, deselect (that is, uncheck) this Automatically Hide and Show the Dock check box to bring it back. The option remains turned off unless you change it or choose Dock⇨Turn Hiding Off from the menu (or press ⌘+Option+D).

Resizing the Dock

If the default size of the Dock bugs you, you can make the Dock smaller and save yourself a lot of screen real estate. This space comes in especially handy when you add your own stuff to the Dock.

To shrink or enlarge the Dock (and its icons) without opening the Dock Preferences window, drag its sizer handle. To make the sizer appear (as shown in the left margin), move your cursor over the thin white line that you find on the right side of the Dock. Drag the sizer down to make the Dock smaller, holding onto the mouse button until you find the size you like. The more you drag this control down, the smaller the Dock gets. To enlarge the Dock again, just drag the sizer back up. Poof! Big Dock! You can enlarge the Dock until it fills your screen from side to side.

Check out the teeny tiny Dock in Figure 3-7.

Figure 3-7:
Here's my
little Dock.

The Dock reduced in size

Chapter 4

I Think Icon! I Think Icon!

*I*f you're going to use a Macintosh, you're going to use icons. Period. They are a fundamental part of what makes a Mac a Mac. I discuss icons a little bit in Chapters 2 and 3, but in this chapter, I get down to the real nitty-gritty and explain them in great detail.

Trust me: By the time you finish this chapter, you'll be so familiar with all the different types of icons that Mac OS X has to offer that you'll probably dream of them tonight.

Introducing . . . Icons!

Icons are those funny little pictographs in your windows. Icons represent things that you work with on your Mac, such as programs, documents, and folders.

Icons come in several shapes and sizes. After you've been around the Macintosh for a while, you get a sixth sense about what an icon contains just by looking at it. The three main types of icons are applications, documents, and folders. Well, there are actually four types — aliases are an icon type in their own right. Don't worry: I show you all four icon types in this section.

TIP

Don't confuse icons with buttons; they're sort of alike but different. When you click a button, something else (such as a file, an application, or a folder) opens. *Buttons* are simply pointers. *Icons* actually represent things on your hard drive, such as folders and applications. You can't move buttons around, but you can move icons. And although you double-click icons to open them, you single-click buttons. The toolbar items in the Finder (which I discuss in Chapter 6) are good examples of buttons. And although calling items in the Dock *buttons* is a stretch, they act like buttons because you single-click them to open them.

Application icons

Application icons are linked to *programs* — the software that you use to accomplish tasks on your Mac. Your word processor is an application. So are America Online (AOL) and Adobe Photoshop. Myth III: The Wolf Age and Quake III: Arena are also applications (and great games to boot).

Application icons come in a variety of shapes. For example, application (that is, program) icons are often square-ish. Sometimes, though, they're diamond-shaped, rectangular, or just oddly shaped. In Figure 4-1, you can see application icons of various shapes.

Figure 4-1: Application icons come in many different shapes.

Document icons

Document icons are files that are created by applications. A letter to your mom, which you create in AppleWorks (formerly known as ClarisWorks), is a document. So are my latest column and my Quicken data files. Document icons are almost always reminiscent of a piece of paper, as shown in Figure 4-2.

Figure 4-2: Typical document icons.

Folder icons

Folder icons are the Mac's organizational containers. You put icons, usually application or document icons, into folders. You can also put folders inside other folders. Folders look like . . . well, folders . . . and can contain just about any other icon. You use folders to organize your files and applications on your hard drive. You can have as many folders as you want, so don't be afraid to create new ones. The thought behind the whole folders thing is pretty obvious — if your hard drive is a filing cabinet, folders are its drawers and folders (duh!). Figure 4-3 shows some typical folder icons.

Figure 4-3: Some run-of-the-mill folder icons.

Aliases

Aliases are wonderful — no, *fabulous* — organizational tools that Apple introduced in the days of Mac OS 7. (Although Mac OS 7 was originally called *System* 7, Apple didn't begin the Mac OS designation until version 7.6.) I like aliases so much, in fact, that I think they deserve their very own section. Read on for more info on this ultra-useful tool.

Aliases: The Greatest Invention Since Sliced Bread

An *alias* is a tiny file that automatically opens the file that it represents. Although an alias is technically an icon, it's actually an icon that opens another icon automatically. You can put aliases in convenient places, such as on the Desktop, to help you easily open programs and files that you access often.

Microsoft stole the alias feature from Apple (if you've used Windows, you may know aliases as *shortcuts*). But what else is new?

An alias is different from a duplicated file. For example, Microsoft Word 2001 uses 9.7 megabytes (MB) of disk space. If I *duplicate* it, I have two files, each using 9+MB of disk space. *Creating* an alias of Microsoft Word, on the other hand, uses a mere 4 kilobytes (KB).

So why do I think that aliases are so great? Well, here are a few good reasons:

- **Convenience:** Aliases enable you to make items appear to be in more than one place, which on many occasions is exactly what you want to do. For example, keeping an alias of your word processor on your Desktop and another on the Dock is convenient. You may even want a third alias of it in your Documents folder for quick access. Aliases enable you to open your word processor quickly and easily without navigating into the depths of your Applications folder each time that you need it.

- **Flexibility:** You can create aliases and store them simultaneously to represent the same document in several different folders. This is a great help when you need to file a document that can logically be stored in any one of several files. For example: If you write a memo to Fred Smith about the Smythe Marketing Campaign to be executed in the fourth quarter, which folder does the document go in? Smith? Smythe? Marketing? Memos? 4th Quarter? All the above?

  With aliases, it doesn't matter. You can put the actual file in any folder and then create aliases of the file, placing them in any other applicable folder. Now you can search for a specific document in several places because whichever pertinent folder you open, you can find the memo.

✔ **Integrity:** Some programs need to remain in the same folder as their supporting files and folders. Many Classic programs, for example, won't function properly unless they're in the same folder as their dictionaries, thesauruses, data files (for games), templates, and so on. Thus, you can't put those programs on the Desktop without impairing their functionality.

Creating aliases

When you create an alias, its icon looks the same as the icon that it represents, but the suffix *alias* is tacked onto its name and a tiny arrow called a *badge* appears in the lower-left corner of its icon. Figure 4-4 shows both an alias and its *parent* icon (that is, the icon that will open if you open the alias).

Figure 4-4: An alias icon (right) and its parent.

To create an alias for an icon, do one of the following:

✔ **Click the parent icon and choose File⇨Make Alias.**

✔ **Click the parent icon and press ⌘+L.**

✔ **Click any file or folder, press and hold down the ⌘ and Option keys, and then drag the file or folder while continuing to hold down the ⌘ and Option keys.**

Presto! An alias appears where you release the mouse button. Better still, aliases created this way don't have that pesky alias suffix tacked onto them.

✔ **Choose Go⇨Favorites, choose File⇨Add to Favorites, or use the keyboard shortcut ⌘+T to automatically create an alias and place it in the Favorites folder so that it appears when you click the Favorites button from the toolbar.**

The same thing happens if you drag an icon onto the Favorites button in the toolbar. The Finder creates an alias of the icon and places it in the Favorites folder.

> ✔ **Click an icon while holding down the Control key and then choose the Make Alias command from the contextual menu that appears.**
>
> The alias appears in the same folder as its parent. (I explore contextual menus — which are very cool — in Chapter 6.)

Deleting aliases

This is a short section because deleting an alias is such an easy chore. To delete an alias, simply drag it onto the Trash icon on the Dock. That's it! You can also Control-click it and choose Move to Trash from the contextual menu that appears or select the icon and use the keyboard shortcut ⌘+Delete.

Deleting an alias does *not* delete the parent item. (If you want to delete the parent item, you have to go hunt it down and kill it yourself.)

Hunting down an alias' parent

Suppose that you create an alias of a file, and later you want to delete both the alias and its parent file — but you can't find the parent file! What do you do? Well, you can use the Finder's Find function (try saying that three times real fast) to find it, but the fastest way to find the parent icon of an alias is to select the alias (single-click) and then choose File⇨Show Original or use the keyboard shortcut ⌘+R.

The temporary alias theory

The Desktop is an excellent place to keep the things that you need most often — whether you use aliases of documents or save the actual files on the Desktop until you figure out where you want to store them. For example, when I first create a file, I save it in its proper folder inside the Documents folder somewhere. If it's a document that I plan to work on for more than a day or two, such as a magazine article, I make an alias of the document (or folder) and plop it on the Desktop. After I finish the article and submit it to an editor, I trash the alias, leaving the original file stashed away in its proper folder.

Of course, you can place that same folder in the Dock as well, so you can use the press-and-hold trick to open its subfolders. But nothing says that you can't have an item appear several places at once for maximum convenience.

Incidentally, you can use a similar technique without the aliases. Just save all your new documents on the Desktop (yourhomefolder/ Desktop). Later, as you finish working with each document, you can file it away in its proper folder.

Playing with Icons

After checking out the different types of icons, it's time to see what you can do with and to them. In the upcoming sections, I show you how to open, rename, get rid of (again), and select icons. In a matter of moments, you'll be an icon pro!

Open sez me! Opening icons

You can open any icon in four ways. (Okay, there are five ways, but one of them belongs to aliases, which I discuss earlier in the section "Introducing . . . Icons!") Anyway, here are the ways:

> ✔ **Click the icon once to select it and then choose File➪Open.**
>
> ✔ **Double-click the icon by clicking it twice in rapid succession.**
>
>   If it doesn't open, you double-clicked too slowly.
>
> ✔ **Select the icon and then press either ⌘+O or ⌘+↓.**
>
> ✔ **Click the icon while holding down the Control key and then use the contextual menu's Open command.**

Of course, you can also open any document icon from within an application — skip ahead to Chapter 8 for more on that.

Getting rid of icons

To get rid of an icon — any icon — merely drag it to the Trash on your Dock. (See Chapter 3 for more info on the Dock and the Trash.)

Playing the icon name game: renaming icons

Icon, icon-a, bo-bicon, banana fanna fo-ficon. Betcha can change the name of any old icon! Well, that's not entirely true. . . .

If an icon is locked (see the upcoming section "Info-mation"), busy (an application that's currently open), or you don't have the administrator's permission to rename that icon (see Chapter 16 for details about permissions), you won't be able to rename it. Similarly, you can't rename certain reserved icons, such as the Library, System, and Desktop folders.

Navigating icons like a supergeek

In addition to the old point-and-click method of navigating icons, you can also move among icons by using the keyboard. In an active window, make sure that no icons are selected and then type the first letter of a file's name. In all views, the first icon that starts with that letter is selected. To move to the next icon alphabetically, press the Tab key. To move to the icon in reverse alphabetical order, press Shift+Tab.

If more than one icon begins with the same letter, type in more than one letter to further restrict the possible results. Suppose that you have three folders in the same window that all begin with *A:* Applications, Abstracts, and Aunt Mary's Stuff. To isolate the Applications folder, type **app**.

If no window is active, typing a letter selects the first icon on the Desktop that starts with that letter. Press the Tab key or press Shift+Tab to work your way through the icon names alphabetically forward or backward, respectively. Finally, pressing ⌘+O or ⌘+↓ opens the selected item.

To rename an icon, you can either click the icon's name directly (don't click the icon itself because that selects the icon) or click the icon and then press Return (or Enter) on your keyboard once.

Either way, the icon's name is selected and surrounded with a box, and you can now type in a new name (as shown in Figure 4-5). In addition to selecting the name, the cursor changes from a pointer to a text-editing I-beam. An *I-beam cursor* (shown in the left margin) is the Mac's way of telling you that you can type now. At this point, if you click the I-beam cursor anywhere in the name box, you can edit the icon's original name. If you don't click the I-beam cursor in the name box but just begin typing, the icon's original name is replaced by what you type.

Figure 4-5:
Change an icon's name by typing over the old one.

untitled folder

If you've never changed an icon's name, give it a try. And don't forget: If you click the icon itself, the icon is selected, and you won't be able to change its name. If you do accidentally select the icon, just press Return (or Enter) one time to edit the name of the icon.

Selecting multiple icons

Sometimes you want to move or copy several items into a single folder. The process is pretty much the same as it is when you copy one file or folder (that is, you just drag the icon to where you want it and drop it there). But you first need to select all the items that you want before you can drag them, en masse, to their destination. You'll find the following method a lot more convenient than selecting and copying files one at a time.

1. **To select more than one icon in a folder, do one of the following:**

   • Click once within the folder window (don't click any one icon) and drag your mouse while continuing to hold down the mouse button. You see an outline of a box around the icons while you drag, and icons within or touching the box become highlighted. (See Figure 4-6.)

   • Click one icon and then hold down the Shift key while you click others. As long as you hold down the Shift key, each new icon that you click is added to the selection. To deselect an icon, click it a second time while still holding down the Shift key.

   • Click one icon and then hold down the Command (⌘) key while you click others. The difference between using the Shift and the ⌘ keys is that using the ⌘ key doesn't select everything between it and the first item selected when your window is in a List or Column view. In an Icon view, it really doesn't make much difference.

   To deselect an icon selected in any of these three ways, click it while holding down the ⌘ key.

2. **When you select all the icons that you want, click one of them (don't click anywhere else or you deselect the icons that you just selected) and drag (or Option+drag) them to the location where you want to move (or copy) them.**

Be careful with multiple selections, especially when you drag icons to the Trash. You can easily and accidentally select more than one icon, so watch out that you don't accidentally put an icon in the Trash by not paying close attention.

If you put something in the Trash by accident, you can almost always return it to whence it came. Just invoke the magical Undo command. Choose Edit⇨ Undo or use the keyboard shortcut ⌘+Z. The accidentally trashed file will return to its original location. Usually.

Unfortunately, Undo doesn't work every time — and it only remembers the very last action that you performed when it *does* work — so don't rely on it too much.

Click here.

Figure 4-6:
Select more
than one
icon with
your mouse.

Drag to here.

Info-mation

Every icon has an Info window that gives you — big surprise! — information about that icon and enables you to choose which other users (if any) that you want to have the privilege of using this icon. (I discuss sharing files and privileges in detail in Chapter 16.) The Info window is also where you lock an icon so that it can't be renamed or dragged to the Trash.

To see an icon's Info window, click the icon and choose File⇨Get Info (or press ⌘+I) The Info window for that icon appears, as in Figure 4-7, which shows the Info window for the QuickTime Player icon.

Documents, folders, and disks each have slightly different Info windows. In this section, I give you highlights on the type of information and options that you can find.

The gray triangles reveal what information for an icon is available in this particular Info window. Figure 4-7 shows the options for the QuickTime Player with the General section expanded. The sections that you see for most icons include the following:

✔ **General:** For information of the general kind, such as

- **Kind:** What kind of file this is — an application, document, disk, folder, and so on

- **Size:** How much disk space this file uses

Figure 4-7:
A typical
Info window
for an
application
(QuickTime
Player, in
this case).

• **Where:** The path to the folder that contains this file

• **Created:** The date and time that this file was created

• **Modified:** The date and time that this file was last modified (that is, saved)

• **Version:** Copyright information and the file's version number

✔ **Name & Extension:** Tells the full name, including the (possibly hidden) extension.

✔ **Preview:** When you select a document icon, the menu offers a Preview option that you use to see a glimpse of what's in that document. You can also see this preview when you select a document icon in Column view — it magically appears in the rightmost column. If you select a QuickTime movie or sound, you can even play it right there in the preview pane without launching a separate application. Neat.

✔ **Languages:** Manages the language that the application uses for menus and dialogs. Note that this option only appears if you're using an Info window to look at certain application programs.

✔ **Ownership & Permissions:** Governs which users have access to this icon. (See Chapter 16 for more about privileges.)

✔ **Comments:** Provides a field in which you type your own comments about this icon.

Other fun things that the Info window offers are

✔ **Open in the Classic Environment check box:** This option is only available for some applications, known as *Carbon apps,* that are developed to run on both OS 9 and OS X. Selecting this check box lets you run the application in the Classic environment.

✔ **The Locked check box:** Enabling this shows you whether you can change an icon's name or drag it to the Trash. When an application is *locked* (this check box will be marked), you can't change its name or drag it to the Trash. (I discuss the Trash in Chapter 3.)

Disks can't be locked by merely marking a check box; documents, folders, and applications can.

Folders can be locked by merely selecting the Locked check box in the Info window. In previous versions of Mac OS, you had to open the Sharing panel of the Info window (formerly known as Get Info), but Mac OS X conveniently allows you to lock a folder by selecting the Locked check box in the General area of the Info window. Yea!

✔ **The Stationery check box:** Document icons sport these. Stationery is a special type of document file that acts as a template. When you open any document for which you've marked this check box, the document opens with all the information in it but it's named Untitled — you have to use Save As to save and rename the file.

The Stationery document remains unchanged even after you open it so that you can use it again and again to open a document with some of its content already in place.

Why would you want to run an app in Classic?

I had a great USB printer (Epson Stylus Photo 750) that wasn't supported in OS X, although it worked fine in Classic. I could do most of my printing from Word and Photoshop in Classic, but every so often, I needed to print a file created by some OS X-only program. I couldn't print from OS X, but I could save the file as a PDF (something almost every OS X program can do because PDF support is built into OS X's Quartz imaging architecture). Then, I used the Open in the Classic Environment feature to tell my copy of Acrobat 5 to open as a Classic application instead of a Mac OS X application, thus allowing me to print the formerly unprintable document from Classic.

Chapter 5

Looking through Finder Windows

● ●

In This Chapter

▶ Checking out the parts of a window

▶ Of gumdrops and windows

▶ Keeping it small with scroll bars (not to be confused with whiskey bars)

▶ Knowing your active windows from your passive windows

▶ Dealing with dealie-boppers in windows

▶ Resizing, moving, and closing windows

● ●

*W*indows are and have always been an integral part of Macintosh computing. Windows on the Desktop show you the contents of hard drive and folder icons; windows in applications usually show you the contents of your documents. Along with the Desktop, Dock, icons, and menus, windows are just part of what makes your Mac a Mac. Knowing how to use them is essential.

This chapter focuses on Finder windows. But after you get the hang of Finder windows, you pretty much know how all the windows that you'll ever see on your Mac work. So relax and don't worry. At the end of this brief chapter, you'll know all you need to operate any Mac window like a pro.

Anatomy of a Window

Like icons, windows are a ubiquitous part of using a Mac. The Finder appears in a window. When you open a folder, it's a window that you see. When you write a letter, the document that you're working on appears in a window, and so on.

For the most part, windows are windows. As you use different programs, you'll probably notice that some of them (Adobe Photoshop or Microsoft Word, for example) take liberties with windows by adding features such as pop-up menus, zoom percentage, and file size to the scroll bar area. Don't let it bug you; that extra fluff is just window dressing (pun intended).

Windows in programs running in the Classic environment look different —
like Mac OS 9 windows. (I cover the Classic environment in Chapter 14.)

And so, without further ado, the following list gives you a look at the main
features of a typical Finder window (as shown in Figure 5-1). I discuss these
features in greater detail in later sections of this chapter.

Figure 5-1:
A typical
Finder
window in
Mac OS X.

✔ **Title bar:** Shows the name of the window.

✔ **Scroll bars:** Used for moving around windows.

✔ **Toolbar:** Where frequently used items live.

✔ **Forward and Back buttons:** Take you to the next or previous folder.

If you're familiar with Web browsers, the Forward and Back buttons in
the Finder work exactly the same way. The first time that you open a
window, neither button is active. But as you navigate from folder to
folder, they remember your path so that you can quickly traverse the
path of folders. Another great thing about them is that you can navigate
this way from the keyboard by using the shortcuts ⌘+[for Back and ⌘+]
for Forward.

If you've enabled the Finder Preference to always open folders in a new
window, the Forward and Back buttons won't work. You need to use
the modern, OS X-style window option — the one that uses a single
window — or the buttons are useless.

✔ **View buttons:** Choose from three exciting views of your window: row,
column, or list.

✔ **Close, Minimize, and Expand (gumdrop) buttons:** Shut 'em, shrink 'em, and make 'em grow.

✔ **Hide/Show toolbar button:** Causes your computer to melt into a puddle of molten silicon slag. Just kidding! This button actually does what its name implies — hides or shows the toolbar of a window.

Top o' the window to ya!

Take a gander at the top of a window — any window. You see three buttons in the upper-left corner and the name of the window in the top center. This section is called the *title bar*. These three buttons (called *gumdrop buttons* by some folks because they look like, well, gumdrops) in the upper-left corner of the window — known as Close, Minimize, and Expand — are colored red, orange, and green (from left to right). Here's what they do:

✔ **Close (red):** Click this button to *close* the window.

✔ **Minimize (orange):** Click this button to *minimize* the window. Clicking Minimize appears to close the window, but instead of making it disappear, Minimize adds an icon for the window on the Dock. To view the window again, click the Dock icon for the window that you minimized. If the window happens to be a QuickTime movie, the movie continues to play, albeit at postage stamp size, in its icon on the Dock. (I discuss the Dock in Chapter 3.)

✔ **Expand (green):** Click this button to make the window larger or smaller, depending on its current size. If you're looking at a standard size window, clicking Maximize *usually* makes it bigger. (I say *usually* because if the window is larger than its contents, clicking this button shrinks the window to the smallest size that can completely enclose the contents without scrolling.) Click Maximize again to return the window to its original size.

A scroll new world

Yet another way to see more of what's in a window is to scroll through it. Scroll bars appear at the bottom and right sides of any window that contains more stuff — icons, text, pixels, or whatever — than you can see in the window. As shown in Figure 5-2, dragging the scroll bar on the right side of the window reveals the items above Clock and below QuickTime Player, depending on whether you scroll up or down. And dragging the scroll bar on the bottom of the window reveals the Date Modified column, which is located to the right of the Kind column.

Simply click and drag a scroll bar to move it either up or down or side to side. And yes, the scroll bars also look a bit gumdrop-like. As best as I can tell, Steve Jobs (Apple's charismatic CEO) has a thing for gumdrops.

Figure 5-2:
Use scroll bars to navigate a window.

Vertical scroll bar

Scroll area

Horizontal scroll bar   Scroll area

Scroll arrows

You can scroll in the following four ways:

- ✔ **Click a scroll bar and drag.** The content of the window scrolls proportionally to how far you drag the scroll bar.

- ✔ **Click in the scroll bar area but not on the scroll bar itself.** The window scrolls either one page up (if you click above the scroll bar) or down (if you click below the scroll bar). If the scroll bar area is white (that is, it doesn't have a blue scroll bar showing), you have no items to scroll to — which means that everything that the window contains is already visible. You can change a setting in your General System Preferences to cause the window to scroll proportionally to where you click. Essentially, this is the same as the OS 9 way, but with a single-click in the place of the click-and-drag.

For what it's worth, the Page Up and Page Down keys function the same as clicking the grayish scroll bar area (the vertical scroll bar only) in the Finder and many applications. But these keys don't work in some programs, so don't get too dependent on them.

- ✔ **Click a scroll arrow at the top or bottom of a scroll area.** The window scrolls a little. Press and hold a scroll arrow, and the window scrolls a lot. Click the up-pointing arrow to scroll toward the beginning and the down-pointing arrow to scroll toward the end.

If you have your General System Preferences set to have the scroll arrows together rather than at top and bottom, they'll be at the bottom and right of the scroll areas, as shown in Figure 5-2. If you don't, you'll see one arrow at each end of the scroll area.

✔ **Use the keyboard.** In the Finder, first click an icon in the window and then use the arrow keys to move up, down, left, or right. Using an arrow key selects the next icon in that direction and automatically scrolls the window, if necessary. In other programs, you may or may not be able to use the keyboard to scroll. The Page Up and Page Down keys work in most programs, but many programs don't use the arrow keys for scrolling their windows. The best advice that I can give you is to try it — either it'll work or it won't.

In the Finder, you can also press the Tab key on the keyboard to select the next icon (in the current window) alphabetically and press Shift+Tab to select the previous icon (in the current window) alphabetically.

(Hyper) Active windows

To work within a window, the window must be *active*. The active window is always the frontmost window, and inactive windows always appear behind the active window. Only one window can be active at a time. To make a window active, click it anywhere — in the middle, on the title bar, or on a scroll bar — it doesn't matter where, with one proviso: You can't click the red, orange, or green gumdrop buttons of an inactive window to activate it.

When you hover your mouse pointer *over* the red, orange, or green gumdrop buttons of an inactive window but don't click your mouse button, the gumdrops light up, thus enabling you to close, minimize, or expand an inactive window without first making it active.

Look at Figure 5-3 for an example of an active window (the Applications window) in front of an inactive window (the Utilities window).

The following is a list of the major visual cues that distinguish active and inactive windows:

✔ The active window's title bar Close, Minimize, and Maximize buttons — the red, orange, and green ones — are, well, red, orange, and green. The inactive windows' buttons are not.

If you move your mouse over an inactive window's gumdrop buttons, they light up in their usual colors so you can close, minimize, or expand an inactive window without first making it active.

✔ Other buttons and scroll bars in an active window look different, too — they're bright. In an inactive window, these features are grayed out and more subdued.

✔ The title bars of inactive windows are also translucent, thus allowing what is behind them to partially show through.

✔ Active windows have bigger and darker drop shadows than inactive windows.

Active window

Inactive window

Figure 5-3:
An active window in front of an inactive window.

Dialog Dealie-Boppers

Dialogs are special windows that pop up over the active window. You generally see them when you select a menu item that ends in an ellipsis (...).

Dialogs can contain a number of standard Macintosh features (I call them *dealie-boppers*), such as radio buttons, pop-up menus, text entry boxes, and check boxes. You see these features again and again in dialogs. Take a moment to look at each of these dealie-boppers in Figure 5-4.

✔ **Radio buttons:** *Radio buttons* are so named because like the buttons on your car radio (assuming that you have a very old car), only one at a time can be active (when they're active they appear to be pushed in, just like with old radio buttons). Radio buttons always appear in a group of two or more; when you select one, all the others are automatically deselected. Eggheads call this setup *mutually exclusive.* Take a look at Figure 5-4 for an example of radio buttons.

As shown in Figure 5-4, the first radio button (Rich Text) is selected. If you were to now select the radio button for Plain Text, you deactivate (deselect) Rich Text. Got it? Good. Moving right along. . . .

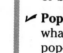

Here's a nifty and undocumented shortcut: You can usually select check boxes and radio buttons by clicking their names (instead of the buttons or boxes). Didn't know that, did you?

✔ **Pop-up menus:** These menus are appropriately named because that's what they do — they pop up when you click them. You can always tell a pop-up menu because it appears in a slightly rounded rectangle and has a double-ended arrow symbol (or, a pair of back-to-back triangles if you like) on the right. For an example, check out Figure 5-4 (the Open and Save pop-up menus both read *Automatic*).

Have you figured out yet what radio buttons and pop-up menus have in common? *Hint:* They both enable you to make a single selection from a group of options.

✔ **Text entry boxes:** In text entry boxes (sometimes called *fields*), you type in text (including numbers) from the keyboard. When a text entry box (or boxes) appears with a selected radio button, only when that radio button is selected can you make an entry. Take a look at Figure 5-4. The Window Width and Window Height options are both text entry boxes.

✔ **Check boxes:** The last dealie-bopper that you see frequently is the check box. You use check boxes to choose items that are not mutually exclusive. In a group of check boxes, you can select or deselect each one individually. Check boxes are selected when they contain a check mark, and they are deselected when they're empty. Unlike radio buttons, which force you to choose one and only one item, check boxes are independent. Each one can be either selected or deselected. In Figure 5-4, you can see several check boxes, four of which are selected and five of which are not.

Radio button — Text entry box   Pop-up menu

Figure 5-4:
This window offers most dealie-boppers that you're ever likely to encounter.

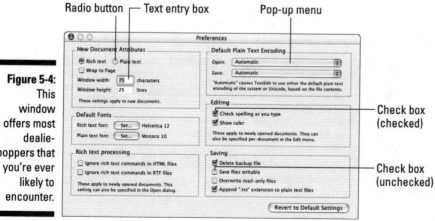

Check box (checked)

Check box (unchecked)

Working with Windows

In this section, I give you a closer look at windows themselves: how you move them, size them, and use them. And although Mac OS X windows are similar to the windows that you've used in other versions of Mac OS, you'll find some new wrinkles.

If you're relatively new to the Mac, you may want to read this section while sitting at your computer, trying the techniques as you read them. You may find it easier to remember something that you read if actually do it. If you've been using your Mac for a while, you probably figured out how windows work by now.

Resizing windows

If you want to see more (or less) of what's in a window, use the sizer in the extreme lower-right corner of a window. (Refer to Figure 5-1 to see the sizer; it has little diagonal grippy lines on it.) Just drag the sizer downward and to the right to make a window larger. Or drag it upward and to the left to make a window smaller. In other words, after you grab the sizer, you can make a window whatever size you like.

Moving windows

To move a window, click anywhere in a window's title bar and drag the window to wherever you want it. The window moves wherever you move the mouse, stopping dead in its tracks when you release the mouse button.

Hunting the seldom-seen Close All command

If you're like me, by the end of the day your Desktop is scattered with open windows — sometimes a dozen or more. Wouldn't you love to be able to close them all at once with a single Close All command? But you don't see a Close All command in any of the menus, do you?

Well, even though Apple (in its infinite wisdom) has hidden this useful command from mere mortals, you can make it come out and play by doing one of the following:

- ✔ Hold down the Option key and click any window's red gumdrop Close button.

- ✔ Hold down the Option key and choose File⇨Close All. (The Close All command usually reads Close Window but becomes Close All when you hold down the Option key. Release the Option key, and it changes back to Close Window.)

- ✔ Press ⌘+Option+W.

Shutting yo' windows

Now that I've gone on and on about windows, maybe I should tell you how to close them. You can close an active window in one of three ways (the last two require the window to be active, by the way):

  ✔ **Click the red Close button in the upper-left corner of the title bar.**

  ✔ **Choose File➪Close Window from the Finder menu.**

  ✔ **Press ⌘+W.**

Hold down Option (and occasionally Control, ⌘, or come combination of the three) and pull down menus in both the Finder and in your favorite application programs. It doesn't always reveal anything interesting in the menu, but sometimes it does. Read through Chapter 6 to discover all things menu!

Chapter 6

A Bevy of Delectable Menus

*L*ike icons and windows, menus are a quintessential part of the Macintosh experience. In this chapter, I start with a few menu basics and then move on to the Finder menus. I try to provide an appropriate level of detail based on the menu item's importance; and in many cases, I direct you to another part of the book where that feature is discussed in greater detail.

Menu Basics

Mac menus are often referred to as *pull-down menus*. To check out the Mac OS X menus, click the Finder button in the Dock to activate the Finder and then look at the top of your screen. From left to right you see the Apple menu, the Finder menu, and six other menus that I discuss throughout this chapter. To use an OS X menu, you click its name to make the menu appear and then pull (drag) down to select a menu item. Piece of cake!

Ever since Mac OS 8, menus stay down after you click their names. They stay down until you either select an item or click outside the menu's boundaries. They also close if you click and hold on a menu for too long — about 15 seconds — without doing anything. Nice touch, eh?

Musical menus

Before you start working with OS X menus, you really, really should know this about menus in general: *They can change unexpectedly.* Why? Well, the menus that you see in the menu bar at the top of the screen always reflect the program that's active at the time. When you switch from the Finder to a program — or from one program to another program — the menus change immediately to match whatever you switched to.

For example, when the Finder is active, the menu bar looks like Figure 6-1. But if you launch TextEdit, the menu bar changes to what you see in Figure 6-2.

An easy way to tell which program is active is to look at the left-most menu with a name (the one just to the right of the Apple menu). When you're in the Finder, of course, that menu reads *Finder*. But if you switch to another program (by clicking its icon on the Dock or by clicking any window associated with the program) or launch a new program, that menu changes to the name of the active program.

Figure 6-1: The Finder menu bar with a typical Mac OS X menu pulled down.

Figure 6-2: Menu bars change to what is active.

I cover only the menus that are part of OS X here in this chapter. The menus that come with other programs are beyond the purview of this book — this chapter alone would be a set of encyclopedias if I tried to cover them all, and there would always be some new program or version that wasn't covered!

Contextual menus: They're sooo sensitive

Contextual menus are a neat feature that Apple introduced in Mac OS 8. A *contextual menu* lists commands that apply to the item that your cursor is over. Contextual menus appear in windows, on icons, and most places on the Desktop when you hold down the Control key and click — what we Mac users like to call a *Control+click*. (Figure 6-3 shows the contextual menu that appears when you Control+click a document icon.)

Figure 6-3:
Only relevant items appear in a contextual menu.

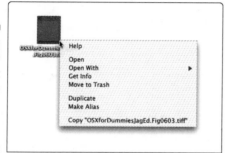

Actions appear in contextual menus only if they make sense for the item that you Control+click. For example, if you Control+click inside a window but not on any icon, the contextual menu contains actions that you perform on a window. By contrast, if you Control+click an icon inside a window, you see a contextual menu for that icon. So, you see, a contextual menu for a document differs from the contextual menu for a window. That's why they call 'em *contextual!*

Don't believe me? Control+click the Desktop (that is, click somewhere that's not in any window and not on any icon), and you'll see a contextual menu appear, bearing different commands.

Contextual menus are also available in many applications. Open your favorite app and try Control+clicking to find out whether they're there. In most cases, using a contextual menu is a quick way to avoid going to the menu bar to choose a command. In some programs, such as AppleWorks 6, contextual menus are the only way to access certain commands.

Get in the habit of Control+clicking items. Before you know it, using contextual menus will become second nature to you.

Disabled options

Menu items that appear in black on a menu are currently available. Menu items not currently available are grayed out, meaning that they're disabled. You can't select a disabled menu item.

In Figure 6-4, the File menu is pulled down while nothing is selected in the Finder; this is why many of the menu items are disabled (in gray). These items are disabled because an item (such as a window or icon) must be selected in order for you to use one of these menu items. For example, the Show Original command is grayed out because it works only if the selected item is an alias.

File	
New Finder Window	⌘N
New Folder	⇧⌘N
Open	⌘O
Open With	▶
Close Window	⌘W
Get Info	⌘I
Duplicate	⌘D
Make Alias	⌘L
Show Original	⌘R
Add to Favorites	⌘T
Move to Trash	⌘⌫
Eject	⌘E
Burn Disc...	
Find...	⌘F

Figure 6-4: Disabled menu items are grayed out.

Submenus

Some menu items have more menus attached to them, and these are called submenus. A *submenu* is just that: a menu under a menu item. You can tell whether a menu item has a submenu if it has a black triangle located to the right of its name.

To use a submenu, click a menu name once to drop down the menu and then slide your cursor down to any item with a black triangle. When the item is highlighted, move your mouse to the right just slightly. The submenu should pop out of the original menu's item. Refer to Figure 6-1 to see the Recent Folders submenu open underneath the Go menu. If you were to release the mouse button while doing exactly what is pictured, a Finder window would pop open, showing you a Finder window displaying your Utilities folder.

The pop-up menus that you see when you click-and-hold or Control+click a Dock icon can also have submenus. In fact, if you were to put your home folder in the Dock, you could access any file in it or its subfolders via the menu and its submenus.

Submenus used to be called *hierarchical* menus, but that's just a mouthful. For a while, people liked to call them *pull-right* menus. But these days, just about everyone refers to them as submenus. If you ever hear folks talk about hierarchical menus or pull-rights, they're talking about submenus.

Keyboard shortcut commands

Most menu items, or at least the most common ones, have *keyboard shortcuts* to help you quickly navigate your Mac without having to haggle so much with the mouse. Using these key combinations activates menu items without using the mouse or by pressing the Command (⌘) key and then pressing another key (or keys) without releasing the ⌘ key. Memorize the shortcuts that you use often.

Some people refer to the Command key as the Apple key. That's because on most keyboards, that key has both the pretzel-looking Command key symbol (⌘) *and* an Apple logo (🍎) on it. To avoid confusion, I'll stick with Command key. Apple's Help system usually refers to it as the Apple key.

Here are four things that you need to know to properly grasp keyboard shortcuts:

✔ **Keyboard shortcuts are shown in menus.** Refer to Figure 6-4 to see that the keyboard shortcut for the Find command appears on the menu after the word Find: ⌘+F. Any menu item with one of these pretzel-symbol-letter combinations after its name can be executed with that keyboard shortcut. Just press the ⌘ key and the letter shown in the menu — *N* for New Finder Window, *F* for Find, and so on — and the appropriate command executes.

✔ **Capital letters don't mean that you have to press Shift as part of the shortcut.** Although the letters next to the ⌘ symbol in the Finder menus are indeed capital letters, you don't have to press the Shift key to use the keyboard shortcut. For example, if you see ⌘+P, just hold down the ⌘ key and then press **P**. Some programs have keyboard combinations that require the use of ⌘+Shift, but these programs let you know by calling the key combination something like ⌘+Shift+S or ⌘+Shift+O. Other programs indicate when you need to use the Shift key with a little up-facing arrow in the shortcut, like the one next to the New Folder command in Figure 6-4.

Of course, there's an exception to every rule, and one of them is Mac Help; you'll get that whole sordid story in a few pages.

✔ **Recognize the funky looking Option key symbol.** You'll see one other symbol sometimes used in keyboard shortcuts: It represents the Option key (sometimes abbreviated in keyboard shortcuts as *Opt*). Check it out next to the Hide Others command, shown in Figure 6-5.

What this freakish symbol means in the Computer menu item (Hide Others in Figure 6-5) is that if you press both the ⌘ and Option keys and *then* press the H key, all applications other than the Finder will be hidden.

Figure 6-5:
Some
keyboard
shortcuts
use the
Option key.

The Option key

✔ **Okay, there was more than one more symbol.** In some programs, developers may even include a caret (an up-pointing arrowhead, ^) as an abbreviation for the Control key.

✔ **If it makes sense, it's probably a shortcut.** Most keyboard shortcuts have a mnemonic relationship to their names. For example, here are some of the more basic keyboard shortcuts:

Command	Mnemonic Keyboard Shortcut
New Finder Window	⌘+N
New Folder	⌘+Shift+N
Open	⌘+O

Command	Mnemonic Keyboard Shortcut
Get Info	⌘+I
Duplicate	⌘+D

It's elliptical

Another feature of Mac menus is the ellipsis after some menu item names. *Ellipses,* in case your English teacher forgot to mention them, are the three little dots (…) that appear in place of missing text. They basically mean that you can reach more options by clicking the menu item.

When you see an ellipsis after a menu item, choosing that item displays a dialog or sheet (I discuss dialogs in Chapter 5 and sheets in Chapter 8) in which you can make further choices. Refer to Figure 6-5 to see that the Preferences command has an ellipsis. If you choose Preferences, the System Preferences window opens.

Choosing a menu item with an ellipsis never actually makes anything happen other than to open a dialog or sheet; from there, you make further choices and then click a button to make things happen.

Underneath the Apple Menu Tree

The Macintosh interface has sported an *Apple* () *menu* since time immemorial (well, the 1980s anyway). So when the Mac OS X Public Beta appeared without one, Mac users everywhere crawled out of the woodwork to express their outrage. The bruised Apple ultimately relented, and now OS X has an  menu, just like every version of Mac OS before it. The following sections discuss the differences between the old  menu and the new and also take you through the main  menu items.

What's in . . . and what's out

The OS X  menu isn't like any  menu before it, though. The biggest differences between it and the OS 9  menu are

> ✔ **The  in the Apple menu is now blue (the default).** Or gray (if you've selected the Graphite appearance in the General System Preference pane); in either case, it's no longer rainbow striped.

✔ **It's not customizable anymore.** You used to be able to add items —
applications, folders, documents, aliases, or whatever your heart
desired — to your menu (desk accessories only before System 7).
You can't do that in the OS X menu. What you see on the OS X
menu is what you get. But it's not a big issue because the OS X Dock
is customizable and does let you add items — applications, folders,
documents, aliases, or whatever your heart desires. (I discuss the Dock
in Chapter 3.)

Tiptoeing through the Apple menu items

You won't find any programs available from the new OS X menu — no
calculator, no scrapbook, no programs at all (other than System Preferences
and the ones in your Recent Items submenu). Instead, the menu provides a
set of useful commands, described here, that are always available no matter
what program is active.

From top to bottom, the Apple menu's items are

✔ **About This Mac:** Choose this item to see what version of Mac OS X
you're running and how much memory your Mac has.

✔ **Get Mac OS X Software:** This launches your Web browser and takes you
to the Apple Web site.

✔ **System Preferences:** Choose this item to open the System Preferences
window (which I discuss in great detail in Chapter 15).

✔ **Dock (submenu):** This lets you mess with, well, the Dock! Scour
Chapter 3 for more info on the Dock.

✔ **Location (submenu):** This enables you to quickly switch network
configurations. I describe locations and network configurations in
Chapter 11.

✔ **Recent Items (submenu):** Your Mac keeps track of the applications and
documents that you've recently used. Expand this menu item to choose
one of them. In versions 10.1 and later, you can set the maximum
number of applications and documents that Recent Items tracks in your
General System Preferences.

✔ **Force Quit:** When a program misbehaves — crashes, freezes, or otherwise
becomes recalcitrant — this is the command for you. Choosing this
brings up the Force Quit Applications dialog from which you choose the
application that you want to quit, as shown in Figure 6-6.

This command is so handy that it has a semi-secret keyboard shortcut:
⌘+Option+Esc. It's not on the menu, although it is displayed on the
Force Quit Applications window (lower-left of Figure 6-6).

Unlike in earlier versions of Mac OS, you don't need to reboot to continue working after you force a program to quit. If a program ever freaks out on you, Force Quit can almost certainly put it out of its misery and allow you to continue using your Mac.

✔ **Sleep:** This puts your Mac into its low-powered sleep mode. I talk more about sleep in Chapter 15. (Yawn!)

✔ **Restart:** Choose this to reboot your Mac, which is essentially the same as shutting down your machine and then turning it back on.

✔ **Shut Down:** Use this to turn off your Mac safely.

✔ **Log Out:** Because OS X is a multi-user operating system, you can have multiple users at one Mac. This command enables you to switch users without restarting or shutting down.

Logging out means that the current user, as identified by username and password, is leaving the scene. The next person to use the Mac (even if it's you) has to enter a username and password to regain entry. All this sharing stuff can be found in Chapter 16.

Figure 6-6:
Use Force
Quit
Applications
to exit a
badly
behaved
program.

Location, location, location

I'm getting a little bit ahead of myself, but because you're probably wondering, a *location* reflects all the settings made in the Network System Preferences pane. They're mostly useful to PowerBook users, who often have different network configurations (locations) for different places where they may need to use their Mac, such as the office (to connect to an Ethernet network), home (to connect to a Digital Subscriber Line [DSL] or cable connection), and out of town (to connect using an internal modem). Each configuration (office, home, and out of town) is a location, and you can switch from one location to another quickly and painlessly by using this menu item. Got it? If not, you will after you read Chapter 11.

Spring-loaded folders have sprung (again)

Spring-loaded folders and windows is a semi-new feature. (This feature *was* in OS 9, then it *wasn't* in OS X 10.0 or 10.1, and now it's back in Mac OS X version 10.2 Jaguar.) This lets you drag items onto closed folders or disks and have them spring open. It's harder to describe than to do, so try it a few times. Open Finder Preferences, mark the Spring-loaded Folders and Windows check box, and then follow these steps:

1. Select any icon (except a disk icon).

2. Drag it onto a folder or disk icon (but don't release the mouse button).

3. Press the spacebar (or just wait a few seconds depending on where you've set the Delay slider).

The window of the folder or disk that you dragged onto springs open. If that's the original icon's final destination, release the mouse button now. Or, if you want to drill down deeper in the folder hierarchy, don't release the mouse button and drag the icon onto any folder or disk icon. *Its* window will spring open. And so on.

Spring-loaded folders clean up after themselves, too. When you release the mouse button, regardless of how many windows you've traversed, all windows except the original (if there was one; if you dragged an icon from the Desktop, there wouldn't be) and the destination folder spring shut again, leaving your screen clean and uncluttered. Spring-loaded folders work in all three Finder window views and also with folder or disk icons in the toolbar. Neat! If you're like me, you'll end up using spring-loaded folders a lot.

Your Constant Companion: The Application Menu

The very first menu on the Mac OS X menu bar is the *Application menu* — so named because it includes commands that you use to control the way lots of things work in the current application. But it's really much more than a command center for the application.

When you have an application open, the Application menu name changes to the name of that application, and the commands available change — but just a little bit. (I discuss this unusual phenomenon in the section "Musical menus" earlier in this chapter.) What makes this cool is that you have access to some standard Application menu items even when you're running an application such as AppleWorks or Internet Explorer. I have more to say about that as I work my way through the Application menu.

The following list overviews the main items in the Application menu, which is called the Finder menu when the Finder is the active application. It's not too long, but it's packed with useful goodies, such as

✔ **About The Finder:** Choose this to find out which version of the Finder is running on your Mac.

Okay, so this menu item isn't particularly useful, or at least not for very long. But when a different application is running, the About The Finder item becomes About *application_name* and usually gives information about the program's version number, the developers (the company and the people), and any other tidbits that those developers decide to throw in. Sometimes these tidbits are useful.

If you click the version number in this window, it changes to the build number (Apple's internal tracking number for versions). Click the build number in this window, and it changes to the serial number of your Mac. Finally, click the serial number of your Mac in this window, and it changes to the version number again. This interesting effect is shown in Figure 6-7. Any or all of this information may come in handy for troubleshooting, repair, upgrades, or who knows what else. At least now you know where to find it.

Figure 6-7:
Click three times on the version number to see this.

✔ **Preferences:** Use choices here to control how the Desktop looks and acts. Choosing Preference opens the Finder Preferences window (see Figure 6-8).

- Select the Show These Items on the Desktop check boxes to choose whether hard drives, CDs, DVDs, and other types of disks appear on the Desktop. OS X selects these options by default (which mimics earlier versions of Mac OS). But if you don't want disk icons cluttering your beautiful Desktop, you have the option of deselecting (clearing) them. If they're deselected, you can still work with CDs, DVDs, and other types of disks. You just have to open a Finder window and click the Computer button.

- You can also choose whether opening a new Finder window displays your Home directory or the Computer window. (Computer is the default.)

- The Always Open Folders in a New Window check box makes OS X work the same way as Mac OS 9.

Try it the OS X way — with windows opening "in place" so that you avoid window clutter. Press ⌘ before double-clicking to force a folder to open in a new window. I've learned to love this new way, although I hated it at first. Now, between this feature and the Column view, I find that I rarely need more than two or three windows onscreen, and I get by most of the time with just a single window in Column view.

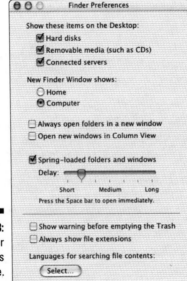

Figure 6-8:
Set Finder preferences here.

- Selecting the Open New Windows in Column View check box tells the Finder that you want each window to be in Column view when you double-click to open it. The default behavior is to use whichever view type the folder was last displaying.

- The Show Warning before Emptying the Trash check box (on by default) allows you to turn off the nagging dialog telling you how many items are in the Trash and asking whether you really want to delete them.

- Finally, selecting the Always Show File Extensions check box tells the Finder to display the little three- or four-character filename suffixes (like `.doc` in `summary.doc`) that make your Mac's file lists look more like those of a Windows user. The Finder hides those from you by default, but if you want to be able to search for files by their extension (Using File⇨Find or ⌘+F), you need to turn this on.

✔ **Empty Trash:** Deletes all items in the Trash from your hard drive — period. I talk about the Trash in Chapter 3 and again in Chapter 4.

I've said it before and I'll say it again: Use this command with a modicum of caution. After a file is trashed and the Trash is emptied, it's gone. (Okay, maybe Norton Utilities can bring it back, but don't bet the farm on it.)

✔ **Services:** One of the really cool features of OS X applications is the accessibility of Services. You can select an e-mail address and create a mail message addressed to that individual, spell-check a document or selection even if the program didn't come with a spell-checker, or calculate exchange rates on currency. Unfortunately, most Carbon-ized applications (including the Finder) don't support Services yet.

Carbon is an Apple API (Application Program Interface): programming technology that allows software developers to make applications originally created for OS 9 run in OS X with a minimum of modification. Some but not all Carbon applications run under both OS 9 and OS X.

Programs written exclusively for OS X that use Apple's latest generation of development tools are called Cocoa applications. Cocoa apps support OS X features such as Services automatically.

From your perspective, there's little or no difference between Carbon and Cocoa apps. Some Carbon apps are awesome; some Cocoa programs stink. It's not about the underlying development environment or APIs used.

But I digress yet again. Cocoa and Carbon are far beyond the scope of this book, but at least I snuck in the extremely abridged version.

✔ **Hide Finder (⌘+H):** Use this command when you've got Finder windows open and they're distracting you. Choosing it makes the Finder inactive (another currently running program becomes active) and hides any open Finder windows. To make the Finder visible again, either choose Show All from the Finder menu (or whatever it's called in the active application — the command should still be there) or click the Finder button on the Dock.

The advantage to hiding the Finder — rather than closing or minimizing all your windows to get a clean screen — is that you don't have to open them all again when you're ready to get the windows back. Instead, just choose Show All or click the Finder button in the Dock.

✔ **Hide Others (⌘+Option+H):** This command hides all windows associated with all running programs except the active program. (This is the Finder in Figure 6-5, but hide/show command items appear in most application's Application menus.) It's also good for hiding distractions so that you can focus on one thing.

✔ **Show All:** Use this as the antidote to both hide commands. Choose this, and nothing is hidden anymore.

You used to find these show and hide commands in the Application menu (the menu on the right side of the menu bar that displays the icon of the active application) of older versions of Mac OS. If you're using the Classic environment or a Classic application (which I discuss in Chapter 14), that's where you'll still find them.

File Management and More: Meet the File Menu

The File menu contains many commands that you use to manipulate your files and folders. I discuss file management in Chapter 10, but here I give you the lowdown on the actual Finder File menu itself.

You'll use these commands frequently, so it would behoove you to memorize their keyboard shortcuts.

✔ **New Finder Window (⌘+N):** Opens a new Finder window. I discuss the Finder window in Chapter 7 and 8 (among other places, such as Chapters 3 and 4).

✔ **New Folder (⌘+Shift+N):** Creates a new, untitled folder in the active window. If no window is active, it creates a new folder on the Desktop.

In every version of Mac OS since the beginning of time, the New Folder keyboard shortcut has been ⌘+N — just like the New Document keyboard shortcut in most applications is also ⌘+N. When creating a shortcut for the New Finder Window command in OS X, Apple decided to add the Shift key to the New Folder keyboard shortcut. I admit that this decision kind of makes sense: Opening a new Finder window and opening a new document both create a new window, whereas creating a new folder simply displays a new icon. But if you're a veteran Mac user, you better get used to adding the Shift key to ⌘+N to create a folder or add the New Folder button to your Finder toolbar. (I discuss customizing the Finder toolbar in Chapter 7.)

✔ **Open (⌘+O):** Opens the selected item, be it icon, window, or folder.

✔ **Open With:** Opens the selected document with an application other than that document's default application. For example, in Figure 6-9, I'm about to open a graphic file. The default application for this document happens to be the Apple Preview app.

Figure 6-9:
Open a document with an application other than its default.

If I double-click this document, it would open in Preview. But that's not what I want. I want it to open it in a graphics editor program such as GraphicConverter because Preview is for displaying graphics, not editing them. This menu item tells the Finder to do just that.

This command is inactive if the selected icon isn't a document.

Using this menu item from the Contextual menu (Control+click the document icon) is often easier than it is to reach all the way up to the menu bar to invoke it, as shown in Figure 6-10.

If you hold down the Option key before you click the File menu, the Open With command changes to Always Open With, as shown in Figure 6-11, which enables you to change the default application for this document permanently.

This Option key trick also works on the contextual menu version of this command!

Figure 6-10:
I prefer the contextual version of this particular menu item.

Figure 6-11:
Hold down
the Option
key before
you pull
down the
File menu to
change
Open With
to Always
Open With.

✓ **Close Window (⌘+W):** Closes the active window. If no windows are open or if none are selected, the Close Window command is grayed out and can't be chosen.

Most menu commands are intuitive. So how did Apple come up with ⌘+W as a shortcut for Close Window? You think Apple would assign the letter *C*, for *Close*. However, ⌘+C is the shortcut for Copy.

If you press the Option key, the Close Window command changes to Close All. This very useful command enables you to close all open Finder windows. But it only shows up if you press the Option key; otherwise, it remains hidden.

✓ **Get Info (⌘+I):** Opens an Info window for the selected icon. (I tell you all about the Info window in Chapter 4.)

If you press the Option key, the Get Info command changes to Show Inspector. The Inspector window is identical to a Get Info window, but it displays information for whatever icon is currently selected in the Finder. If you click a different icon, the Inspector window updates to show you information about that item.

A Get Info window, on the other hand, is static. Each one is connected to one item.

It's good to have choices; sometimes one is more convenient to use for a particular task than the other, and sometimes you use them both.

✓ **Duplicate (⌘+D):** Makes a copy of the selected icon, adds the word *copy* to its name, and then places the copy in the same window as the original icon. You can use the Duplicate command on any icon except a disk icon.

You can't duplicate an entire disk onto itself. But you can copy an entire disk (call it Disk 1) to any other disk (call it Disk 2). Just drag the Disk 1 onto Disk 2's icon. The contents of Disk 1 will be copied to Disk 2 and will appear in a folder named Disk 1.

✓ **Make Alias (⌘+L):** Creates an alias for the selected icon in the same folder as the selected icon (or on the Desktop if the selected icon is on the Desktop). I cover aliases in detail in Chapter 4.

- **Show Original (⌘+R):** Switches to the folder that contains the parent icon. Suppose that you make and use an alias, you put it on your Desktop or in your Favorites folder, and everything's peachy. But now you want to delete or move the original file or folder as part of a little spring-cleaning. Where is that original? You've been using the alias so long that you can't remember. To find it, click the alias and then choose File⇨Show Original. Quick as a flash, the Finder window switches to the folder that contains the parent icon. You can now delete, copy, move, or change the parent icon.

- **Add to Favorites (⌘+T):** Creates an alias of the selected item and puts it in the Favorites folder. You can now reach the item by clicking the Favorites button on the Finder window toolbar. And remember, the Favorites folder is easily available from both Open and Save sheets (see Chapter 8), thus making it even more useful.

- **Move to Trash (⌘+Delete):** Moves the selected icon to the Trash.

   The icon (that is, the item that the icon represents) that you move to the Trash is not deleted from your hard drive until you choose the Empty Trash command from the Finder menu, the Trash pop-up menu, or the contextual menu.

- **Eject (⌘+E):** Ejects the selected removable disk (such as a CD, DVD, floppy, or Zip).

- **Burn Disc:** Burns data to a CD or DVD. If you have a compatible CD-RW or DVD-R drive and you've prepared the media, choosing this command tells the Finder to finish the job and actually burn the data to the CD or DVD. I cover burning CDs and DVDs in Chapter 9.

- **Find (⌘+F):** Finds a file or folder on your hard drive. Use the File⇨Find command when you can't remember where you put it in a file or folder. This command is a Mac OS X feature that really kicks some butt. I discuss finding files in detail in Chapter 12.

The Edit Menu (Which Shoulda Been Called the Clipboard Menu)

In contrast to the File menu, which has commands that mostly deal with file management and are exclusive to the Finder window, the Edit menu's commands and functions are available in almost every Macintosh program ever made.

Because almost every program has an Edit menu and because almost every program uses the same keyboard shortcuts on its Edit menu, it behooves you to know the Edit menu keyboard shortcuts by heart, even if you remember no others.

Personally, I think that the Edit menu should have been called the Clipboard menu because most of its commands deal with the Macintosh Clipboard. Well, I used to think that until Mac OS X version 10.1 came out. With 10.1, Apple included one of the few things that people really like about Windows. You can now use Copy and Paste commands in the Finder in order to copy files from one directory to another.

Comprehending the Clipboard

The *Clipboard* is a holding area for the last thing that you cut or copied. That copied item can be text, a picture, a portion of a picture, an object in a drawing program, a column of numbers in a spreadsheet, or just about anything that can be selected. In other words, the Clipboard is the Mac's temporary storage area.

The Clipboard commands in the Edit menu are enabled only when they can actually be used. If the currently selected item can be cut or copied, the Cut and Copy commands in the Edit menu are enabled. If the selected item can't be cut or copied, the commands are unavailable and are dimmed (gray). And when nothing is selected, the Cut, Copy, Paste, and Clear commands are also dimmed.

Copying or cutting to the Clipboard

To cut or copy something to the Clipboard, select the item and then choose Cut or Copy from the Edit menu or use the keyboard shortcuts ⌘+X (cut) or ⌘+C (copy). Choosing Cut *deletes* the selected item and puts it on the Clipboard; choosing Copy *copies* the selected item to the clipboard but does not delete the selected item.

As a storage area, the Clipboard's contents are temporary. *Very* temporary. When you cut or copy an item, that item remains on the Clipboard only until you cut or copy something else. When you do cut or copy something else, the new item replaces the Clipboard's contents and in turn remains on the Clipboard until you cut or copy something else. And so it goes.

Of course, whatever's on the Clipboard heads straight for oblivion if you crash, lose power, log out, or shut your Mac down, so don't count on it too heavily.

Pasting from the Clipboard

To place the item that's on the Clipboard, click where you want the item to go and then paste what you've copied or cut (choose Edit⇨Paste or use the keyboard shortcut ⌘+V). Pasting does *not* remove the item from the Clipboard; the item remains there until you cut or copy another item.

Pasting doesn't purge the contents of the Clipboard. In fact, an item stays on the Clipboard until you cut, copy, clear, crash (these used to be called the four Cs of Macintosh computing, but Mac OS X almost never crashes), restart, shut down, or log out. This means that you can paste the same item over and over and over again, which can come in pretty handy at times.

Almost all programs have an Edit menu and use the Macintosh Clipboard, which means that you can usually cut or copy something in a document in one program and paste it into a document from another program. Usually.

Checking out the main Edit menu items

The previous sections give you probably 75 percent of what you need to know about the Edit menu. Still, because I get paid to be thorough and because the Finder's Edit menu has a few commands that aren't Clipboard-related, in this section, I go through the Edit menu's commands one by one.

- ✔ **Undo/Redo (⌘+Z):** This command undoes the last thing you did. For example, if you change the name of a folder and then choose this command, the name of the folder resorts back to what it was before you changed it.

  The Undo command toggles (that is, switches back and forth) between the new and old states as long as you don't do anything else. For example, if you rename a file from _Do Me_ to _Undo Me_ and then choose Edit➪Undo, the file name reverts to _Do Me_. If you pull down the Edit menu now, the Undo command reads Redo instead of Undo. Select Redo, and the name of the file changes back to _Undo Me._ You can continue to Undo and Redo until you click somewhere else.

  Don't forget about this command because it can be a lifesaver. Almost every program has an Undo command. Now for the bad news: The Undo command is ephemeral, like the Clipboard: You can only use Undo to reverse your last action. As soon as you do something else — even just clicking a lousy icon — you lose the ability to undo the original action. At least, this is true in the Finder. Some programs, such as Microsoft Word, BBEdit, and Adobe Illustrator, allow multiple Undo's.

  Here's a cool feature — the Undo command works with certain actions that it never worked with before, such as moving icons. That's way cool because sometimes you drag an icon somewhere and drop it accidentally. Finding it is a hassle. Now you can just undo the move. Kewl beans.

  As you find out more about your Mac and OS X, you'll no doubt discover actions that you can't undo. Still, Undo is a great command when available, and I urge you to get in the habit of trying it often.

- ✔ **Cut (⌘+X):** This command removes the selected item and places it on the Clipboard. You can then paste the item from the Clipboard to another document, text box, or other valid destination. For more info on Cut and the Clipboard, see the earlier section "Copying or cutting to the Clipboard."

✔ **Copy (⌘+C):** This command makes a copy of a selected item and places it on the Clipboard. However, the original is not removed like it is when you cut something. For more info on Copy and the Clipboard, see the earlier section "Copying or cutting to the Clipboard."

✔ **Paste (⌘+V):** This command places the contents of the Clipboard at the place you last clicked. For more info on Paste and the Clipboard, see the earlier section "Pasting from the Clipboard."

✔ **Select All (⌘+A):** This command selects all icons in the active window. Or, if no window is active, using Select All selects every icon on the Desktop. If a window is active, choosing Select All selects every icon in the window, regardless of whether you can see them onscreen.

The Select All command has nothing whatsoever to do with the Clipboard, so why is it on the Edit menu? Is it because selecting is an editing operation and that's why the menu is called Edit? Who knows? The Powers That Be at Apple put it there once upon a time, and there it remains.

✔ **Show Clipboard:** This command summons the Clipboard window, which lists the type of item (such as text, picture, or sound) on the Clipboard and a message letting you know whether the item on the Clipboard can be displayed.

A View from a Window: The View Menu

The View menu controls what the icons and windows look like, how icons and windows are arranged and sorted, and the look of your windows. The View menu affects the icons in the active window; if no window is active, it affects the icons on the Desktop.

The following list gives you a brief description of each of the menu items on the View menu:

✔ **As Icons:** Using Icon view is the traditional Macintosh view — the one most closely associated with the Macintosh experience. In my humble opinion, however, this view is one of the two least useful views because those big horse-y icons take up far too much valuable screen real estate. I discuss Icon view in Chapter 7.

✔ **As List:** In List view, you can copy or move items from different folders with a single motion without opening multiple windows. In either Icon view or Columns view, on the other hand, moving files from two or more different folders requires opening several windows and two separate drags or the use of Copy and Paste introduced in version 10.1.

- **As Columns:** This changes the active window to Columns view. Choosing Columns view is a new way (added in Mac OS X) to view your files in a Finder window where the folders on your computer are displayed in a column at the left of the Finder window and the contents of those folders are displayed in a larger window pane on the right. See Chapter 7 for more info on Columns view.

- **Clean Up:** Choose this to align icons to an invisible grid; you use it to keep your windows and Desktop neat and tidy. (If you like this invisible grid, don't forget that you can turn it on or off for the Desktop and individual windows by using View Options.) Clean Up is available only in Icon view or when no windows are active. If no windows are active, the command instead cleans up your Desktop. (To deactivate all open windows, just click anywhere on the Desktop.)

If you're like me, you've taken great pains to place icons carefully in specific places on your Desktop. Cleaning up your Desktop destroys all your beautiful work and moves all your perfectly arranged icons. And alas, cleaning up your Desktop is not undo-able.

- **Arrange:** This rearranges your icons in your choice of five different ways: alphabetical order (by Name); modification date (by Date Modified); creation date (by Date Created); Size; or Kind. Like Clean Up, it's only available for windows viewed as icons, and it's not undo-able.

- **Hide/Show Toolbar (⌘+B):** This shows or hides the buttons on the toolbar of the active window. Suppose that you want to see more files and fewer buttons. Because the buttons on this toolbar are also available from the Go menu (see the next section "Going Places"), you're safe in hiding them. Just choose Hide Toolbar to make the toolbar go away or Show Toolbar to bring it back. (As I detail in Chapter 5, the gray oval button in the upper-right corner of every Finder window does the same thing.)

When the toolbar is hidden, opening a folder opens a *new* Finder window rather than reusing the current one (which is what happens when the toolbar is showing unless you've changed this preference in Finder Preferences). Go to Chapter 7 for more about the toolbar in Finder windows.

- **Customize Toolbar:** This one is way cool — use it to design your own Finder window toolbar. Find out more about this nifty feature in Chapter 7.

- **Hide/Show Status Bar:** This shows or hides the status bar for Finder windows. The status bar tells you how many items are in each window, how much space is available on the hard drive containing this window, and what permissions you have for this window's contents. (Read about permissions in Chapter 16.)

- **Show View Options (⌘+J):** Here's where you can soup up the way any (or all) of your windows looks and behaves. You can do this either globally (so that all windows use the same view when opened) or on a window-by-window basis. I discuss Show View Options more in Chapter 7.

Going Places

The Go menu is chock full of shortcuts. The items on this menu take you to places on your Mac — many of the same places that you can go with the Finder window toolbar — and a few other places.

Checking out Go menu items

The following list gives you a brief look at the items on the Go menu.

See the next section for info on some menu items that aren't listed here, such as Computer, Home, iDisk, and Favorites.

✔ **Back (⌘+[):** Use this menu option to return to the last Finder window that you had open. It's equivalent to the Back button in the Finder toolbar, in case you have the toolbar hidden.

Think of this command as a breadcrumb trail that moves backward through every folder you open. For example, suppose that you open seven folders to get to the destination folder that you desire — call them folders 1, 2, 3, 4, 5, 6, and 7. Each time that you select the Back command, the previous folder appears — 6, 5, 4, 3, 2, and 1.

✔ **Forward (⌘+]):** This is the opposite of using the Back command, moving you forward through every folder you open. Picking up from the previous example, suppose that you're in folder 1. Each time you select the Forward command, you move forward through those folders — 2, 3, 4, 5, 6, and 7.

✔ **Recent Folders:** Use this submenu to quickly go back to a folder that you recently visited. Every time you open a folder, Mac OS X creates an alias to it and stores it in the Recent Folders folder. You can open any of these aliases from the Recent Folders command in the Go menu.

✔ **Go to Folder (⌘+~):** This summons the Go to Folder dialog, as shown in Figure 6-12. Look at your Desktop. Maybe it's cluttered with lots of windows, or maybe it's completely empty. Either way, suppose that you're several clicks away from a folder that you want to open. If you know the path from your hard drive to that folder, you can type the path to the folder that you want in the Go to the Folder text box (separating each folder name with a forward slash [/]) and then click Go to move (relatively) quickly to the folder that you need.

The first character that you type must also be a forward slash, as shown in Figure 6-12, unless you're going to a subdirectory of the current window.

This particular window is clairvoyant, trying to guess which folder you mean by the first letter or two that you type. For example, in Figure 6-12, I typed the letters *U* and *T,* and the window guessed the rest *(ilities)* and filled it in for me. (The letters I *didn't* type are highlighted in Figure 6-12.)

✔ **Connect to Server (⌘+K):** If your Mac is connected to a network or to the Internet, use this command to reach these remote resources.

Figure 6-12:
Go to a
folder by
entering
its path.

Go menu: Keyboard shortcuts at a glance

Note that the Go menu lists keyboard shortcuts for commands that you also find on the Finder window toolbar and your iDisk. I cover these in detail in Chapter 7 as buttons, and the commands do the same things. But if you want to know the commands and keyboard shortcuts to these commands, here ya go:

Command	Keyboard Shortcut
Computer	⌘+Option+C
Home	⌘+Option+H
iDisk	⌘+Option+I
Favorites	⌘+Option+F
Applications	⌘+Option+A

The Go menu also has a Favorites menu item that parallels the use of the Favorites button on the Finder toolbar. The submenu shows your favorite items — the ones that you mark by using the Add to Favorites command from the File menu — but it shows them as a submenu instead of in a window, as the Finder's Favorites button does. It's up to you whether you like the menu better than the button, but I think they both have their moments. And if you prefer the window approach, select the Favorites menu item (⌘+Shift+F) instead of the Favorites submenu.

Window Dressing

Again with the windows! I spend a lot of pages in Chapter 5 giving you the scoop on how to work with windows. The commands on the Window menu provide you with tools that you can use to manage your windows. Here is a brief look at each of the menu items on the Window menu.

✔ **Zoom Window:** This is the same as clicking the green gumdrop on your Finder window.

✔ **Minimize Window (⌘+M):** Use this command to unclutter your Desktop. It's the same as clicking the orange gumdrop.

With a Finder window selected (the command will be unavailable — grayed out — if you don't have an active Finder window), using the Minimize Window command makes a file disappear, as it were: The file or folder is still open, but it's not active, and you don't see it on your screen. You do see, however, an icon representing it in the Dock. (Read all about the Dock in Chapter 3.)

✔ **Bring All to Front:** In previous versions of Mac OS, when you clicked a window belonging to an application, *all* that application's windows came to the front. That is, windows moved within layers and as layers. Under OS X, windows interleave. For example, you could have a Finder window, a Word window, a Photoshop window, a Word window, and another Finder window in a front-to-back order. Choosing Bring All to Front enables you to have all the Finder windows move to the front of those belonging to other applications (while keeping their own relative ordering). This essentially allows an emulation of the layering to which Mac (and Windows) users are accustomed.

If you hold down the Option key when you pull down the Window menu, the Minimize Window changes to the Minimize All Windows, and the Bring All to Front command changes to the useful Arrange in Front, which arranges all your Desktop windows neatly starting in the upper-left corner of the Desktop, as shown in Figure 6-13.

Figure 6-13:
The Arrange in Front command stacks up your windows neatly in the corner.

✔ **Other items:** The remaining items on the Window menu are the names of all currently open Finder windows. Click a window's name to bring it to the front.

  The names of windows that you minimize (the ones with icons appearing on the Dock) remain on the Window menu. You can view the window by choosing its name from the Window menu.

Not Just a Beatles Movie: Help and the Help Menu

One of the best features about all Macs since System 7.x is the system's excellent built-in help. And Mac OS X doesn't cheat you on that legacy: This system has online help in abundance. When you have a question about how to do something, the Mac Help Center is the first place that you should visit (after this book, of course).

The sole item in the Help menu — Mac Help (⌘+?) — opens the Mac Help window, as shown in Figure 6-14.

  ✔ The one exception to the rule that I mention earlier in this chapter — that you don't have to press Shift for capital letters in a keyboard shortcut on a menu — is the keyboard shortcut for Help. This shortcut appears on the Help menu as ⌘+?, and you do have to hold down the Shift key to type the question mark. In fact, if you press ⌘+/ (the Command key and a front slash, which is what you get when you type a lowercase question mark), nothing happens. This is different from earlier versions of Mac OS.

  In other words, the shortcut for Help *should be* ⌘+Shift+/ even though the menu says ⌘+?. Got it? If you're wondering why this is, you'll have to ask Apple. Personally, I think it's lame.

To use Mac Help, simply type a word or phrase into the text field at the top right and then press Enter or Return. In a few seconds, your Mac provides you with one or more articles to read, which (theoretically) are related your question. Usually. For example, if you type **Menus** and press Return, you get 50 different help articles, as shown in Figure 6-15.

Although you don't have to be connected to the Internet to use Mac Help, you do need an Internet connection to get the most out of it. That's because OS X installs only certain help articles on your hard drive. If you ask a question that isn't answered by the help articles on your hard drive, Mac Help will connect to Apple's Web site and download the answer (assuming that you have an active Internet connection). This can sometimes be inconvenient, but it's also smart. This way, the help system can be updated at any time by Apple without requiring any action from you.

Figure 6-14:
Mac Help is
nothing if
not helpful.

Furthermore, after you've asked a question and Mac Help has grabbed the answer from the Apple Web site, the answer remains on your hard drive forever. If you ask for it again (even in a later date), your computer won't have to download it from the Apple Web site again.

Figure 6-15:
You got
questions?
Mac's got
answers.

Part II
Rounding Out Your Basic Training

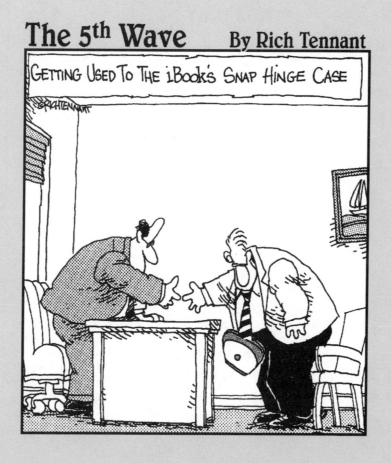

The 5th Wave   By Rich Tennant

GETTING USED TO THE iBook's SNAP HINGE CASE

In this part . . .

Peruse the chapters in this part to discover how to perform important hands-on tasks. But don't get all worked up: This stuff is easy. In fact, I think of this part as "The Lazy Person's How-To Guide."

First I show you each and every OS X menu, in full and loving detail. Then, it's time to learn more about the all-important Finder, followed by a pair of all-important skills: saving and opening files. You'll also discover how to use removable media with your Mac — a good thing to know!

You're gonna love it!

Chapter 7

New-Fangled Finder

*B*elieve it or not, all the stuff on your Mac can fit in one window — the Finder window. In this window, you can double-click your way to your favorite application, your documents, or out onto the Internet. In fact, the Finder is the place you are when you haven't yet gone any place at all. The Finder window appears on the Desktop when you start up your Mac, and it's always available. And if you close the Finder, you can get it back easily. Even if you're an old hand with Mac OS, I show you how to get the most from the OS X Finder in this chapter.

The Finder is, among other things, a window. A very talented window, but a window just the same. For the lowdown on windows in general, see Chapter 5.

Getting to Know the Finder

A Finder window is a handy friend. And the Finder is indeed a window (or multiple windows) in OS X. Use the Finder to navigate through files, folders, and applications on your hard drive or to connect to other Macs and Internet servers — right from your Desktop.

Hey, I know you!

If you're an experienced Mac user, you know the Finder well. Every version of Mac OS before Max OS X has included the Finder, and its appearance is pretty much the same since the Mac was introduced in 1984. What's new in Mac OS X is that you can use a single window in the Finder — instead of multiple windows — to view just about everything stored on all your hard drives and removable disks. Instead of opening a new window for each folder, the Finder can display everything in the same window, shifting your view of items as you click or select them with buttons in the window.

You still have the option to use multiple windows: When you open an application, for example, it has its own menu bar and windows — just as it always has.

One thing that you won't find is the venerable Chooser. It's gone in OS X, replaced by the Print Center application (which you can read about in Chapter 12) and the Connect to Server menu option (covered in Chapter 6).

If you *really* like multiple Finder windows onscreen the way that many long-time Mac users do, you can tell the Mac to give you what you want so that you don't have to haggle with the above methods of opening a new Finder window. Just hold down the ⌘ key when you double-click any folder, and it'll open in a separate window (with the toolbar hidden). Alternatively, you could just set your Finder Preferences to open a new window when you double-click a folder.

Note: If you've hidden the toolbar by clicking a Finder window's Hide/Show Toolbar button, new windows open automatically when you open a folder — you don't have to hold down the ⌘ key at all. It can be disconcerting when the Finder suddenly starts behaving differently. If you want to use the new one-window approach when you've hidden the toolbar or set your Finder Preferences, hold down the Option key when you double-click a folder. It'll open in the same window as if you had never hidden the toolbar.

In Figure 7-1, you can see a typical Finder window, including the following major features:

- ✔ **Toolbar:** From here you can open frequently used items.
- ✔ **Forward and Back buttons:** Click these to go to the last or next folder, respectively, that you viewed in this window. This is sort of like how a Web browser works. However, clicking this Back button takes you back one folder instead of one Web page. Click the Forward button, and you traverse forward in the order that you opened the folders.

    Folders are often referred to as *directories* in OS X parlance.

- ✔ **Icons:** Click these to open your stuff — applications, files, folders, and remote resources, such as Web sites.
- ✔ **Status bar:** Just below the toolbar is the *status bar,* which tells you the amount of space available on this hard drive and the number of items in the current folder.

You can turn the status bar on and off by choosing View➪Show Status Bar (which toggles to View➪Hide Status Bar when the status bar is showing).

✔ **Search field:** You can now search for files in a folder (just enter some descriptive text) right from any window's toolbar. (Its toolbar must be showing, of course.)

✔ **View buttons:** The Finder toolbar also sports three view buttons (located to the right of the Forward and Back buttons). Use these buttons to view the contents of your Finder window by icons, list, or columns. Read about these views in the section "Customizing Finder Windows with Views" later in this chapter.

Figure 7-1:
The contents of the imaginatively named Macintosh HD disk.

Belly Up to the Toolbar

Right below the title bar, you find the Finder window toolbar (refer to Figure 7-1). On it are buttons that take you to all sorts of places, whether you're on your own hard drive, in the wider world of the Internet, or on a network (if you're connected to one). To activate a toolbar button, click it once.

You say you don't want to see the toolbar at the top of the window? Okay! Just choose View➪Hide Toolbar or click the little gray gumdrop-looking thing in the upper-right corner of every Finder window, and it's gone. If only life were always so easy!

If you've customized your toolbar, as you discover later in this chapter, it won't look exactly like this. But, from left to right, here's the lowdown on the toolbar's default buttons:

Finding the Finder

If you don't see the Finder window on the Desktop when your Mac finishes the start-up process, you probably closed it the last time that the Mac was on. So how do you find the Finder window again?

✔ Choose File➪New Finder window (or use the keyboard shortcut ⌘+N), and a Finder window appears. New Finder windows always open up showing the top level of your drives. In other words, they open up labeled Computer, the same as if you choose Go➪Computer or clicked the Computer button in the toolbar.

Note: In Finder Preferences, you can change where your New Finder window opens — but only to automatically open to your Home directory. Home or Computer; those are your choices. If you prefer Documents or Macintosh HD, you're out of luck. It could be worse, though — you could have no choices at all.

You'll probably open a lot of new windows, so consider memorizing this keyboard shortcut: ⌘+N. This shortcut is good to know because most software programs use the ⌘+N shortcut to create a new document. If your memory is bad, use this mnemonic device: N is for New.

I'm almost over it, but since time immemorial (or at least since before Mac OS X 10.0), ⌘+N was the New Folder shortcut in the Finder. If you came to OS X via OS 9, the change will take some digital (the finger kind) retraining. If you never used 9, the change shouldn't bother you a bit (you never learned it the old way).

In Mac OS X, pressing ⌘+N spawns a New Window and pressing ⌘+Shift+N spawns a New Folder.

✔ Click the Finder icon in the Dock. (It's the left-most one, with a smiley Mac face on it.)

✔ **Forward and Back buttons:** Clicking the Forward and Back buttons displays the directories that you've viewed in this window in sequential order. If you've used a Web browser, it's just like that.

The keyboard shortcuts ⌘+[for Back and ⌘+] for Forward are more useful (in my opinion) than using the buttons. For more on this nifty navigation device, see the "Hither and yon: The Forward and Back buttons" section later in this chapter.

✔ **View buttons:** The three view buttons change the way that the window displays its contents. Stay tuned for an entire section on views coming up in just a few pages.

✔ **Computer:** Click this button to see what hard drives, CD/DVD-ROM or Zip drives, and servers are connected to your Mac. Or maybe you just want to see everything that you have in one place. Either way, click here to see the list of your mounted disks (see Figure 7-2). You can double-click any of the drives or disks that you see to get to their contents.

Figure 7-2:
Click the
Computer
button to
show your
computer's
storage
devices and
servers.

The icons in Figure 7-2 are, from left to right:

- **Macintosh HD:** This Mac's internal hard disk.

- **Network:** Resources and servers available to me (the current user) on the network.

- **Storage:** A FireWire drive connected to this Mac.

- **Warcraft III:** An educational CD-ROM in this Mac's CD-RW drive.

- **Ztorage:** A remote volume connected to another Mac on the network.

✔ **Home:** There's no place like it, is there? At least no place *I* know. The Home button leads to your private folder on the Mac. (Think of it as your own personal storage facility.) You find other folders there, including Desktop, Documents, Library, Movies, Music, Pictures, Public, and Sites. Use these folders to store your personal stuff, and you'll never lose track of it because it's conveniently located within folders that are always available with just a single click in the Finder. And if you ever get confused, use the keyboard shortcut ⌘+Shift+H, and Home magically appears on screen.

Go to Home if you've lost your bearings while cruising around your Mac in the Finder window. You may or may not share your Mac with others, but every user who works on this computer has his or her own Home folder. Rest easy, though — only your folders and your files appear when you click the Home button on a shared Mac. Read all about sharing Macs in Chapter 16.

You can set up a portion of your Home folder so that others can drop stuff in or take stuff out. In fact, Apple starts you out with a Public Folder containing a Drop Box folder for just that purpose.

✔ **Favorites:** Click the Favorites button to see items that you use a lot, such as files, folders, or links to Web sites. You can quickly add items to a folder with the Add To Favorites command on the File menu (or press ⌘+T). See Chapter 6 for more on the Add To Favorites command or if you need more info on menus in general.

Favorites are *aliases*: that is, pointers that you double-click to open items that are stored somewhere else on your Mac. When you install Mac OS X, Documents is already in your Favorites folder.

✔ **Applications:** Click the Applications button on the toolbar to reach the Applications folder, which contains applications that come with Mac OS X. In this folder, you can (and probably should) put any new applications that you install so that you can easily keep track of them. I discuss most of these programs in various places throughout the rest of the book, and I discuss folders in particular in Chapter 10.

If you share a computer with others, you'll need appropriate permissions to add things to the Applications folder; if you're the only one who uses your computer, you're the administrator by default and can add all the programs that you like to it. If that doesn't make sense to you at this time, read Chapter 16, which is all about sharing.

✔ **Search:** The toolbar's Search field is a nifty new way to search for files within the current folder. Just type a word or even just a few letters and then press Return or Enter. After a few seconds, the window will fill with a list of files that match, as shown in Figure 7-3.

Performing a search this way finds files in the current folder or in any of its subfolders. To clear the contents of the Search field, click the little X-in-a-circle on the right side of the Search field. Click the Back button to return to the folder that you were viewing before you searched.

For searches using multiple criteria or to search for a word within a document (meaning within the text of the document rather than in its file name), use the more powerful, new Find command. I take a closer look at it in Chapter 10.

Figure 7-3: Searching Macintosh HD for *Snapz* finds 17 files.

Navigating the Finder: Up, Down, and Backwards

In addition to the toolbar icons described previously and some good old-fashioned double-clicking, the Mac OS X Finder window offers a nifty new navigation tool: the aptly named Back button in the toolbar. But first I discuss the current folder pop-up menu, which is essential for understanding where you are in the big scheme of things.

Like a roadmap: The current folder drop-down menu

In the center of the window's title bar is the name of the folder that you're viewing in this window — the highlighted folder. To see a roadmap to this folder from the top level (Computer), press ⌘+click and hold on the folder's name (Utilities) in the title bar, as shown in Figure 7-4.

A drop-down menu appears with the current folder (Utilities) at the top.

Select any folder in the menu, and it becomes the highlighted folder in the current window.

Figure 7-4: Traverse folders from this convenient drop-down menu.

Put another way, in Figure 7-4, Utilities is the highlighted (or active) folder; Applications will be the highlighted/active folder when I release the mouse.

Use this pop-up menu to move from your current folder all the way to the Computer folder. Now click the Back button. Hey, you're right back where you were before you touched that pop-up menu.

If you like this feature a lot, use the Customize Toolbar command (in the View menu) to add a Path button to your toolbar. It displays the menu of folders previously described without having to hold down the ⌘ key.

Hither and yon: The Forward and Back buttons

Suppose that you're fiddling around in a Finder window, opening stuff, and maybe even looking for a particular file. You realize that the item you want is in the folder that you just left. D'oh! What to do? Click the Back button — yes, just like with a Web browser. The Back button (shown on the left in the margin) is the left-pointing arrow at the left end of the Finder window toolbar. If you want to move to the last folder you were at, just click the Back button, and there you are! If you use a Web browser (and who doesn't these days?), you're probably a pro at this already.

Here's an example of how the Back button works. Say you're in your Home folder, you click the Favorites button, and then a split-second later you realize that you actually need something in the Home folder. Just a quick click of the Back button and poof! You're back Home.

As for the Forward button, well, it moves you the opposite direction through folders that you've visited in this window.

Play around with them both — you'll find them invaluable. And don't forget even more invaluable keyboard shortcuts — ⌘+[and ⌘+] for Forward and Back, respectively.

Customizing Finder Windows with Views

You have three ways to view a window — Column view, Icon view, and List view. Some people like columns, some like icons, and others love lists. To each her own. Play with the three Finder views to see which one works best for you. For what it's worth, I prefer Column view.

The following sections give you a look at each view.

Column view

The Column view is new in Mac OS X; previous versions of Mac OS didn't have anything like it. It's quickly become my favorite way to display windows in the Finder.

 To display a window in the Column view, click the Column view button in the toolbar (as shown in the margin), choose View⇨As Columns from the Finder's menu bar, or use the keyboard shortcut ⌘+3.

You can have as many columns in a Column view window as your screen can handle. Just use the window sizer in the lower-right corner to enlarge your window horizontally so that new columns have room to open. Or click the green Maximize gumdrop to expand the window to its maximum width instantly. (See Chapter 5 for details about the window sizer and Maximize gumdrop . . . er, button.)

 You can use the little grabber handles at the bottom of a column to resize the column widths. When you drag this handle left or right, all columns resize equally *unless* you hold down the Option key — then only the column to the left of the handle resizes. See what a Finder window displayed in Column view looks like in Figure 7-5.

Figure 7-5:
A Finder window in Column view.

Icon view: The ol' stick-in-the-mud view

If there's a view that's a dead-ringer for the old Finder interface, it's Icon view. In all fairness, I must say that many perfectly happy Macintosh users love Icon view and refuse to even consider anything else. Fine. But as the number of files on your hard drive increases (as it does for every Mac user), screen real estate becomes more and more valuable. Too, the only advantage that the Icon view has over the Column or List views is the capability to arrange the icons anywhere you like within the window. Big deal.

I offer this solution as a compromise. If you still want to see your files and folders in Icon view, make them smaller so that more of them fit in the same space onscreen.

To change the size of a window's icons, choose View⇨Show View Options (or press ⌘+J). In the View Options window that appears, click the Window tab. Drag the Icon Size slider that you find there to the left. This makes the icons in the active window smaller. Conversely, you could make 'em all bigger by dragging the Icon Size slider to the right. Bigger icons make me crazy, but if you like them that way, your Mac can accommodate you.

If you want to make the icons in *every* window bigger or smaller, click the All Windows radio button in the View Options window and drag the Icon Size slider right or left. This affects all windows displayed in Icon view. (Read more on the View Options window coming up in a page or two. . . .)

Note: If you like Icon view, consider purchasing a larger monitor — I hear that monitors now come in a 24-inch size.

Here's how it works: When I click the Macintosh HD icon in the left-most column, its contents appear in the column to the right. When I click the Applications folder in the second column, its contents appear in the third column. When I click the Utilities folder in the third column, its contents appear in the fourth column. When I click the Java folder in the fourth column, its contents appear in the fifth column. Finally, when I click Applet Launcher in the fifth column, a big icon plus some information about this file appears (it's an application, 264K in size, created on July 29, 2002, and so on).

This rightmost column displays information about the highlighted item to its left, but only if that item is not a folder or disk. (If it were, its contents would be in this column, right?) That's the preview column. For most items, the picture is an enlarged view of the file's icon, as shown in Figure 7-5. But if that item is a graphic file saved in a format that QuickTime can interpret (most graphic file formats), a preview picture appears instead of an icon, as shown in Figure 7-6.

Almost everyone who I've talked to about this view thinks it's a darn handy way to quickly look through a lot of folders at once.

Figure 7-6:
The preview
of a graphic
file is a
picture
instead of
an icon.

Icon view

Icon view is a free-form view that allows you to move your icons around within a window to your heart's content. Check out the Finder window in Figure 7-7 to see what Icon view looks like.

To display a window in the Icon view, click the Icon view button in the tool-bar (as shown in the margin), choose View⇨As Icons from the Finder's menu bar, or use the keyboard shortcut ⌘+1.

Figure 7-7:
Icon view is
pretty and
very Mac-
like but
wastes
valuable
screen real
estate.

List view

Finally, I come to the view that I loved and used most in Mac OS 9 (but have forsaken since meeting the Column view): the List view (as shown in Figure 7-8). The main reason why I liked it so much was the little triangles to the left of each folder, known as *disclosure triangles*, which let you open a folder without actually opening a folder. The Documents folder is shown in its disclosed state in Figure 7-8.

 To display a window in List view, click the List view button in the toolbar (as shown in the margin), choose View➪As List from the Finder's menu bar, or use the keyboard shortcut ⌘+2.

Figure 7-8: A window in List view.

Easy copying and moving in List view

Here's a slick advantage for viewing folders and files in List view with the disclosure triangles. Because you can easily see folders and files with just one window open, you can copy or move items from separate folders with a single dragging motion. You're spared from having to open multiple windows, as you must do in the Icon view or Column view. In those views, moving files from two or more different folders requires opening several windows and two separate file-dragging motions.

It's easier to do than to explain, but here goes. In Figure 7-8, you can move any or all three files in the Documents folder into the Desktop, Library, Movies, Music, Pictures, Public, Sites, or zzMine folders without opening another window. Further, if you've clicked the disclosure triangle for say, Pictures, you can even move the files into a subfolder of Pictures or move files from the Documents and Pictures folder to another folder with one drag.

A little triangle-shaped arrow appears next to the name of the selected column in a List view window. (In Figure 7-9, you can see the arrow in the Size column.) If this little arrow points up, the items in the corresponding column sort in descending order; that is, the biggest item in the Size column appears first. When you click the header (Size) once, the arrow now points down, and the items show up in the opposite (ascending) order, as shown in Figure 7-10. This behavior is true for all columns in List view windows.

Figure 7-9:
Sort items in descending order in List view . . .

Figure 7-10:
. . . but click the Size header, and items are now in ascending order.

To change the order in which columns appear in a window, press and hold on a column's name and then drag it to the left or right until it's where you want it. Release the mouse button, and the column moves. The exception to this (isn't there *always* an exception?) is that the Name column always appears first.

Showing those View Options

To customize the way Finder windows look, use the View Options window. When you choose View⇨Show View Options from the Finder menu bar (or use the keyboard shortcut ⌘+J), you see the View Options window, as shown in Figure 7-11.

Figure 7-11:
Set the
appearance
of Finder
windows
here.

Sharp-eyed readers may notice that the View Options window shown in Figure 7-11 reads `Applications` in its title bar. That's because the View Options window always bears the name of the active window (the one that will be affected if you mark the This Window Only radio button instead of the All Windows radio button).

Start by selecting the All Windows radio button at the top of the View Options window. Now, whatever choices you set in this window affect *all* Finder windows for which you haven't specified explicit options (by using the This Window Only radio button, which I'll get to in a moment).

First decide whether you want to modify the All Windows Icon, List, or Column view by displaying the window in that view. If you choose Icon view, your options apply to all windows in Icon view; if you choose List view, your choices apply to all windows in List view. Because there are no This Window Only choices for Column view, your choices in View Options for Column view always apply to all Column view windows.

The choice that you make determines what options you see in the View Options window. The following sections describe your choices.

Icon view All Windows options

So you just can't kick that icon habit, eh? Okay . . . here's how to make global settings so that all your windows look the same. (If this concept excites you, you really need to get out of the house more!)

In the window, select the All Windows radio button. Now you're really living on the edge — oooh. Now you can set how big you want your icons, how to arrange them in windows, and whether you want to insert a picture as a background for your folder windows (yup, *all* folders).

The following list describes the View Options that you see after you choose Icon view:

- **Icon Size:** Use the Icon Size slider to make icons larger or smaller. To save valuable screen real estate space, I recommend that you keep your icons small. The largest icon size is nothing short of huge. *Hint:* Have a Finder window open in which icons are visible as you move the slider so that you can monitor icon size as they shrink or grow, depending on how far you move the slider.

- **Text Size:** What it says . . . the size of the icon's name. Just enter the point size that you want in the list box here.

- **Label Position:** Select either the Bottom or the Right radio button here to set where the icon's name appears — below it or to its right.

- **Icon arrangement:** Set here whether those icons should be penned up or free range with these check boxes:

  - **Snap to Grid:** Creates nice, straight lines of icons.

  - **Show Item Info:** Adds a line of text below the icon's name with info about the file (or folder).

  - **Show Icon Preview:** Got me. Nobody I know has figured this one out yet. It doesn't seem to do anything. If you know what it does, please let me know.

  - **Keep Arranged By:** Lets you specify the sort order for your icons from the pop-up menu below. Your choices are Name, Date Modified, Date Created, Size, and Kind.

- **Background:** From this list of radio buttons, you can pick a color or picture for your windows or opt for none at all. Look at Figure 7-12 to see what a folder looks like with a picture in its background. I'm not sure that windows should have pictures in their backgrounds, but if you like them, this is how it's done.

Whatever you choose — insert a picture, choose a color, or neither — appears in each of your windows if you've chosen the All Windows radio button in the View Options window.

Figure 7-12:
All windows
now have a
faux fur
Apple logo
as their
background.

List view All Windows options

Suppose that you prefer List view (instead of Icon view) and want to set global options for viewing your items this way. With your Finder window in List view, choose View➪Show View Options from the Finder menu bar and then select the All Windows radio button from the View Options window that appears. In Figure 7-13, you see a cluster of check boxes beneath the Show Columns heading. Select as many of these check boxes as you like to adjust your List view. When you view a window in List view, those columns will appear.

Most of the options here tell Mac OS X which fields to display or hide. The choices depend on what information you want displayed, such as

- ✔ Date modified
- ✔ Date created
- ✔ Size
- ✔ Kind
- ✔ Version
- ✔ Comments

Select the ones that you want to see and then decide whether you like the view that you selected. You can always change your selections later if you find that you aren't using a particular field.

Figure 7-13:
Choose
which fields
to display in
List view.

Here are two more options that may prove useful. Near the bottom of this
window are these two check boxes:

✔ **Use Relative Dates:** Select this check box, and Mac OS X intelligently
substitutes relative word equivalents — such as *yesterday* or *today* — for
numerical dates.

When you set your clock back a day and look at files that you updated
that day before setting your clock back, the relative date reads
tomorrow. Curious but true.

✔ **Calculate All Sizes:** Selecting this check box instructs Mac OS X to do
just that — calculate all sizes. Select this view to see how much stuff is
in each folder when you look at it in List view. The items (including folders) in the active window are sorted in descending order from biggest to
smallest when you sort by size.

If you don't select the Calculate All Sizes check box, items other than
folders are sorted by size, with all folders — regardless of their size —
appearing at the bottom of the list.

Near the top of the View Options dialog box, you find the Icon Size radio buttons. Select from these two radio buttons here to choose between small and
large icons in your List views. For my money, I think the smallest ones make
windows appear noticeably faster; your mileage may vary.

One last thing. Spring-loaded folders have been resurrected in OS X version
10.2 Jaguar. They work in all the views and with icons in the toolbar.

If you were among the millions who requested that Apple bring them back,
I'm happy to report that Apple did and that Jaguar's spring-loaded folders are
better than ever. I'll show you why they're so cool in Chapter 10.

Being really finicky and choosing your views window by window

Perhaps choosing a global look for your Finder windows is just too big of a commitment for you, or you have a setup that you like but need a special view for a particular window. Here's how to adjust your window view settings individually.

1. **Open the window that you want to set up.**

2. **Choose View➪Show View Options from the menu bar.**

3. **Select the This Window Only radio button in the View Options window.**

4. **Choose View➪As List or View➪As Icons to get the view that you want to set.**

The options are conveniently the same as the global options that I describe earlier, so have at it and make this special window look just the way you like it.

Chapter 8

Mastering the Save Sheet and the Open Dialog

· ·

In This Chapter

▶ Saving your document

▶ Discovering the differences between Save and Save As

▶ Mastering the Open dialog

▶ Discerning the subtle differences between the Open dialog and Save sheets

▶ Knowing what the Open dialog doesn't show you

· ·

Mark my words, this could well be the most important chapter in this book. If you don't understand the Open dialog and Save sheets, you'll never quite get the hang of your Mac. (Actually, there are two Save sheets: Save and Save As sheet, which you see when you choose File⇨Open or File⇨Save, respectively, in most programs.) Yet, mastering these essential techniques is perhaps the biggest problem that many Mac users have. Ask any long-time Mac user whether he's ever heard, "Well, I saved the file and now I don't know where it went." It happens all the time with new users.

This chapter is the cure-all for your Save, Save As, and Open woes. Hang with me and pay attention; everything will soon become crystal clear. And keep saying to yourself, "The Save sheets and the Open dialog are just another view of the Finder," as I explain in this chapter.

 You work with Open dialogs and Save sheets within applications. You only see them after you launch your favorite application or work within an open or newly created document. For more on launching applications, read through Chapter 4 on icons; for more on creating and opening documents, see the documentation for the program that you're using.

Saving Your Document Before It's Too Late

You can create as many documents as you want, but all is lost if you don't save them to a storage device like your hard drive or some other disk. When you *save* a file, you're committing a copy to a disk — either one mounted on your Desktop, one available over a network, or wherever.

In this section, I show you how to save your masterpieces. Prevent unnecessary pain in your life by developing good saving habits. If you take my advice, you'll save your work:

- ✔ Every few minutes
- ✔ Before you switch to another program
- ✔ Before you print a document
- ✔ Before you stand up

If you don't heed this advice and the program that you're using crashes while switching programs, printing, or sitting idle (which, not coincidentally, are the three most likely times for a crash), you lose everything that you did since your last save.

The keyboard shortcut for Save in almost every program I know is ⌘+S. Memorize it. See it in your dreams. Train your finger muscles to do it unconsciously. Use it (the keyboard shortcut) or lose it (your unsaved work).

Checking out the Save sheet

When you choose to save a file for the first time (by choosing File⇨Save or pressing ⌘+S), a Save sheet appears in front of the window that you're saving, as shown in Figure 8-1. You navigate folders in the Save sheet the same way that you navigate folders in the Finder — by opening them to see their contents. The Save sheet works like the Column view in the Finder. That is, you click an item on the left to see its contents on the right and then you click a folder to open it and display its contents on the right. (See Chapter 7 for more info about navigating in Column view.)

Before you can navigate the columns in a Save sheet, you need to click the downward-pointing disclosure triangle (to the right of the Where menu, just above the Save button in Figure 8-1) to expand the sheet. Otherwise, you're stuck with the small, less functional version of the Save sheet that you see in Figure 8-1. Click the disclosure triangle and the sheet expands, as shown in Figure 8-2.

Hiding your stuff under the right rock

If you've used previous versions of Mac OS, the rules about where to store things were a lot looser. Storing everything within your Documents folder wasn't at all important. But Mac OS X arranges its system files, applications, and other stuff a bit differently than older versions did.

I *strongly* advise you to store all your document files and the folders that contain them in the Documents folder within your Home folder. Files that you place outside the Documents folder are very likely to get lost while you navigate through a maze of aliases and folders that belong and make sense to certain programs or parts of the system software — and not to you as a user.

If other people besides you use your Mac (and they had changed privilege settings to give you access to their directories — see Chapter 16), you could even save a file in another user's folder by accident, in which case you'd *never* find it again.

So, trust me when I say that the Documents folder is the right place to start, not only because it's easy to remember but also because it's only a menu command (Go⇨Favorites⇨ Documents) away, wherever you're working on your Mac.

Figure 8-1:
Basic Save
sheets can
look like
this.

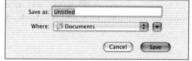

Figure 8-2:
Expanded
Save sheets
can look
like this.

Like the Column view in a Finder window, you can enlarge the Save sheet to see more. Just drag the lower-right corner of the sheet to the right. Then, when you click items in the current right column of the Save sheet (note that you must have the columns showing to have any columns to deal with here), their contents appear in a new, third column.

After you've saved a file once, choosing File⇨Save or pressing ⌘+S doesn't bring up a Save sheet anymore. It just saves the file again without any further intervention on your part. Get in the habit of pressing ⌘+S often. It can't hurt and just may save your bacon someday.

In Figures 8-1 and 8-2 you see, respectively, the Save sheet for the TextEdit program, default and expanded. In programs other than TextEdit, the Save sheet may contain additional options, fewer options, or different options, and therefore may look slightly different. Don't worry. The Save sheet always *works* the same, no matter what options there are.

In Mac OS X, you can move the window and Save sheet around the screen (just as you can any window) by dragging the window's title bar around. Just click the title bar and then hold down the mouse button while you drag the window wherever you desire. The Save sheet moves right along with the window. And, unlike the Save dialog in earlier versions of Mac OS, a Save sheet doesn't prevent you from using other programs or windows when it's onscreen.

Wherefore art thou, Where pop-up menu?

Take some time and get to know the Where pop-up menu. It's a great navigation aid but a bit confusing for new users. With it, you can quickly move to a location on your hard drive and open or save a file stored there. Consider the Where pop-up menu a shortcut menu to frequently used folders, your Favorites, and recent folders that you've used.

The Where pop-up menu looks a lot like the drop-down menu that appeared at the top of the Open/Save dialogs in earlier versions of Mac OS. But instead of tracing the folder path (as it did in versions of yore, and as the Finder window's pop-up menu still does), the Where pop-up menu lists four main places where you may save your files (Desktop, Home, iDisk, or Favorite Places) as well as more folders (under the Recent Places heading) where you have saved files recently, as shown in Figure 8-3. Therefore, if you move downward into a folder hierarchy and want to back up one, you have to choose an item on the pop-up menu (such as Documents, for example) and move back down the list from there. Yes, that is a pain, but understanding the Where menu can make it a little less confusing.

With three ways to navigate to your target folder — the mouse, the Where menu, and the arrow keys — you should always be able to get to your target folder (for saving the document) with just a few clicks or keystrokes.

In this section, I run down the parts of the Where pop-up menu. In the process, I show you why it's best to store your files in certain places on your Mac. Finally, I'll show you how to use the Where menu to quickly reach your favorite folders.

Figure 8-3:
Use the
Where pop-
up menu to
select from
these
frequently
used folders
when you
save a
document.

The Where menu works the same — whether or not you've expanded the Save sheet (by clicking the disclosure triangle).

Saving to the active folder

In the Save sheet, the name at the top in the Where pop-up menu is the name of the active item (be it a folder, a drive, or the Desktop). In Figure 8-4, the active folder is Folder 2.

Figure 8-4:
Saving a file
in Folder 2.

Think of the active item in a Save sheet as akin to the active window on the Desktop. That's where your file is saved by default if you click the Save button without changing the destination folder at all. This concept is important. In other words, if the Documents folder is the active item (as it is in both Figures 8-1 and 8-2), your document is saved in the Documents folder when you click the Save button. If Folder 2 is the active item (as it is in Figure 8-4), your document is saved in Folder 2 when you click the Save button. And so on.

The best places to save

Mac OS X includes your Documents folder in the Favorite Places section by default, and you can add folders as Favorites by using the Add to Favorites button of the Save sheet. The four main storage areas that Mac OS X gives you are described in the following list:

- **Home:** This is your Home folder on a Mac running Mac OS X. All users have their own Home folder that contains all their stuff — their documents, their preferences, their applications — everything that belongs to them. You can save documents to your Home folder, which is named for you. To do this, choose Home from the Where menu and then click the Save button.

  I don't, however, recommend saving most of your stuff to your Home folder. It quickly gets overcrowded and unmanageable. I find it easier to organize and find files in the Documents folder, away from the Library, Pictures, Music, and other folders that live in Home already.

- **Documents:** Located within your Home folder, the Documents folder is the best place to store your files (in my humble opinion). You can organize stuff inside your Documents folder by creating sub-folders with meaningful names. For example, in my Documents folder, you'd find subfolders named Letters, Databases, Finances, Public Relations, Templates, Articles, and Books.

- **Desktop:** This is a good place to save files (until you figure out where to put them) or leave those files that you plan to work on again soon. When you save a file to the Desktop, you'll see it appear in two places: in the Desktop folder in your Home folder and on the Desktop itself (the picture or pattern behind Finder windows where disc and other icons can often be found).

  If that sounds redundant to you, it is — but with good reason. Because OS X is a multi-user operating system and each user has a personal Home folder, your Desktop folder is how Mac OS X ensures that the icons that you see on the Desktop are *your* icons and not some other user's.

  Again, the Desktop is not a great place to store stuff long-term. I like to save the file in the appropriate folder, create an alias for it, and then drag that alias to the Desktop or to the Dock. (I cover aliases in Chapter 4.) When I'm done working on the file, I trash the alias on the Desktop and move on to the next task. The original document is tucked away safe and sound in the appropriate folder that I mentioned earlier.

- **iDisk:** If you use a Mac and you pay the fee for .Mac, Apple gives you a 100MB virtual disk, called an *iDisk*, at no cost to you. Your iDisk resides on an Apple server and can only be used if you have an active Internet connection. I don't think it's a particularly good place to store the only copy of an important document because you have to have a live Internet connection to access it. Thus, if your Internet connection goes down, you won't have access to files that you've saved on your iDisk.

On the other hand, one excellent use for your iDisk is to copy important files to it so you that have a back-up copy if anything awful should happen to your hard drive or your Mac.

For more information — and to create your own iDisk — visit www.mac.com.

✔ **Favorite Places:** When you designate a folder as a Favorite, it appears in the Where pop-up menu. Just select the Favorite folder where you want to store a file, and it opens in the Save sheet's right-most column.

About Recent Places

When you save a file by using the Save sheet, the folder containing it is added to the list of recent places. Check out the Recent Places sub-menu after you save files to several folders, and you'll see them all on the list in the menu.

Getting active with the Save As field

When a Save sheet first appears, the Save As field is active and ready for you to type a name into it. When you press the Tab key, the Save As field becomes inactive, and the file list box below (the one with the columns in it) becomes active. That's because the file list box and the Save As field are mutually exclusive. Only one can be active at any time. You either navigate the folder hierarchy or you name a file.

Look at Figure 8-5. In the left-hand screen, the Save As field is active; in the right-hand screen, the file list box is active. You can tell which item is active by the thin blue or gray border around it.

Active (has border)   Inactive (no border)   Inactive (no border)   Active (has border)

Figure 8-5:
Check the
borders to
see active
and inactive
fields.

When you want to switch to a different folder to save a file, click anywhere in the file list box to make it active. In Figure 8-5, it's displaying the folders (Desktop, Documents, Library, and so on) in my Home folder in the middle column and the contents of the Documents folder (the active folder) in the far-right column.

Either the Save As field or the file list box is active at any given time; they can never both be active at the same time.

The following lists are some things to help you get a hold of this whole active/inactive silliness:

- ✔ Look for the thin border that shows you which part of the Save sheet is active. It's around the Save As field in Figure 8-5 (left side) and the file list box in Figure 8-5 (right side).

- ✔ If you type while the file list box is active, the list scrolls and selects the folder that most closely matches the letter(s) that you type. It's a little strange because you won't see what you type: You'll be typing blind, so to speak. Go ahead and give it a try. For example, typing the letters **pu** in the file list box of Figure 8-5 (right side) selects the Public folder.

  Or at least it should. It only works sometimes. Alas, typing blind in Save sheets to select an item is unreliable at best. It's been that way since OS X version 10.0, but with luck, it'll work properly every time by the time you read this.

- ✔ When the file list is active, the letters that you type don't appear in the Save As field. If you want to type a file name, you have to activate the Save As field again to type in it.

- ✔ Regardless of which box or field is active at the time, when you press the Tab key on your keyboard, the other becomes active. So if the Save As field is active, it becomes inactive when you press Tab, and the file list box becomes active. Press Tab again, and they reverse — the Save As field becomes active again.

If you don't feel like pressing the Tab key, you can achieve the same effect by clicking either the file list box or the Save As field to make it active. Try it yourself and notice again how visual cues let you know which is active. When the file list is active, it displays a border; when the Save As field is active, the file list has no border, and the Save As field displays a border and is editable.

Putting your finger on the button

Most Save sheets contain the following four buttons (New Folder, Add to Favorites, Cancel, Save) and a Hide Extension check box. I describe them all briefly in the following list.

- ✔ **New Folder:** The New Folder button is a nice touch. Click this button, and you create a new folder inside the active folder. You first get the opportunity to name the folder; then you can save your document there.

- ✔ **Add to Favorites:** If you find yourself saving a lot of files to a certain folder, it could very well become one of your favorite folders. Click the Add to Favorites button to designate the active folder as a favorite. After you do, you can quickly get to that folder from anywhere, but most especially from the Where pop-up menu in a Save sheet. Just select the folder from the Favorite Places section of the menu to open it.

✔ **Cancel:** Clicking this button dismisses the Save sheet without saving anything anywhere. In other words, the Cancel button returns things to the way they were before you displayed the Save sheet.

The keyboard shortcut for Cancel is ⌘+. (⌘+ a period). Pressing the Esc key usually (but not always) does the same thing. This shortcut is a good command to memorize because it cancels almost all dialogs, and it also cancels lots of other things. If a program is dragging — your spread-sheet is calculating or your database is sorting or your graphics pro-gram is rotating, for example, and it's taking too long — try pressing either Esc or ⌘+. (period). (They work — usually.)

✔ **Save:** Click this button to save the file to the active folder.

But wait! What if the Save button is grayed out? This happens when the Save As field is blank; typing even one character will activate the Save button again.

Make sure that the folder you want to save your document in is high-lighted. If you're not sure and you click the Save button, *you* could be the next one to say, "Well, I saved the file and now I don't know where it went."

✔ **Hide extension:** Marking this check box turns off the display of file name extensions, such as `.rtf` or `.txt`, in Save sheets.

It looks like Save and it acts like Save, so why is it called Save As?

The Save As command, which you can find in the File menu of almost every program ever made, lets you resave a file that has already been saved by giving it a different name.

Why would you want to do that? Here's a good (albeit kind of rude) example:

Suppose that you have two cousins, Kate and Zelda. You write Kate a long, chatty letter and save this document with the name `Letter to Kate`. At some point afterward, you decide that you want to send this same letter to Zelda, too, but you want to change a few things. So you change the part about your date last night (Zelda isn't as liberated as Kate) and replace all references to Kevin (Kate's husband) with Zeke (Zelda's husband). (Aren't computers grand?)

So you make all these changes to `Letter to Kate`, but you haven't saved this document yet. And although the document on your screen is actually a letter to Zelda, its file name is still `Letter to Kate`. Think of what would happen if you were to save it now without using the Save As feature: `Letter to Kate` reflects the changes that you just made (the stuff in the letter meant for Kate is blown away, replaced by the stuff that you write to Zelda). Thus, the file name Letter to Kate is inaccurate. Even worse, you would no longer have a copy of the letter that you sent to Kate!

To rename this file Letter to Zelda, use Save As. From the File menu, choose Save As. A Save sheet appears, in which you can type a different file name in the Save As field. You can also navigate to another folder, if you like, and save the newly named version of the file there.

Now you have two distinct files: Letter to Kate and Letter to Zelda. Both contain the stuff they should but both started life from the same file. *That's* what Save As is for.

Open Sez Me

If you've read the earlier parts of this chapter, you probably already know how to use the Open dialog — you just don't yet know that you know. Open dialogs are so much like Save sheets that it's scary. To summon an Open dialog, launch your favorite program and choose File⇨Open (or use the keyboard shortcut ⌘+O, which works in 98 percent of all programs ever made).

Check out a typical Open dialog in Figure 8-6.

Figure 8-6:
The Open
dialog in all
its glory.

Knowing the differences between Open dialogs and Save sheets

After you master navigating the Save sheet, you should have smooth sailing when using an Open dialog. They work the same except for a few minor differences:

Getting there with the Go To field

Check out the Go To field, near the bottom of the Open dialog. Use this field to navigate through your folders by typing their folder names (separated by forward slashes — and make sure to include the initial forward slash) and then clicking the Open button (lower-right of this window). For example, typing **/Macintosh HD/Users/ bobl/Documents/Folder 2** into the Go To field and clicking Open moves me directly to Folder 2, regardless of what's displayed when the Open dialog appears.

Make sure to include the initial forward slash. It won't work without one.

Given the graphical nature of the Mac interface, I think this is kind of a lame feature (all that typing!). But if you know the path for your files and don't mind the keystrokes, just type the path into the text field and click the Open button to instantly view the folder or file that you want. If you're a wicked-fast and accurate typist and want to get to a folder quick, this is one way to do it.

✔ **No Save As field:** A Save As field isn't needed in an Open dialog because it's the one you see when you want to open a file! Because you're not saving or naming a file here, you don't need the Save As field.

✔ **No Where pop-up menu:** In the Open dialog, you find the From pop-up menu instead. Why? Because you're opening a file *From* a certain folder, rather than telling your Mac *Where* to save it. The From menu has the same basic job as the Where menu, and you see the same folders in it that you see in the Where menu.

✔ **No New Folder button:** Why? Well, you can't open something that you haven't yet created, right? You don't need to create new folders when you're opening a file, basically.

You may notice a couple of other differences between the Save sheet and the Open dialog. At the bottom of the Open dialog (refer to Figure 8-6), note the Plain Text Encoding pop-up menu and the Ignore Rich Text Commands check box. These are specific to TextEdit and have to do with the format that TextEdit uses to save text files. Don't worry about these for now. Just remember that many applications add special items to their Open dialogs and Save sheets that help you to select formats and other options specific to those programs.

Navigate through the Open dialog just as you would a Save sheet. Don't forget the mantra, "The Open dialog and the Save sheet are just another view of the Finder."

Knowing what the Open dialog doesn't show you . . .

When you use a program's Open dialog, only files that the program knows how to open appear enabled (in a bold font) in the file list. In other words, the program filters out files that it can't open, so that you barely see them in the Open dialog. This method of selectively displaying certain items in Open dialogs is a feature of most applications. Therefore, when you're using TextEdit, its Open dialog will dim all your spreadsheet files because TextEdit can only open text, rich text, and picture files. Pretty neat, eh?

Some programs such as AppleWorks, Microsoft Word, and Adobe Photoshop have a Show menu in their Open dialogs. This menu lets you specify what type(s) of files that you want to see in the Open dialog. (Check it out in Figure 8-7.) You can often open a file that appears dimmed by choosing All Documents in the Show menu.

Figure 8-7:
Microsoft
Word's
Show menu
offers to
show you
many
different
types of
files.

All Readable Documents
✓ All Office Documents
All Word Documents
Word Templates
Rich Text Format (RTF)
Text Files
Unicode Text Files
Web Pages
AppleWorks 5 & 6
Microsoft Excel 3.x Worksheet
Microsoft Excel 4.x Worksheet
Microsoft Excel 5.x Worksheet
Microsoft Excel 97–2002 and X Worksheet
Recover Text from Any File
All Documents

Chapter 9

Haggling with Removable Media

· ·

· ·

*I*n this chapter, I show you disk basics: how to format them; how to format them so that our less-fortunate Windows-using brethren (and sisteren) can use them; how to eject them; how to copy or move files between disks; and much more. Onward!

Now, some of you with iMacs (or other Macs that don't have a floppy disk drive, which these days is all Macs) may be thinking, "My Mac doesn't even have a floppy drive. Why should I read a whole chapter about disks?" Well, I'll tell ya. In this chapter, I tell you lots of info that applies to every Mac user, including folder management and moving or copying files. I also show you how to work with other types of removable magnetic media, such as Zip, Orb, and Jaz, and optical media such as CD-R, CD-RW, DVD-R, DVD-RW, DVD-RAM, and SuperDisk disks, which many Mac owners also use. If you have a Power Mac G4, for example, you've probably got a Zip drive or a DVD-R drive. And lots of Mac owners add SuperDisk drives, which read both standard 1.4MB floppies and 120MB SuperDisks, so that they can easily copy files for friends or move their files between home and work.

Comprehending Disks

You should think of the disk icons that appear on the Desktop (and in the Finder window called Computer) as if they were folders. That's because disks are nothing but giant folders. When you double-click them, their contents appear in the Finder window, just like a folder. You can drag stuff in and out of a disk's window, and you can manipulate the disk's window in all the usual ways, just like a folder. In fact, for all intents and purposes, disks are folders.

Is that a disk or a disc?

So how do you spell this critter, anyway? Sometimes you see it spelled d-i-s-k; other times you see it spelled d-i-s-c. If you're wondering what's up with that, here's the skinny. In the good old days, the only kind of disk was a disk with a *k:* floppy disk, hard disk, Bernoulli disk, and so on. Then one day, the compact disc (you know, a CD) was invented. And the people who invented it chose to spell it with a *c* instead of a *k*, probably because it's round like a *discus* (think track and field). From that time on, both spellings have been used more or less interchangeably.

Now some people will tell you that magnetic media (floppy, hard, Zip, Jaz, Orb, and so on) are called *disks* (spelled with a *k*). And that optical media — that is, discs that are read with a laser (such as CD-ROMs, audio CDs, DVDs, and CD-RWs) — are called *discs* (spelled with a *c*). Maybe that's true, but the two terms have been used pretty much interchangeably for so long that you can't depend on the last letter to tell you whether a disk is magnetic or optical.

The bottom line is that I'm going to compromise and use the word *disk* in this chapter. If you're offended that I call CD-ROMs, audio CDs, DVDs, CD-RWs, and such *disks* instead of *discs*, I'm sorry.

My editors made me do it.

The only exception to the disks-are-folders rule that I can think of is that you can't use the Duplicate keyboard shortcut (⌘+D) on a disk, although you can use it on a folder.

Making Sure Your Disks are Mac Disks

Brand-new disks sometimes need to be *formatted* — prepared to receive Macintosh files — before they can be used. (This is especially true for floppy disks, if your Mac has a floppy drive.) I say *sometimes* because you can buy new disks that are preformatted. Formatting a disk takes only a few minutes to do, so don't pay a whole lot more for preformatted disks unless you really believe that time is money.

When you insert a floppy disk, your Mac may take a bit (or sometimes quite a while) before it recognizes that a disk is present and displays it on your Desktop or in the Computer window. Be patient with floppies; they're old and slow.

When you pop in any type of unformatted disk, your Mac pops up a dialog that asks whether you wish to format it, but your Mac usually calls this *initializing* rather than formatting. If you choose to format the disk, the Disk Utility program starts, and you can initialize the disk from the Erase tab.

The Erase command defaults to using Mac Extended as the format. If you're formatting a floppy disk, don't use Mac Extended — switch to Mac Standard. You should probably mark the check box to include OS 9 drivers as well if you or anyone who may need the floppies is using OS 9 or earlier.

Moving and Copying Disks

Moving an icon from one disk to another works the same as moving an icon from one folder to another with one notable exception: When you move a file from one disk to another, you automatically make a copy of it, leaving the original untouched and unmoved. If you want to move a file from one disk to another, you need to delete the original by dragging it to the Trash.

Copying the contents of a removable disk (Zip and SuperDisk, among others) to your hard drive works a little differently. To do this task, click the disk's icon and while holding down the Option key, drag it onto the icon or window for the destination media (for example, your hard drive icon, your hard drive's open window, or onto any other folder icon or open folder window). If you don't hold down the Option key, all you get is an alias to the disk.

When the copy is completed, a folder bearing the same name as the copied disk appears in the destination folder. The new folder now contains each and every file that was on the disk of the same name.

Surprise: Your PC Disks Work, Too!

One of the most excellent features of Mac OS X (if you have friends unfortunate enough not to own Macs and you want to share files with them) is that it reads both Mac- and DOS-formatted disks without any user intervention. *DOS disks* are formatted for use with personal computers (PCs) that run DOS or Windows. If a friend has a Windows computer, you can read his or her disks by just sticking them in your disk drive. Your unfortunate friend, on the other hand, can't do diddly squat with your Mac-formatted disks — yet another reason why Macs are better.

Although PC-formatted disks will work in your Mac, the files on them may or may not. If the files are documents, one of your Mac programs can probably open them. This applies also to other types of disks, including CD-ROMs, Zip, Jaz, Orb, and SyQuest.

But if the files are Windows programs (these often sport the .exe suffix, which stands for executable), your Mac won't be able to do anything with 'em without additional software.

That additional software is the almost-magical Virtual PC from Connectix (`www.connectix.com`). This program emulates a Pentium-based PC on your Mac so that you can run genuine Microsoft Windows operating systems (Windows XP Professional or XP Home, Windows 2000, Windows Me, and Windows 98) on your Mac.

So with a copy of Virtual PC (around $200), your Mac can run those `.exe` files (and most Windows programs as well). Unfortunately, because emulating a Pentium processor and PC video card demands a lot from your Mac, it's slower than even the cheapest PC sold today. So although it's useful for most Windows applications (including Web browsers, which run remarkably well under Virtual PC), games are mostly unplayable. Bummer.

Burning CDs and DVDs

Apple, or at least Steve Jobs, refers to the Macintosh as "your digital hub" and has been doing so since January 2001 at Macworld Expo (before Intel started touting the Pentium 4 as the "center of your digital world"). With Mac OS X (10.1 or later), this means that you can play, create, and publish audio and video. If your Mac is equipped with a CD-RW or SuperDrive, just insert a blank CD-R, CD-RW, DVD-R, or DVD-RW disc and you'll see the alert, as shown in Figure 9-1, that asks you what you want to do with the disk.

Figure 9-1:
Insert a
blank CD in
your CD-RW
drive and
get ready
to feel
the burn.

Name the disk and choose from the Action pop-up menu. The default choice is Open Finder, unless you've changed that default in your CD/DVD System Preferences.

The other choices are Open iTunes and Open Disk Copy. If you choose either one, that program automatically opens when you insert a blank CD, and you won't even see the disk icon on your Desktop.

Click OK, and your blank CD mounts on the Desktop just like any other removable disk but with a distinctive icon telling you that it's a recordable CD, as shown in Figure 9-2. From that point on, just copy files onto it until you have it the way you want it. When you're ready to create your CD, start to drag the icon, and the Trash will turn into a Burn button (looks like the warning for radioactivity to me), as shown in Figure 9-3.

Figure 9-2: Recordable optical discs get a distinctive, labeled icon.

Alternatively, you could Control+click the disk's icon and choose Burn Disc (yes, Apple spells it with a *c*) from the contextual menu or select the icon and choose Burn Disc from the File menu. If you choose Eject, either from the contextual menu or from the File menu, you'll be asked whether you want to burn the disk first.

Figure 9-3: Just drag the icon to the Burn Disc button when you're ready to burn your CD.

The Trash icon turns into a Burn Disc icon.

MP3 players play files in the order that they're written, which will be alphabetically. So, if you want them to play in a particular order, be sure to name them with sequential numbers at the beginning. Fortunately, iTunes makes that easy with the Create File Names with Track Number option in your Importing preferences.

If you're blessed with a SuperDrive — the cool drive that is a combination DVD-R/DVD-RW/CD-R/CD-RW drive — you can even burn data and video DVDs from the Desktop — just like CDs — when you insert a blank DVD-R disk.

Getting Disks out of Your Mac

You now know almost everything there is to know about disks except one important thing: how to eject a disk. Piece of cake, actually. Here are several ways, all simple to remember:

✔ Click the disk's icon to select it, and then choose File➪Eject (or use the keyboard shortcut ⌘+E).

✔ Drag the disk's icon to the Trash. You'll notice that when you drag a disk's icon, the Trash icon in the Dock changes into an Eject icon, like that shown in the left margin here.

The preceding method of ejecting a disk is something that used to drive me (and many others) crazy before Mac OS X. In the olden days, the Trash icon didn't change into an Eject icon. And this confused many new users, who then asked me the same question (over and over and over): "But doesn't dragging something to the Trash erase it from your disk?"

✔ Click the disk icon while holding down the Control key and then choose Eject from the contextual menu.

Chapter 10

File Management without Tearing Your Hair Out

● ●

● ●

*I*n other parts of this book, you can discover the basics about windows and icons and menus. Here, you begin a never-ending quest to discover the fastest, easiest, and most trouble-free way to manage the files on your Mac. And, along the way, you'll discover what some of the special folders (most notably the multiple Library folders) in Mac OS X are all about.

I've been wrangling with Macintosh files and folders for more than 14 years now, and I've learned a lot about what works and what doesn't — for me, that is. And although Mac OS X is very different from earlier versions of Mac OS, the fundamentals of organizing files and folders haven't changed that much. So this chapter spares you at least part of my 14-year learning curve.

Remember that I'm talking about Mac OS here, and so, just like the Mac interface, I encourage you to develop your own personal style. I don't preach (much) about the right way to organize your files. After you've read this chapter, you'll have all the ammunition that you need to organize your files into a Mac environment designed by you, for you.

I won't pretend to be able to organize your Mac for you. Organizing your files is as personal as your taste in music. You develop your own style with the Mac. So in this section, I give you some food for thought: some ideas about how I do it as well as some suggestions that should make organization easier for you, regardless of how you choose to do it yourself.

Working with Files and Folders

Before I go any further, you first need to understand a bit about files and folders: the difference between a file and a folder, how you can arrange and move files and folders around, and how to nest folders. Then you can concentrate on becoming a savvier — and better organized — Mac OS X user.

Then, after I discuss *your* files and folders, I offer more about the folders that Mac OS X creates (and requires). In other words, by the end of this chapter, you'll not only know all about *your* files and folders, you'll also know about the files and folders that Mac OS X creates when you install it and what they do.

Files versus folders

When I speak of a *file*, I'm talking about any icon except a folder or disk icon. A file can be a document, an application, an alias of a file or application, a dictionary, a font, or any other icon that *isn't* a folder or disk. The main distinction is that you can't put something *into* a file icon.

When I talk about *folders*, I'm talking about, well, folders. They look like folders and they can contain files or other folders *(subfolders)*. You can put any icon — any file or folder — into a folder.

Here's an exception: If you put a disk icon into a folder, you get an alias to the disk (as I explain in Chapter 9) unless you hold down the Option key. Remember that you can't put a disk icon into a folder on itself. In other words, you can only copy a disk icon to a different disk. Or, put another way, you can never copy a disk icon into a folder that resides on that disk.

Finally, *disks* are nothing more than big folders. A disk icon is, for all intents and purposes, the same as a folder icon. (Look in the margin to see a typical folder icon.)

File icons can look like practically anything. If the icon doesn't look like a folder or one of the numerous disk icons, you can be pretty sure that it's a file.

Creating new folders

So you think that Apple has already given you enough folders? Can't imagine why you'd need more? Think of creating new folders the same way that you'd think of labeling a new folder at work for a specific project. New folders help you keep your files organized, enabling you to reorganize them just the way you want. Creating folders is really quite simple.

To create a new folder, just follow these steps:

1. **Decide which window you want the new folder to appear in and then make sure that the window is active; or, if you want to create a new folder right on the Desktop, make sure that no windows are open or active.**

   You can make a window active by clicking it, and you can make the Desktop active if you have windows onscreen by clicking the Desktop itself.

2. **Choose File⇨New Folder (or press ⌘+Shift+N).**

   A new, untitled folder appears in the active window with its name box already highlighted, ready for you to type a new name for it.

3. **Type a name for your folder.**

   If you accidentally click anywhere before you type a name for the folder, the name box will no longer be highlighted. To highlight it again, select the icon (single-click it) and then press Return once. Now you can type its new name.

   Name your folders with relevant names. Folders with nebulous titles like *sfdghb* or *Stuff* — or worst of all, *Untitled* — won't make it any easier to find something six months from now.

Navigating Nested Folders

Folders within other folders are often called *nested folders*. To get a feel for the way nested folders work in Mac OS X, check out Figure 10-1. You can see the following from the figure:

   ✔ Folder 1 is one level deep.

   ✔ Folder 2 is inside Folder 1, which is one level deeper than Folder 1, or two levels deep.

   ✔ Folder 3 is inside Folder 2 and is three levels deep.

   ✔ The files inside Folder 3 are four levels deep.

If the previous list makes sense to you, you're golden. What's important here is that you are able to visualize the path to Folder 3. That is, to get to files inside Folder 3, you open Folder 1 and then open Folder 2 to be able to open Folder 3. Understanding this concept is important to understanding the relationships between files and folders. Keep reviewing this section and eventually the concept will click — you'll slap yourself in the head and say, "Now I get it!"

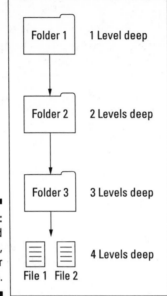

Figure 10-1:
Nested
folders,
going four
levels deep.

Moving files and folders

You can move files and folders around within a window to your heart's content as long as that window is set to the Icon view. Just click and drag any icon to its new location in the window.

Some people spend hours arranging icons in a window so that they're just so. But because using Icon view wastes so much screen space, I avoid using icons in a window.

You can't move icons around in a window that's viewed as a list or as columns, which makes total sense when you think about it. Well, you can move them to put them in a different folder in List or Column view, but that's not moving them around, really.

As you may expect from Apple, the King of Having Lots of Ways to Do Anything, you have choices for how you move one file of folder into another folder. You can use these techniques to move any icon — folder, document, alias, or program icon — into folders or onto other disks.

✔ **Drag an icon onto a folder icon:** Drag the icon for one folder (or file) onto the icon for another folder (or disk) and then release when the second folder is highlighted (see Figure 10-2). The first folder is now inside the second folder. Put another way, the first folder is now a subfolder of the second folder.

This technique works regardless of whether the second folder's window is open.

✔ **Drag an icon into an open folder's window:** Drag the icon for one folder (or file) into the open window for a second folder (or disk), as shown in Figure 10-3.

Figure 10-2: Placing one folder into another.

If you try to move an item from one disk to another disk, it's only copied — not moved. If you want to *move* a file or folder from one disk to another, you have to trash the original manually after the copying is complete.

Figure 10-3: You can also move a file or folder by dragging it into the open window of another folder.

That is, unless you're using Mac OS X version 10.1 or later. If so, there's a great new trick: If you hold down the ⌘ key when you drag an icon from one disk to another, it's moved instead of copied, and the original is deleted automatically. The little Copying Files window even changes to read Moving Files. Nice touch, eh?

Copying files or folders

What if you want to *copy* an icon from one place to another, leaving the icon in its original location and creating an identical copy in the destination window? No problem — all it takes is the addition of the Option key.

If you're wondering why anyone would ever want to do that, trust me: Someday you will. Suppose that you have a file called Long Letter to Mom in a folder called Old Correspondence. You figure that Mom has forgotten that letter by now, and you want to send it again. But before you do, you want to change the date and delete the reference to Clarence, her pit bull, who passed away last year. So now you need to put a copy of Long Letter to Mom in your Current Correspondence folder.

Read about how to make a copy of a file by using Save As in Chapter 8. This technique yields the same result.

When you copy a file, it's wise to change the name of the copied file. Having more than one file on your hard drive with the same name is not a good idea, even if the files are in different folders. Trust me, having 10 files called Expense Report or 15 files named Randall's Invoice can be confusing, no matter how well-organized your folder structure is. Add distinguishing words or dates to file and folder names so that they're named something more explicit, such as Expense Report 10-99 or Randall's Invoice 10-30-99.

You have four ways to copy a file or folder, as follows:

- ✔ **Drag an icon from one folder icon onto another folder icon while holding down the Option key.**

  Drag the icon for one folder onto the icon for another folder and then release when the second folder is highlighted (refer to Figure 10-2). This technique works regardless of whether the second folder's window is open.

  When you copy something by dragging and dropping it with the Option key held down, the mouse pointer changes so that it includes a little plus sign (+) next to the arrow as shown in the margin. Neat!

- ✔ **Drag an icon into an open window for another folder while holding down the Option key.**

  Drag the icon for the file or folder that you want to copy into the open window for a second folder (or removable media, such as a floppy disk), as shown in Figure 10-3.

- ✔ **Copy an icon and paste it in another folder's window.**

> Introduced to the Mac with the OS X 10.1 release, you can now click an icon, choose Edit⇨Copy (or press ⌘+C), click where you want the icon to go, and then choose Edit⇨Paste (or press ⌘+V) — it's done.

> ✔ **Choose File⇨Duplicate or Control+click the file or folder that you want to duplicate and then select Duplicate from the contextual menu that appears.**

> For more about the Duplicate command, check out Chapter 6.

You can have lots of files with the same name *on the same disk* (although, as I mentioned earlier, it's probably not a good idea). But your Mac won't let you have more than one file with the same name *in the same folder*.

Everything that I've discussed so far in this chapter works at least as well for windows using the List or Column views as it does for windows using the Icon view. (You gotta love those disclosure triangles in the List view! I sure do.) In other words, I only used the Icon view in the previous examples because it's the best view to show you what's going on. For what it's worth, I find moving and copying files easiest in windows when using the List view.

Opening files with drag-and-drop

Macintosh drag-and-drop is usually all about dragging text and graphics from one place to another. But there's another angle to drag-and-drop — one that has to do with files and icons. I tell you the real deal in this section.

You can open a document by dragging its icon onto the proper application. In other words, you can open a document that you created with Microsoft Word by dragging the document icon onto the Microsoft Word application's icon. The Word icon will highlight, and the document will launch. Of course, it's usually easier to just double-click a document's icon to open it. The proper application opens automatically when you do. Or at least it does most of the time. This brings me to why I'm explaining this drag-and-drop thing here.

If you try to open a file and Mac OS X can't find a program to open the file, Mac OS X prompts you with an error window, as shown in Figure 10-4. You can either click OK (and abort the attempt to open the file) or pick another application to open it.

Of course, you can click the Choose Application button and pick another program from a regular Open File dialog (see Chapter 8 for details). If you click the Choose Application button, a dialog appears (conveniently opened to your Applications folder, and shown in Figure 10-5). Applications that you can't use to open the file are dimmed. For a wider choice of applications, choose to view All Applications instead of Recommended Applications from the Show pop-up menu.

Figure 10-4:
Oops! Mac
helps you
find the
correct
application.

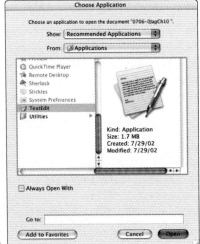

Figure 10-5:
Choose an
application
to open
a file.

Here is a better way: Use drag-and-drop to open a file using a program other than the one that would ordinarily launch when you open the document. To do so, just drag the file onto the application's icon (or alias icon or Dock icon), and presto — the file opens in the application.

If the icon doesn't highlight and you release the mouse button anyway, the document will be dropped into the folder that contains the application (with the icon that didn't highlight.)

If that happens, don't forget that the OS X Finder, unlike previous Finders, offers Undo. This is a case where it's a godsend. Just choose Edit⇨Undo (or press ⌘+Z), and the mislaid document magically returns to where it was before you dropped it. Just remember — you can't do anything else after dropping the file, or Undo may not work.

You can't open every file with every program. For example, if you try to open an MP3 (music) file with Microsoft Excel (a spreadsheet), it just won't work — you'll get an error message or a screen full of gibberish. Sometimes you just have to keep trying until you find the right program; other times, you won't have a program capable of opening the file.

TIP

Only applications that *might* be able to open the file will highlight when you drag the document on them. That doesn't mean the document will be usable, just that the application *can* open it.

Suffice it to say that Mac OS X is smart enough to figure out which applications on your hard drive can open what documents and to also offer you a choice.

You're usually best off clicking the Choose Application button and sticking to the Recommended Applications choice in the Choose Application dialog. But if that doesn't work for you, at least you now know another way — drag the file onto an application's icon and see what happens.

Assigning an application to a document or document type

I don't know about you, but people send me files all the time that were created by applications I don't use . . . or at least that I don't use for that document type. Mac OS X lets you specify the application in which you want to open a document in the future when you double-click it. More than that, you can specify that you want all documents of that type to open with the specified application. "Where is this magic bullet hidden?" you ask. Right there in the file's Show Info window.

Suppose, for example, that you want all PictureViewer-created JPEG files to open with GraphicConverter (one of my favorite pieces of OS X-savvy shareware) so that you don't have to launch Classic. Just click one of these files in the Finder and then choose File⇨Get Info (⌘+I). In the Info window, choose Open with Application from the pop-up menu to display the Info window shown in Figure 10-6.

Figure 10-6:
Set a
default
application
for this
document or
document
type here.

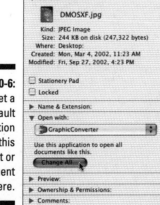

Click and hold on the icon button, and a menu appears of the applications that Mac OS X believes will open this document type. Choose one (in my case, GraphicConverter). If you close the Info window now, GraphicConverter will be the application for this particular document; however, you can click the Change All button at the bottom of the window to make Graphic Converter the default application for all documents owned by PictureViewer.

Organizing your stuff with subfolders

As I mention earlier in this chapter, you can put folders inside other folders to organize your icons. I call a folder that's inside another folder a *subfolder*.

Create subfolders based on a system that makes sense to you. Here are some organizational topic ideas and naming examples for subfolders:

- **By type of document:** Word-Processing Documents, Spreadsheet Documents, Graphics Documents
- **By date:** Documents May–June, Documents Spring '99
- **By content:** Memos, Outgoing Letters, Expense Reports
- **By project:** Project X, Project Y, Project Z

When you notice your folders swelling and starting to get messy (that is, becoming filled with tons of files), subdivide them again by using a combination of these methods that makes sense to you. For example, suppose that you start by subdividing your Documents folder into multiple subfolders, as shown in Figure 10-7. Later, when those folders begin to get full, you may subdivide them even further, as shown in Figure 10-8.

Figure 10-7:
Organize a folder with subfolders.

My point (yes, I do have one!): Allow your folder structure to be organic, growing as you need it to grow. Let it happen. Don't let any one folder get so full that it's a hassle to deal with. Create new subfolders when things start to get crowded.

Figure 10-8:
Further
subdivide a
growing
folder.

Creating subfolders . . . or not

How full is too full? When should you begin creating subfolders in a folder? That's impossible to say, but having too many items in a folder can be a nightmare, as can having too many subfolders with just one or two files in them. My guideline is this: If you find more than 15 or 20 files in a single folder, begin thinking about ways to subdivide it.

On the other hand, some of my bigger subfolders contain things that I don't often access. For example, my Bob's Correspondence 1992 folder contains more than 100 files. But because I want to keep this folder on my hard drive just in case I do need to find something there — even though I don't use it very often — it's overcrowded condition doesn't bother me. Your mileage may vary.

Here are some tips to help you decide whether to use subfolders or just leave well enough alone:

✔ **Don't create subfolders until you need them.** In other words, don't create a bunch of empty folders because you think that you may need them someday. Wait to create new folders until you need them to prevent opening an empty folder when you're looking for something else — a complete waste of time.

✔ **Let your work style decide the file structure.** When you first start working with your Mac, you may want to save everything in your Documents folder for a week or two (or a month or two, depending on how many new documents that you save each day). After a decent-sized group of documents accumulates in the Documents folder, at that point consider taking a look at them and creating logical subfolders for them.

If you want to monkey around with some subfolders yourself, a good place to start is the Documents folder — it's inside your home folder (that is, it's a *subfolder* of your home folder). I'll start your look at getting organized here.

If you use a particular folder a great deal, make an alias of it and then move the alias from the Documents folder to the Dock, your home folder, or to your Desktop (for more info on aliases, see Chapter 4) to make the folder easier to access. For example, if you write a lot of letters, you could keep an alias to your Correspondence folder in your home folder, in the Dock, or on your Desktop for quick access. (By the way, there's no reason you can't have a folder appear in all three places if you like. That's what aliases are all about, aren't they?)

If you put the Documents folder in the Dock, you can click and hold on it (or Control-click) to reveal its subfolders, as shown in Figure 10-9.

Figure 10-9:
It's super
convenient
to have your
Documents
folder in
the Dock.

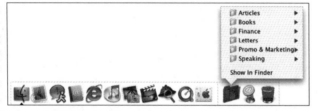

Spring-loaded folders

Spring-loaded folders have been resurrected in Mac OS X version 10.2 Jaguar, and they work in all views and with all folder or disk icons in the toolbar. Because you just got the short course on folders and subfolders and various ways to organize your stuff, you're ready for your introduction to one of my favorite ways to get around my disks, folders, and subfolders.

Here's how they work: Select any icon except a disk icon and drag it onto any folder or disk icon but don't release the mouse button. The folder or disk icon will highlight to indicate that it's selected.

I call this *hovering* because you're doing just that — hovering the cursor over a folder or disk icon.

In a second or two, the highlighted folder or disk will flash once or twice and then spring open right under the cursor.

You can continue to traverse your folder structure this way until you release the mouse button. When you do, the icon that you've been dragging will be dropped into the active folder at the time. That window will remain open but all the windows that you traversed will close.

You can toggle spring-loaded folders on or off in the Finder's Preference window. There's also a setting for how long the Finder waits before it springs open these spring-loaded folders. If you're impatient, you can spring a folder open instantly by pressing the Space bar as you hover your mouse over it.

Finally, to cancel a spring-loaded folder, drag the cursor away from the folder icon or outside the boundaries of the sprung window — the folder will pop shut.

After you get used to them, you'll wonder how you ever got along without them. They work in all three window views, and they work with icons in the toolbar. Give 'em a try and you'll be hooked.

Getting Up to Speed with the Mac OS X Folder Structure

In addition to your personal files and folders, your Mac OS X system has its own folder structure. These folders contain the system software that runs the Mac, as well as folders that include system preferences, fonts, and other files that are used by everyone with access to this Mac. These shared files include applications, programs, utilities, and other software.

Also, each person who uses the Mac has his or her own set of folders that contain documents, preferences, and other information that's used by only that person. If you're the sole person who accesses your Mac, you have only one user. Regardless, the folder structure that Mac OS X uses is the same, whether you have one user or ten.

I realize that a lot of people don't share their Macs with others. And if you're one of these folks, you may wonder why I keep mentioning sharing and multiple users and the like. Well, Mac OS X is based on the UNIX operating system, which is a multi-user operating system that's used by high-end servers and workstations that are often shared by several people. Mac OS X has both the benefit of this arrangement and a bit of the confusion caused when a single user like you fires up a computer that could be set up for several people. That's why Mac OS X folders are organized the way that they are — with different hierarchies for each user and for the computer as a whole.

All these files are stored in a nested folder structure that's a bit tricky to understand at first. This structure makes more sense after you spend a little time with it and learn some basic concepts.

In this section, I walk you through these different folder structures one by one, starting with the place where you'll spend most of your time — your home folder.

The Mac OS X folder structure in depth

I start with the Computer folder, which is the top level of the folder hierarchy. The Computer folder shows all the storage devices (hard drives, CD- or DVD-ROM, Zip disk, and so forth) that are currently connected to your Mac. Figure 10-10 shows a hard disk and a Network icon, with which you can access servers or shared Macs on your network. (Don't quite know what file sharing is all about? Read Chapter 16 for the whole scoop on sharing files with other Macs and sharing your Mac with other users.)

Figure 10-10:
Contents
of the
Computer
folder.

To find the Computer folder, use the keyboard shortcut ⌘+Shift+C or click its icon in the toolbar of any Finder window.

You may have more or fewer icons in your Computer folder than the two that you see in Figure 10-10 (depending upon how many disks that you have mounted), but I'm going to drill down on the one that holds your Mac OS X stuff. In Figure 10-10, that hard drive is called *Macintosh HD* — of course, I have no idea what yours is called; if you haven't changed it, it's probably called *Macintosh HD,* too. Double-click that icon to open it.

Inside your boot disk icon (the one with OS X installed on it; the one called *Macintosh HD* in Figure 10-10) is everything on that disk. You should see at least four folders (unless you've added some — if you installed the Developer Tools CD, for example, or an OS 9 System Folder, you'll have more). I'll go through each of them for you.

Applications

The Applications folder, located at the root level of your boot drive (the one with OS X installed on it), is accessible with a click of the Application button on the toolbar, from the Go menu, or by using the keyboard shortcut ⌘+Shift+A. In this folder, you find all the applications that Apple includes with Mac OS X.

All users of a given Mac have access to the items in this Applications folder. Read more about the Applications folder in Chapter 13 and more about the toolbar in Chapter 6.

Library

The Library folder at the root level of your Mac OS X hard drive is like a public library because it stores items that everyone with access to this Mac can use. You'll find two different library folders on your hard drive — the one at the root level of your OS X disk and another in your home folder.

Okay, I wasn't entirely truthful but only for your own good: There's actually a third Library folder inside the System folder, which I discuss in a page or two. But for now, heed this warning: **Leave this folder alone** — don't move, remove, or rename it or anything within it. It's the nerve center of your Mac. In other words, you should never have to touch this third Library folder.

Think of the Library folder inside your home folder like a library in your own house (have you ever actually been in a house with its own library?) and the one at root level as a public library. I talk more about these Library folders in the upcoming sections.

You find a bunch of folders inside the Library folder at root level (the public Library folder). Most of them contain files that you never need to open, move, or delete. (For what it's worth, just about all of them are preferences of one kind or another.)

The Library folder that most users will work with is the Fonts folder, which houses all the fonts installed on the Mac. Fonts can either be available to everyone who uses the Mac (stored here) or only to a single user (stored in that user's Library folder, the one in their home folder). I discuss fonts more in Chapter 12. Some other subfolders that you may use or add to are the Internet Search Sites folder (where you put Sherlock plug-ins), the Printers folder (where you install new printer drivers), the Scripts folder (which houses AppleScripts accessible to all users), and Desktop Pictures (where you can place pictures to be used for Desktop pictures).

Leave the Library folder pretty much alone unless you're using the Fonts folder or know what you're adding to one of the other folders. Don't remove, rename, or move any files or folders. Mac OS X uses these items and is very picky about where they're kept and how they're named.

Note: Under most circumstances, you won't actually add or remove items from folders in this Library yourself. Software installers do the heavy lifting for you by placing all their little pieces into appropriate Library folders. You shouldn't need to touch this Library often, if ever. That said, knowing what these folders are and who can access their contents may come in handy down the road a-piece.

If you want to add something to a Library, it's usually best to add it to your Home/Library.

Mac OS 9

If you have Mac OS 9.2.2 installed on the same disk as OS X, this folder contains your Mac OS 9.2.2 System folder (which the Classic environment requires) as well as the System Disk program (which enables you to choose to boot your Mac from Mac OS 9.2.1 or OS X).

You can read more about Classic in Chapter 14.

System

The System folder includes the files that Mac OS X needs to start up and keep working. **Leave this folder alone** — don't move, remove, or rename it or anything within it. It's a part of the nerve center of your Mac.

If you've used any previous version of Mac OS, you should notice two things:

✔ The System folder doesn't include the same items or the same arrangement of files and folders.

✔ This folder is now simply called System rather than System Folder.

Also gone are the System file and Finder file that have been around since the first Mac. Located here instead are a large number of files that make up the Mac OS X system.

Users

When you open the Users folder, you see a folder for each person who uses the Mac as well as the Shared folder.

In the next section, I drill down from the home folder bob1 to see what's inside. If user bob1 logs onto this Mac using his username, his home folder (bob1) opens when he clicks the Home button.

The Shared folder that you see in the Users folder allows everyone who uses the Mac to use the files stored there. If you want other people who use your Mac to have access to a file or folder, this is the place to stash it.

Enough with the big picture folder structure! Read on as I dig into how to work with the folders and files in Mac OS X.

There's no place like home

Your home folder is the most important folder to you as a user — or at least the one where you'll probably spend most of your time — but it's only part of

Mac's higher-level folder structure. I walk you through this configuration so that you understand where your home folder fits in and so that you'll be able to find applications and other items shared by everyone who uses your Mac. It's kind of complicated, especially if you're an old-time Mac user who's used to arranging things pretty much the way you want. Take heart, though: After you get the hang of the new way of arranging things, it makes sense.

I strongly recommend that you store all the files that you create or work with in one of the folders of your home folder, whether in the Documents folder or in another folder that you create. The advantage of using the Documents folder is that you can quickly locate the folder from the Go menu or with the keyboard shortcut ⌘+Shift+H — *H* for *home*, of course.

When you open your home folder, you see a Finder window with your username in the title bar. (I discuss this name in Chapter 15.) Seeing your username in the Finder window's title bar tells you that you're in your home folder. Every user has a home folder named after their username in the Users folder. In Figure 10-11, you can see that my home folder is named bobl — that's the nickname I used when I first set up my Mac.

Figure 10-11:
My home
folder.

Your home folder has several folders inside it created by Mac OS X. You can create more if you like — in fact, every folder that you *ever* create (at least every one that you create on this particular disk or volume) should be within your home folder. I'll explain this as I describe the other main folders on your hard drive.

Your home folder contains eight folders by default. The following four are the most important ones:

 ✓ **Desktop:** If you put items (files, folders, applications, or aliases) on the Desktop, they appear on the Desktop. The files themselves, however, are actually stored in this folder.

✔ **Documents:** This is the place to put all the documents (letters, spread-sheets, recipes, and novels) that you create. For more on the Documents folder, check out Chapter 8.

✔ **Library:** Preferences (files containing the settings that you create in System Preferences and other places) are stored in the Library folder, along with fonts (ones that are only available to you, as described previously in this chapter), links to your favorite items, Internet search sites, and other stuff used by you and only you.

✔ **Public:** If you share your Mac, you can't work inside other users' folders. But you can share files with others by storing them in the Public folder of your home folder. (Read more about Public folders in Chapter 16.)

If you decide that you don't want an item on the Desktop anymore, delete it by dragging its icon from the Desktop folder to the Trash or by dragging its icon from the Desktop itself to the Trash. Both techniques yield the same effect — the file is in the Trash, where it remains until you empty the Trash.

In previous versions of Mac OS, there was no Desktop folder. Items stored on the Desktop appeared on the Desktop, and that same Desktop was seen and used by everyone that used this Mac. In Mac OS X, each user has his or her own Desktop, and the items there are stored in the user's Desktop folder.

✔ The other four folders that you may see in your home folder are Movies, Music, Pictures, and Sites. All these folders except Sites are empty until you put something in them; Sites contains a few files that your Mac needs if you enable Web Sharing (in the Sharing System Preferences pane, as I describe in Chapter 15).

Your Library card

The Library subfolder of your home folder is the repository of everything that Mac OS X needs to customize your Mac to your tastes. You won't spend much time (if any) adding things to the Library folder or moving them around within it, but it's a good idea for you to know what's in there. In the "Library" section earlier in this chapter, I discuss the Library folder that's used to specify preferences for the Mac as a whole. But *this* Library folder is all about you and your stuff.

Be cautious with the Library folder because OS X is very persnickety about how its folders and files are organized. As I discuss in the "Library" section earlier in the chapter, you can add and remove items safely from most Library folders, but **leave the folders themselves alone.** If you remove or rename the wrong folder, you could render OS X inoperable. It's like the old joke about the guy who said to the doctor, "It hurts when I do that," and the doctor replies, "Then don't do that."

To find the Library folder, click the Home icon in the toolbar of any Finder window and then open the Library folder. You should see several folders there. The exact number of folders in the Library folder depends on the software that you install on your Mac — for example, if you have an e-mail account, you should see a folder called Addresses (if not, it won't be there). Some of the more important standard folders in the Library folder include the following:

- **Assistants:** When you first set up your Mac or your Internet connection, an assistant helps you along. (See Chapter 13 and this book's Appendix for more on setting up your machine.) The actual files that the assistant uses to do its thing are contained in this folder. This folder is quite likely to be empty.

- **Favorites:** When you add an item to your list of Favorites, an alias of it goes here. (Scope out Chapter 4 for more about aliases.) If you choose Favorites from the Go menu or click the Favorites button on the Finder window's toolbar, this is the folder that you see. If you decide that a particular item is no longer a favorite of yours, you can open this folder and drag the no-longer-loved item to the Trash.

- **Fonts:** This folder is empty unless you install your own fonts here. The fonts that come with Mac OS X aren't stored here but rather in the Library folder at root level for everyone who uses this Mac. I discuss this earlier in this chapter in the "Library" section. If you want to install fonts that only you have access to, put them in the Fonts folder of *your* Library folder.

To install a font, drag its icon to this folder. It will only be available when you're logged in; other users won't be able to use a font stored here. To install a font that's available to anyone who uses this Mac, drag it onto the public Library folder, the one that you see when you open your hard disk's icon.

If your Mac is set up for multiple users, only users with Administrator (admin) privileges can put stuff into the public Library folder. (For more information on admin privileges, check out Chapter 16.)

- **Internet Search Sites:** The files in this folder are used by Sherlock to contact and search Internet sites. Read through Chapter 11 for the basics on Sherlock. Besides the big batch of Internet search sites that come with Mac OS X, you can use search engine files that you can download from the Internet. Store them here and use them with Sherlock.

- **Preferences:** The files here hold the information about things that you customize in Mac OS X. Whenever you change a system or application preference, that info is saved to a file in the Preferences folder.

Don't mess with the Preferences folder! You should never need to open or use this folder unless something bad happens — like you suspect that a particular preference file has become corrupted (that is, damaged). My advice is to just forget about this folder and let it do its job.

Part III
Doing Stuff with Your Mac

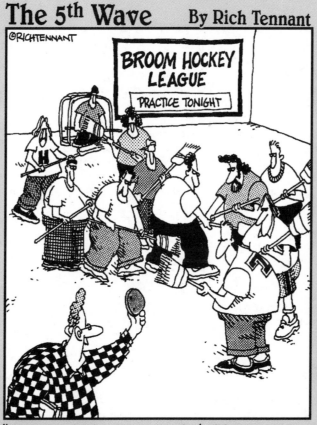

The 5th Wave   By Rich Tennant

@RICHTENNANT

BROOM HOCKEY
LEAGUE

PRACTICE TONIGHT

"Hey you bunch of loser jocks! This happens to
be an AirPort, and I got it to go with my iBook,
and you wouldn't even know what to do with it!"

In this part . . .

Moving right along, Part III comprises how to do stuff
with your Mac. In this section, it's off to the
Internet first — how to get it working and what to do with
it after you do. Next, I help you decipher the myriad Print
options to better help you become a modern-day
Gutenberg. You'll also learn about the applications that
come with OS X, the Classic Environment, and how to
make your OS X look and feel the way you want it.

It's an excellent section if I do say so myself . . . one you
definitely don't want to miss.

Chapter 11

Internet-Working

● ●

In This Chapter

▶ Getting an overview of the Internet

▶ Pre-surfing with the Internet Setup Assistant

▶ Surfing the Web with Internet Explorer (IE)

▶ Searching with Sherlock

▶ E-mailing with Mail

▶ About the .Mac (dot-Mac) services

▶ Chatting with iChat

● ●

*S*imply put, use the Internet to connect your Mac to a wealth of information residing on computers around the world. Lucky for you, Mac OS X has the best and most comprehensive Internet tools ever shipped with a Mac operating system. In this chapter, I cover the top two: the *World Wide Web* (that's the *www* you see so often in Internet addresses) and *e-mail* (which stands for *electronic mail*). Okay, with Apple's release of iChat, I'm adding a third one: *live chatting.*

This chapter covers only the barest minimum of stuff that you need to know to connect to the Internet. If you're interested in knowing more about Macs and the Internet, look for *The Internet For iMacs For Dummies* by Bob LeVitus and Natanya Pitts (published by Hungry Minds, Inc.) at fine bookstores everywhere. In all fairness, I have to admit that this book was written before OS X came along and doesn't have any OS X-specific content. Still, it does cover the Internet in full and loving detail far beyond what I can provide in this chapter.

A Brief Internet Overview

The *Internet,* which is a giant conglomeration of connected computers, offers innumerable types of services. Sometimes referred to as the *Information Superhighway*, the Internet is a giant worldwide network of computers. With an Internet connection, you can view text and graphics on your computer, even if the text and graphics are sitting on a computer in Tokyo. Via the Internet, you can send and retrieve messages and computer files to and from almost anywhere in the world — in milliseconds.

Other Internet services include bulletin board discussions called *newsgroups*, File Transfer Protocol (FTP), and video conferencing. After you have your connection set up (I discuss this process in the "Setting Up for Surfing" section later in this chapter), I urge you to check out these nifty features. Unfortunately, although these other features are pretty cool, going into much detail about them is also beyond the purview of this book.

The most interesting part of the Internet, at least in my humble opinion, is the Web. This is the part of the Internet in which you traverse (that is, surf) to Web sites and view them on your computer with software called a *Web browser*.

Mac OS X offers built-in Internet connectivity right out of the box. For example, your machine comes with

- ✔ Its own built-in **Point-to-Point Protocol** (PPP) client for making modem connections to the Internet

  If you don't even know what a modem is, don't worry. Skip ahead to the upcoming section "Setting Up for Surfing," and all will become clear.

- ✔ Microsoft **Internet Explorer** (a Web browser with which you to navigate the Web, download remote files via FTP, and more)

- ✔ The **Mail** application (for e-mail)

- ✔ **iChat** (Apple's live online chatting client that works with other iChat users and people using AOL Instant Messaging, AIM, clients)

Because most Mac users like things to be easy, Mac OS X includes a cool feature in its Setup Assistant to help you find and configure an account with an Internet Service Provider (ISP). After your Internet connection is up and running, you can use Internet Explorer, which is included with OS X, to cruise the Internet.

But before I can talk about browsers, e-mail software, and chatting, I first have to help you configure your Internet connection. When you're finished, you can play with Internet Explorer and Mail to your heart's content.

Setting Up for Surfing

Before you can surf the Internet, you need to do a few things first. In this section, I walk you through them all.

If you're a typical home user, you need three things to surf the Internet:

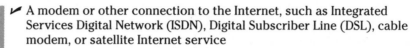

✔ A modem or other connection to the Internet, such as Integrated Services Digital Network (ISDN), Digital Subscriber Line (DSL), cable modem, or satellite Internet service

If you use any technology other than a regular (analog) modem to connect your computer to the Internet, your network administrator (the person who you run to at work when something goes wrong with your computer) or ISP will have to help you set up your Mac because setting up those other configurations is beyond the scope of this book.

✔ An account with an ISP (an Internet Service Provider such as EarthLink) or America Online (AOL)

As I write this chapter, America Online has finally released a version of its software that works with OS X.

✔ Mac OS X default installation

It starts with the modem

A *modem* is a small, inexpensive device that turns data (that is, computer files) into sounds and then squirts those sounds across phone lines. At the other end, another modem receives these sounds and turns them back into data (that is, your files). All current Macs include an internal 56 Kbps modem.

Now plug a phone line into the modem. On Macs with internal modems, that simply means plugging one end of the phone cable into the phone plug-shaped port on the side or back of your Mac and the other end into a live phone outlet (or the phone jack on a surge suppressor that has a phone line running to your phone outlet). If you have an external modem, plug the phone cable into the modem and plug the modem cable into a USB port. Finally, plug the modem into an AC power source.

  The modem port on Macs with internal modems looks a lot like the Ethernet port, but it's smaller. You could plug a phone cable into the Ethernet port, but it wouldn't fit right and it wouldn't get you connected to the Internet. The modem port is the smaller of the two — look for the phone icon next to it. Conversely, the Ethernet port is the larger of the two. Look for an icon that looks something like this: <• • •>. Check out the differences: Both ports and their icons appear in the margin (the Ethernet port is on the left).

Just in case you visit a store populated by computer geeks, a phone connector is called an RJ-11, and an Ethernet connector is called an RJ-45.

High-speed connections

If you have a cable modem, digital subscriber line (DSL), or other high-speed Internet connection — or are thinking about getting any of these — you can use them with your Mac. In most cases, you connect your Mac to the Internet via a cable plugged into the Ethernet port of your Mac and into an external box, which is either connected to a cable or phone outlet, depending on what kind of access you have to the Internet. Your cable or DSL installer-person should set everything up for you. If they don't, you'll have to call that service provider for help — troubleshooting your high-speed connection is, as they say, "beyond the purview of this book."

Your Internet service provider and you

After you make sure that you have a working modem, you need to select a company to provide you with access to the Internet. These companies are called *Internet Service Providers* (ISPs). Just like when choosing a long-distance company for your phone, the prices and services that ISPs offer vary, often from minute to minute. After you make your choice, you can launch and use Internet Explorer, Mail, iChat, or any other Internet application. Keep the following in mind when choosing an ISP:

✔ If you're using a cable modem, your ISP is your cable company. In most cases, the same applies to DSL — except that your provider is either your local phone company or an ISP that you've chosen to get your service connected. In that case, your ISP usually contacts the phone company and arranges for installation and setup for you.

✔ If you subscribe to AOL, you don't need to do anything more than install the AOL software and log on to AOL. You can ignore the rest of this chapter except for the parts about surfing with Internet Explorer, Apple's .Mac (dot-Mac) offerings, and preferences. You don't need Mail (the e-mail program included with OS X) if you get your mail exclusively through AOL, but if you've opted for a .Mac account, you can still use Mail to access it.

In addition to AOL, check out dedicated Internet service companies such as EarthLink and AT&T. Also investigate what your local cable or phone company offers. In other words, it pays to shop around for the deal that works best for you.

The going rate for unlimited access to the Internet, using a modem, is $10–$23 per month. If your service provider asks for considerably more than that, find out why. *Note:* If you have a cable modem, DSL, or other high-speed connection, you'll probably pay at least twice that much.

When you installed OS X (assuming that you did, and that it didn't come pre-installed on your Mac), the Installer program asked you a bunch of questions about your Internet connection and then set everything up for you. This process is detailed at the end of the book in the Appendix. If you didn't have an Internet connection (an ISP) at that time, you'll need to configure the

For those who don't care for Internet Explorer (or Microsoft)

You can use any Internet browser you choose — such as Netscape, Mozilla, OmniWeb, iCab, Opera, or Chimera — but these browsers are not installed automatically with OS X like Internet Explorer. Instead, you'll have to download and install them first. You'll find the latest version of each by visiting www.versiontracker.com/macosx and searching for *browser*.

If you don't like Internet Explorer or Netscape, I recommend OmniWeb. Unlike IE and Netscape, OmniWeb was designed exclusively for Mac OS X — and in my opinion, renders the best-looking pages. For more info, visit www.omnigroup.com.

The newest browsers on the OS X scene are Chimera, iCab, and Opera. All three were unfinished when I wrote this, but working beta versions are always available and usually work fairly well.

Frankly, all the browsers — even the unfinished ones — are pretty darned good, and there's no penalty for installing a second (or third or fourth) one on your hard disk. So if you're not totally satisfied with the included Internet Explorer browser, try some of the others to decide which you like best.

Network System Preferences pane yourself. Although I cover the Network System Preferences pane in depth in Chapter 15, how to configure it so that your Mac will work with your ISP is something you'll have to work out with that ISP. If you have questions or problems not answered by this book, your ISP should be able to assist you.

And if your ISP can't help, it's probably time to try a different ISP.

Browsing the Web with Internet Explorer

In this chapter, I concentrate on IE because it's installed and ready to go on your Mac by default. (And, because I prefer it at this time.) Apple includes Microsoft Internet Explorer (IE) with Mac OS X. Also, it's no problem to install and use more than one Web browser on your hard drive if you so desire.

Getting up and running with IE

Before you can browse the Web, the first step is to open your Web browser. No problem. As usual, there's more than one way. You can launch Internet Explorer by

✓ Clicking the Internet Explorer icon on the Dock (look for the big blue lowercase *e*)

✓ Double-clicking the Internet Explorer icon in your Applications folder

✓ Double-clicking a link document representing a Web page

When you first launch IE, it automatically connects you to the Internet and displays Apple's Web page (see Figure 11-1).

If a dialog pops up asking whether you'd like to set Internet Explorer as your default browser, click Yes. If you later change your mind and would prefer a different browser to be your default, you can change it in the Internet System Preference pane (covered extensively in Chapter 15).

I don't have room in this book to describe everything about IE, but I'll hit the highlights from the top of the IE screen.

"What's this button do?"

The buttons along the top of the window — Back, Forward, Stop, Refresh, Home, and so forth — do pretty much what their names imply. Play with them a bit, and you'll see what I mean.

Figure 11-1:
The Apple
Web page.

Below the Address field are some more buttons that take you directly to pages that may interest you, such as the Apple Web site (unless you've surfed to another site, that's what you're looking at), your Live Home Page (see Figure 11-2), the Apple tech support Web site, the Apple .Mac Web site, the Apple Store, and others. Clicking any of them transports you instantly to that page.

I just clicked the Live Home Page button, which moves me from the Apple Web page that I was viewing to the My Netscape Live Home Page, as shown in Figure 11-2.

Why Netscape? Last year Apple used Excite as its Live Home Page vendor, but Excite ran into some well-publicized financial difficulties. Not long after that, Excite was out, and Netscape was in.

Click any of the four Personalize buttons near the top of the page to customize the look and contents displayed on your Live Home Page.

Figure 11-2:
Your very
own Live
Home Page.

"Address me as Sir, rodent!"

Beneath the top row of buttons is the Address field. This is where you type Web addresses, or *URLs* (Uniform Resource Locators), that you want to visit. Just type one in and press Return to surf to that site.

Web addresses almost always begin with `http://www`. But Internet Explorer has a cool trick: If you just type a name, you usually get to the appropriate Web site that way without typing **http**, **//**, or **www**. For example, if you type **apple** in the Address field and then press Return, you go to `http://www.apple.com`. Or if you type **boblevitus**, you're taken to `www.boblevitus.com`. Try it; it's pretty slick.

"Get me a Tab, would you dahling?"

IE gives you five tabs down the left side of the browser window that let you look at two things at once. In the case of the Favorites tab (which I briefly discuss in the "Playing Favorites" section later in the chapter), you view a Web site in the main page on the right and the Web sites you like to visit most often on the left.

You just click a tab to open a pane on the left of your screen. Explore all the tabs if you want to get the most from Internet Explorer. Following is a brief description of each tab:

- ✔ **Favorites:** Otherwise known as *bookmarks,* this tab is where you save the addresses of your favorite Web sites.
- ✔ **History:** This tab holds links to all the Web pages that you've visited recently.
- ✔ **Search:** Click this tab to hunt for sites and people on the Web.
- ✔ **Scrapbook:** Use this tab to saves pages exactly as they are when you put them in the scrapbook. Because Web pages can change from day to day (or even more frequently), this is convenient if you want to save a page for future reference but you aren't sure that it'll still be the same if you just bookmark it.
- ✔ **Page Holder:** With this tab, you can copy a page to browse its links without using the Back button. The linked pages come up in the main window on the right when you click them in the Page Holder window on the left.

Change the size of the left window by clicking on the vertical bar between it and the right pane and then dragging it to move the border.

To close the left window, just click the tab that corresponds to it.

Playing Favorites

Clicking the Favorites tab (top-left; next to Netscape Network logo in Figure 11-2) shows your favorites on the left while the page that you're viewing remains on the right, as shown in Figure 11-3. You can open a Favorite by clicking it. To open a folder full of Favorites (they're the same favorites and folders on the Favorites menu), just click the disclosure triangle to the left of its heading.

Click to open a Favorites folder.

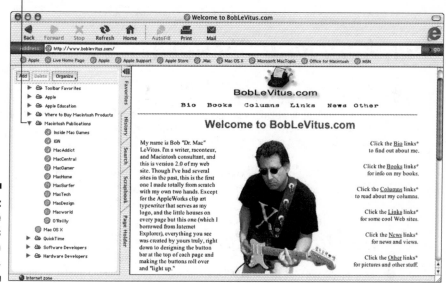

Figure 11-3: The Favorites tab in action.

Your copy of IE comes with some pointers — known as *favorites* (they're called *bookmarks* in Netscape) — that take you to other nifty Mac sites to check out.

TIP

Bookmarks are favorites, and favorites are bookmarks. Both words describe the same exact thing — shortcuts to Web sites. In this chapter, I use the words interchangeably. But be careful not to confuse Internet Explorer's Favorites with Mac OS X's Favorites. They serve a similar purpose: Both are shortcuts to something you use often, but they are *not* interchangeable. In other words, even though they're both called favorites, your OS X favorites are not used by Internet Explorer, and your Internet Explorer favorites are not used by OS X.

To manage your favorites, choose Favorites⇨Organize Favorites. A window listing your favorites and the folders containing them appears. You can move your favorites, create and remove folders, and otherwise treat favorites just like files in the Finder. You can even place these favorites and folders of favorites on the Internet Explorer toolbar. To delete a favorite, just select it and then press Delete or Backspace.

You'll find favorites links to Apple sites, hardware and software vendors, Mac publications, and more. Take a look at the list of great Web pages that your pals at Apple have put together. Choosing any item from the Favorites menu takes you to that Web page. Be sure and explore all the included Favorites when you have some time; most, if not all, are worth knowing more about.

Searching with Sherlock

Looking for something on the Internet? Check out *Sherlock,* an application included with Mac OS X that can help you locate stuff on the Internet. You can scour general-purpose Internet search engines with the options under the Internet button or get more specific with one of the nine other Internet buttons.

In this section, you discover how to find Sherlock, how to use it to search the Internet, and how to get help with it when all else fails.

Starting Sherlock

You have two ways to invoke Sherlock:

- ✓ **Double-click the Sherlock icon in your Applications folder.**
- ✓ **Click the Sherlock icon on the Dock.** (Read more about the Dock in Chapter 3.)

Whichever way you choose, the Sherlock window appears, as shown in Figure 11-4.

A quick look at Sherlock's features

Before you use Sherlock, I'd like to point out a few of its more important features.

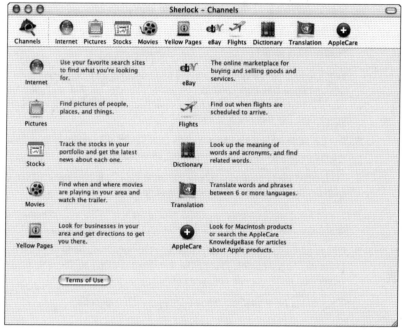

Figure 11-4:
It's
Sherlock's
Channels
screen.

The top of the Sherlock window sports a series of buttons. From left to right they are Channels, Internet, Pictures, Stocks, Movies, Yellow Pages, eBay, Flights, Dictionary, Translation, and AppleCare. You click the button that best represents what you're searching for. If you're looking for a Web site, click Internet. If you want to find where and when a movie is playing near you, click Movies. If you want to look up a word's meaning, click Dictionary. And so on.

The bottom part of the Sherlock window changes, depending on which button you've clicked (before a search). Then, it displays the results of your search (after you search, of course).

Searching with Sherlock

You use Sherlock to find things on the Internet. In this section, I first show you how to search with Sherlock.

Although I use an Internet search in the steps, you follow the same steps to search in any of the other channels. After you know how to search the Internet with Sherlock, you know how to search any Internet channel with Sherlock. To use Sherlock, follow these steps:

1. **Start Sherlock (I describe how in the previous section).**

2. **Click one of the ten Internet buttons to choose a channel.**

   Figure 11-5 shows the Internet channel.

   Yes, I know there are actually 11 icons, but the leftmost icon just describes what the 10 real search icons do, as you can see in Figure 11-4. The 10 to the right of the little dividing line are the actual buttons that you click for Internet searches.

3. **In the text entry field beneath the Sherlock search buttons, type a word or a phrase that you want to search for.**

4. **To begin your search, press Return or click the magnifying glass button to the right of the text entry field.**

   Sherlock passes your request along to the Web search engines and then displays a list of search results, similar to Figure 11-5.

5. **Click any search site listed along the bottom of Sherlock's window (About, Ask Jeeves, Best Site 1st, and so on) to launch your Web browser and access the search engine directly.**

   To start a new search, repeat Steps 2 through 5.

Figure 11-5: Searching for myself by using Sherlock's Internet search.

Some channels are slightly different in the way they look, such as the Movies channel shown in Figure 11-6, which doesn't let you search for movies by name but rather asks for your city and state or ZIP code and then displays the movies in a three-column browser.

The Movies channel offers some nifty extras not found in other channels, including the movie poster and a QuickTime preview (lower-right pane of Figure 11-6) and the Buy Tickets button (lower-left pane of Figure 11-6). Slick!

Checking out Help Center

I need to use another weasel-out here. I could write an entire chapter about using Sherlock, but one of the rules we *For Dummies* authors must follow is that our books can't run 1,000 pages long. So I'm going to give you the next best thing: Open the Help Center (by choosing Help⇨Sherlock Help from the Sherlock menu bar). A special Sherlock Help window appears; you can search for any topic here.

Figure 11-6:
The Movies channel works a bit differently than some of the others.

Getting Your E-Mail with Mail

Mail is a program that comes with Mac OS X that you use to send, receive, and organize your e-mail. You can also use Mail to access an address book that includes the addresses of your friends and family.

You can use other applications to read Internet mail. Netscape, for example, has a built-in mail reader, as does Microsoft Office (Entourage). But the easiest and best mail reader around (meaning, the best one on your hard drive by default) is probably Mail. And you can't beat the price; it's free!

Mail is fast and easy to use, too. Click the Mail icon on the Dock to send and receive mail; the Mail icon looks like a cancelled postage stamp.

Mail's main window looks like Figure 11-7.

Figure 11-7:
Mail's main window.

Composing a new message

Here's how to create a new e-mail message:

1. Choose File⇨New Message or press ⌘+N.

A new window appears; this is where you compose your e-mail message, as shown in Figure 11-8.

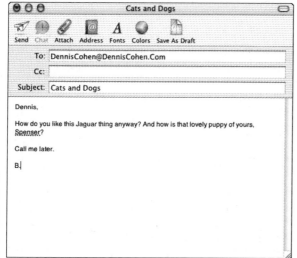

Dennis,

How do you like this Jaguar thing anyway? And how is that lovely puppy of yours, Spenser?

Call me later.

B.

Figure 11-8:
Composing
an e-mail
message.

2. **Place your cursor in the To field and type someone's e-mail address.**

   Use my address (boblevitus@boblevitus.com) if you don't know anyone else to send mail to.

   After you finish addressing a mail message, you can add the recipient to your address book. After you add an address to your address book, all you have to do is type the first few letters of the recipient's name, and Mail fills in the entire address for you. Neat, huh? (Choose Help➪Mail Help to find out more about this feature.) You can even have Mail add the name and address of people who sent you mail by choosing Message➪ Add Sender to Address Book (press ⌘+Y) when you're reading the mail from them.

3. **Press the Tab key twice to move your cursor to the Subject text field and then type a subject for this message.**

4. **Click in the main message portion of the window (refer to Figure 11-8) and type your message there.**

5. **When you're finished writing your message, click the Send button to send the e-mail immediately or choose File➪Save as Draft to save it in the Drafts folder so that you can work on it later.**

   If you do save your message to the Drafts folder (so you can write more later, perhaps), you can send it when you're ready by opening the Drafts folder, double-clicking the message, and then clicking the Send button.

Checking your mail

How do you check and open your mail? Easy. Just click the Get Mail button at the top of the main Mail window.

You can configure Mail to send and receive your mail every *x* minutes by choosing Mail⇨Preferences and then clicking the Accounts icon at the top of the window. Pull down the Check Accounts for New Mail pop-up menu and make a selection — every 1, 5, 15, 30, or 60 minutes — or choose Manually if you don't want Mail to check for mail automatically at all. The default setting is to check for mail every five minutes.

Dealing with spam

E-mail is a wonderful thing, but some people out there try to spoil it. If you think you get a lot of junk mail in your regular mailbox, just wait until some purveyor of electronic junk mail gets hold of your e-mail address. These lowlifes share their lists — and before you know it, your e-mail box is flooded with get-rich-quick schemes, advertisements for pornographic Web sites and chat rooms, and all the more traditional buy-me junk mail.

Mail comes with a Junk Mail filter that analyzes incoming message subjects, senders, and contents to determine which ones are likely to contain bulk or junk mail. Apple calls its initial configuration *training mode*. While training Mail to recognize which of its selections aren't junk, click the Not Junk button in the brown bar informing you that Mail thinks it found a piece of junk mail.

If a piece of junk mail slips past Mail's filters, select it in your Inbox and click the Junk button in the Mail window's toolbar.

After a few days (or weeks, depending upon your mail volume), Mail should be getting it right almost all the time. When you reach that point, choose Mail⇨Junk Mail⇨Automatic, and Mail will start moving junk mail automatically out of your Inbox and into a Junk folder where you can scan the items quickly and trash it when you're ready.

If, for some reason that escapes me, you prefer to receive and manually process your junk mail, you can turn Junk Mail processing off by choosing Mail⇨Junk Mail⇨Off.

Changing your preferences

Actually, Mail's Preferences are more than you may expect from the name. This is the control center for Mail where you: create and delete e-mail accounts; determine which fonts and colors are used for your messages;

decide whether attachments (such as pictures) are downloaded and saved; decide whether you send formatted mail or plain text; decide whether the spell checker is turned on; decide whether you have an automatic signature appended to your messages; and even establish rules to process mail that you receive.

As I've said before, space limitations make much of this beyond the scope of this book, but you should find everything perfectly straightforward, possibly with the assistance of Help⇨Mail Help. If you really want to tap the power of Mail, learn to set *Rules*. These little snippets let you automatically tag messages with a color, file them in a specific mailbox, reply to/forward/redirect the message (handy when you're going to be away for a while), or just delete the message *(kill-filing)* without even bothering to look at it.

Adding an item to your address book

If you have a fair number of contacts — relatives, friends, or the odd enemy that you keep in touch with for self-punishment purposes — you may want to check out the nifty Address Book application that comes with Mac OS X. You can enter new contacts in the Address Book application or while you're working in Mail or iChat (or any other program that interfaces with the Address Book).

Follow these steps to create a new entry in the Address Book:

1. **Launch the Address Book application by double-clicking its icon in the Applications folder or clicking its Dock icon.**

   The Address Book appears. The first time that you open Address Book, you see an empty address book.

2. **To create a new entry, click the Plus button at the bottom of the Address Book's Name column.**

   An untitled address card appears. The First name text field is initially selected. (You can tell by the border it now has, as shown in Figure 11-9.)

3. **Type the person's first name in the First text field.**

   I am entering my info into Address Book, so I type **Bob**.

4. **Press Tab.**

   Your cursor should now be in the Last text field.

   You can always move from one field to the next by pressing Tab. And, in fact, this shortcut works in almost all Mac programs that have fields like these. Furthermore, you can move to the previous field by pressing Shift+Tab.

5. Type the last name for the person who you're adding to your Address Book.

Continue this process, filling in the rest of the fields shown in Figure 11-10.

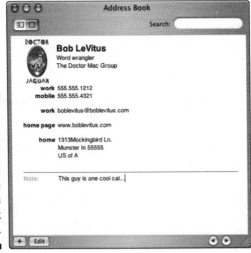

6. When you're done entering information, click in either of the other two Address Book columns.

The contact that I just created for myself appears in Figure 11-9.

The little contact card is called a *vCard* (virtual business card).

To add more info about any Address Book entry, select the name in the Name column (<No Name> in Figure 11-9; you can tell when a name is selected because it has a gray field behind it), click the Edit button at the bottom of the Address Book window, and then make your changes.

You can do some pretty neat stuff with Address Book that I just don't have room to cover in this book. For example, you can organize your contacts into groups so that you can e-mail everyone in a group (that you define) with one click. You can create a blank e-mail message to a contact by clicking and holding the label next to the e-mail address and choosing Send Email from the pop-up menu that appears, as shown in Figure 11-11.

Figure 11-11:
Sending
e-mail to
someone
in your
Address
Book is as
easy as
clicking
here.

And much more.

A Quick Overview of .Mac

.Mac is a set of Internet-based services provided by Apple. Although .Mac isn't specifically a Mac OS X feature (most of them are still available to Mac OS 9 users and have been since before Apple released Mac OS X), I'd be remiss if I didn't at least mention them and give you some background so you can check them out.

The seven .Mac services at the time of this writing are

- **Mac.com and Webmail:** An e-mail service run by Apple that lets you have an e-mail address in the form of `yourname@mac.com`. For OS X users, Apple has added IMAP support and an SMTP server (is that enough geek-speak for you?). What this means is that you can now maintain your messages on the Apple server, and you don't have to use your ISP's server to send mail any longer. You can also access your Mac.com e-mail account from any computer with an Internet connection and a Web browser (that's called *Webmail.*)

- **iDisk:** Your own personal 100MB Internet-based virtual disk.

- **HomePage:** The easiest way I know of to build your own home page.

- **Backup:** A utility to back up folders on your hard disk to either your iDisk or a CD-R or DVD-R disk.

- **iCards:** Electronic greeting cards that you can e-mail to your friends.

- **Anti-Virus:** A copy of the Virex virus-scanning and protection utility, including regular updates.

- **Support:** A consolidated link to a variety of support services, such as Network Status, online discussion boards concerning Apple hardware and software products, the AppleCare Knowledge Base, and Apple's customer Feedback page.

The first two services — Mac.com and iDisk — are beautifully integrated with OS X. For example, the aforementioned Mail program is set up to work perfectly with a Mac.com e-mail account. All you have to do is supply your username and password. And iDisk is a choice in the Finder's Go menu, although you can't use it until you visit the Apple Web site and create your own Mac.com account ($100/year). Even better, Apple keeps a folder there that doesn't count against your 100MB, full of software for you to download and try out. If you want more than 100MB, Apple will lease you space — find out all about it on the Mac.com Web pages.

So what are you waiting for? To sign up, surf to `http://www.Mac.com`.

Communicating via iChat

Instant messaging and chat rooms provide for interactive communication between users all over the world. If you're into instant messaging, iChat gives you immediate access to all the other users of AOL Instant Messaging (AIM) and .Mac. All you need is their screen name and you're set to go. You can even join any AOL chat room just by choosing Go To Chat from the File menu and typing its name, as shown in Figure 11-12.

Figure 11-12:
Entering an
AOL chat
room.

OS X 10.2's built-in Rendezvous support makes it even better. With Rendezvous, which offers configuration-free connections, you don't have to do anything to be part of a Rendezvous network because your Mac configures itself and joins up automatically. For example, with Rendezvous enabled, if you take your AirPort-equipped PowerBook to a location with an AirPort network, you can communicate via iChat with anyone on that network without any network configuration. Just choose Rendezvous from the Window menu and select the person with whom you want to chat from the Rendezvous window.

Your chats can be one-to-one or they can be group bull sessions. Each participant's picture (or icon) appears next to anything he says, which is displayed in a cartoon-like thought bubble, as shown in Figure 11-13.

Figure 11-13:
A chat with
myself (I
have two
Macs on
the same
network.)

If you've attached a picture to a person in your Address Book, you'll even see that picture when you iChat with that person. Neat!

If you find the thought bubbles a little too childish, you can turn them off from the View menu.

iChat even lets you transfer files, giving you a very convenient way to share photos or documents without resorting to file sharing or e-mail. Just drag the document's icon to the message box, as demonstrated in Figure 11-14, press Enter or Return, and the file will zip across the ether.

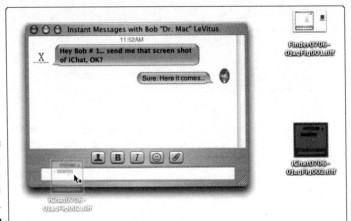

Figure 11-14:
Transferring
a file with
iChat.

iChat is integrated with the Address Book, so you don't have to enter your Buddies' information twice. It also communicates directly with the Mail application. Just select a Buddy in iChat's Buddy List, click the Compose Email button at the bottom of the window, and Mail will address a new message for you.

Chapter 12

Publish or Perish: The Fail-Safe Guide to Printing

*P**rinting* is the process of getting what's on your screen onto paper. I know you probably know that, but my editor insisted I start this chapter by defining printing. And so I have.

Printing under OS X should be as simple as pressing the keyboard shortcut ⌘+P and then pressing the Return or Enter key. Happily, that's usually how easy printing something is. When it isn't, however, printing turns into a raging nightmare. If you configure your printer and printing software properly, though, printing is as easy as can be. And that's pretty darn simple. In this chapter, I scare away the bogeymen to help you avoid any printing nightmares. I'll walk you through the entire process as if you just unpacked a new printer and plugged it in.

If you're upgrading from a 9.*x* version of Mac OS, you probably want to work through these steps because things have changed in OS X.

Before Diving In . . .

Before I even start talking about hooking up printers, you should know a few things. So here's a little list that tells you just what those things are:

❘ ✔ **Read the documentation that came with your specific printer.**
Hundreds of different printer makes and models are available for the Mac, so if I contradict something in your printer manual, follow your

manual's instructions first. If that effort doesn't work, try it my way — use the techniques that you'll be reading about in the rest of this chapter.

✔ **The Print and Page Setup sheets differ slightly from program to program and from printer to printer.** Although the examples that I show you in this chapter are representative of what you will probably encounter, you may come across sheets that look a bit different. For example, the Print and Page Setup sheets for Microsoft Word include choices that I don't cover in this chapter, such as Even or Odd Pages Only, Print Hidden Text, and Print Selection Only. If you see commands in your Print or Page Setup sheet that I don't explain in this chapter, they're specific to that application; look within its documentation for explanation.

✔ **I use Apple's bare-bones word processor, TextEdit, for the examples in this chapter.** If you want to follow along, you'll find TextEdit in your Applications folder.

✔ **Don't forget about Mac OS Help.** Many programs support this excellent Apple technology, which can be the fastest way to figure out a feature that has you stumped. So don't forget to check the Help menu before you panic. (I cover the Help menu way back in Chapter 6.)

So, with those things in mind, get ready, set, print!

Ready: Connecting and Adding Your Printer

Before you can even think about printing something, you have to connect a printer to your Mac and then tell OS X that the printer exists. Here's how.

Connecting your printer

Once again, I must remind you that there are thousands of printer models that you could connect to your Mac. And each one is a little different from the next. In other words, if what you're about to read doesn't track with the printer that you're trying to connect, I again implore you to RTFM (that's *Read The Fine Manual*, in case you're wondering.) It should tell you how to load your ink or toner cartridges.

Remove all the packing material and little strips of tape, some of which you won't even see if you don't know where to look.

That said, here are some very general steps to connect a printer:

1. **Connect the printer to your Mac with the cable snugly attached at both ends (printer and machine).**

   For your printer to work, you have to somehow connect it to a data source. (Think of your phone — you can't receive calls without some sort of connector between the caller and the callee.)

2. **Plug the AC power cord printer cord into a power outlet (yup, the regular kind in the wall or on a power strip).**

   Some printers require you to plug one end of the AC power cord into the printer; others have the AC power cord attached permanently. The point is that your printer won't work if it's not connected to a power source.

3. **Turn on your printer (check out your manual if you can't find the switch).**

4. **If your printer came with software, install it on your hard drive, following the instructions that came with the printer.**

5. **Restart your Mac.**

   That's it!

Any port on a Mac

You need to plug the printer cable into the appropriate port on the back of your Mac. Therein lies the rub. Mac technology has changed dramatically since the previous editions of this book, when I used to say, "Begin by connecting the printer to the Printer port on the back of your Mac (with both the Mac and the printer turned off, of course — but you knew that, didn't you?)." Now I tell you, "You need to plug the printer cable into the appropriate port. . . ." Why am I being so vague? Because I have to be. You see, these days, printers don't always connect to the same port. Some printers connect to the Ethernet port or to an Ethernet hub (which is, in turn, connected to the back of your Mac). Others connect through the Universal Serial Bus (USB) port. I've even seen a few that connect via the FireWire port. So

read the instructions that came with your printer and plug your printer into the appropriate hole (port) for your Mac.

Typically, your printer connects to your machine with a USB, Ethernet, or FireWire cable. Don't confuse this with your printer's AC power cord (the kind you find on everyday appliances). If your printer didn't come with a cable that fits into one of the ports on your Mac, contact your printer manufacturer and ask for one; it's cheesy not to provide the proper cable with a printer. Unfortunately, some manufacturers make printers with different kinds of connectors on the back (to sell them to those poor souls stuck using Windows) and expect you to buy your own cable. Asking one of these manufacturers for a cable will be an exercise in futility.

Setting up a printer for the first time

After you connect your computer and printer with a compatible cable, provide a power source for your printer, and install the software for your printer, you need to configure your Mac so that it and your printer can talk to each other.

The Print Center application, which I am about to discuss, is the tool that you use to tell your Mac what printers are available. Note that many of the steps involving Print Center require that your printer is turned on and warmed up (that is, run through its diagnostics and start-up cycle).

Follow these steps to set up a printer for the first time:

1. **Launch Print Center.**

   You'll find Print Center in the Utilities folder, which is inside your Applications folder. Click the Applications button in the toolbar of any Finder window to open the Applications folder. Now open the Utilities folder and double-click Print Center.

2. **Choose Show Printer List from the Printers menu.**

3. **From the Printer List window that appears (see the upcoming Figure 12-1), click the Add button in the window's toolbar.**

   Most printers are either connected directly to your Mac via a USB port — or over a network, using AppleTalk.

4. **In the sheet that appears, click the pop-up menu to select your printer's connection type.**

   Many USB printers (such as most of the compatible printers from Epson, Canon, and Hewlett-Packard) will be recognized immediately without you having to perform this step.

   For my example, I choose USB because the printer I'll be working with is a Canon USB printer, connected to the Mac via a USB cable.

AppleTalk and USB are by far the most common kinds of printer connections for Macs. Another option available in the Add Printer window is IP Printing. If your printer is on a Transmission Control Protocol/Internet Protocol (TCP/IP) network, you need to configure the printer by using its network address. IP printers are almost always found on large corporate networks. Fortunately, such large networks are almost always maintained by a network administrator, who should be able to help you set up an IP printer.

If you encounter trouble setting up a printer for Mac OS X, you may want to contact your printer's manufacturer about getting the latest, greatest driver. Many printer manufacturers are offering new drivers with enhanced functionality. You may find new drivers for your printer on the Web or a major Internet Service Provider, such as America Online. Apple often includes such new drivers in the Software folder on your iDisk. And Disk 2 of the Mac OS X 10.2 Installer disks has additional printer drivers as well. Check with your printer manufacturer for details.

After you choose your printer connection type, you see the names and kinds of available printers in the Printer List window. In Figure 12-1, my USB printer, named *S830D*, appears.

Figure 12-1:
Available printers with the specified connection type appear here.

Checking for AppleTalk if you don't see your printer

If you have an AppleTalk printer but don't see it on the list when you click the AppleTalk option from the pop-up menu (look for the pop-up reading USB in Figure 12-1), check in System Preferences to see whether AppleTalk is active. (I cover System Preferences in Chapter 15, but here's how you check this.)

1. **Choose System Preferences from the Apple menu or by clicking its icon in the Dock.**

   The System Preferences window opens.

2. **Open the Network Preferences pane by clicking the Network icon in the System Preferences window.**

   The System Preferences window turns into the Network pane.

3. **Click the AppleTalk tab of the Network pane and check to see whether the Make AppleTalk Active check box is selected.**

4. **If the AppleTalk Active check box is not marked, check (select) it. You may have to click the padlock icon on the bottom left of the window and enter an Administrator password to do this.**

5. **After you make AppleTalk active, quit System Preferences and go back to the Print Center application (click its icon on the Dock; or, if you quit or restarted, launch it — it's in the Utilities folder inside your Applications folder) and add your Apple Talk printer. (See the section "Setting up a printer for the first time" where I detail adding your AppleTalk printer.)**

6. **When you've added and configured a printer, you can quit Print Center.**

5. **Click the name of the printer that you want from the list and then click the Add button.**

   This window closes and the Printer List window reappears, containing the printer that you just added. If you've added printers before, they appear here, too.

   Now you can print your first document! Make sure, though, that you have the document set to look how you want it to print. Read through the section "Set: Setting Up Your Document with Page Setup" later in this chapter for more info.

Set: Setting Up Your Document with Page Setup

After you set up your printer, the hard part is over. You should be able to print a document quickly and easily — right? Not so fast, Buck-o. Read here how the features in the Page Setup sheet can help you to solve most basic printing problems.

Become familiar with Page Setup — you may not need to use it right this second, but it's a good friend to know.

Almost every program that can print a document has a Page Setup command on its File menu. Note that some programs use the name *Page Setup*, and others use *Print Setup*. (Print Setup is the quaint, old-fashioned term, more popular in the System 6 era and in Windows than on today's Macs.) Either way, in this sheet you can choose paper size, page orientation, and scaling percent (see Figure 12-2).

Figure 12-2:
The Page
Setup sheet
in TextEdit.

Users of network printers or PostScript printers may see slightly different versions of the Print and Page Setup sheet. The differences should be minor enough not to matter.

Click the little question mark in the lower-left corner at any time for additional help with the Page Setup sheet. Page Setup help will open immediately in the Help Viewer if you do.

The options within the Page Setup sheet are as follows:

- ✔ **Settings:** When the default Page Attributes displays in this pop-up menu, you see what configuration options are available. In that same pop-up menu, you can also choose

    - *Custom Paper Size:* Define a paper size other than one supported directly by your printer driver as described under Paper Size in this list

    - *Summary:* Get a list of the options that apply to the current document, based on what you've set up in the Page Setup sheet

- ✔ **Format For:** In this pop-up menu, you find the name of the active printer. If you have several printers configured, you can choose any of them from this list. As you see in Figure 12-2, the Canon S830D printer that I set up earlier in this chapter (see the "Ready: Connecting and Adding Your Printer" section) is on the menu.

- ✔ **Paper Size:** Use options in this pop-up menu to choose the type of paper currently in the paper tray of your printer or to choose the size of the paper that you want to feed manually. The dimensions of the paper that you can choose appear below its name.

Page Setup sheet settings remain in effect until you change them. For example, when you print an envelope, don't forget to change back to Letter before trying to print on letter-sized paper.

- ✔ **Orientation:** Choose from options here to tell your printer whether the page that you want to print should be portrait oriented (like a letter, longer than it is wide) or landscape oriented (sideways, wider than it is long). Click the icons of the little person for the following (from left to right): Portrait, Landscape facing left, and Landscape facing right. You can see them in Figure 12-2 to the right of the Orientation heading.

- ✔ **Scale:** Use the Scale control percentages to enlarge or reduce your image for printing. Just type a new value into the Scale text entry box, replacing the default number 100 (shown in Figure 12-2).

Some programs also offer additional Page Setup choices. To see them (if your program offers them, of course), they'll usually appear in the Settings pop-up menu in the Page Setup sheet. Adobe Photoshop and Microsoft Word have them; TextEdit doesn't. The additional settings for Microsoft Word appear in Figure 12-3.

Page Setup

Settings: [Microsoft Word ▼]

Custom page size
☐ Use custom page size
Width: [8.5"] ↕   Height: [11"] ↕

Feed Method: [🖹] [🖹] [🖹]

◉ Face up
○ Face down   (Reset)

Apply Page Setup settings to: [Whole document ▼]

(Margins...)   (Default...)   (Print...)

⑦   (Cancel) (OK)

Figure 12-3:
The
additional
Page Setup
options in
Microsoft
Word.

Go: Printing with the Print Sheet

After you connect and configure your printer and then set up how you want your document to print, you come to the final steps before that joyous moment when your printed page pops out of the printer. Navigating the Print sheet is the last thing standing between you and your output.

Although most of the Print sheets that you see look like the figures that I show in this chapter, others may differ slightly. The features in the Print sheet are strictly a function of the program with which you're printing. Many programs choose to use the standard-issue Apple sheet as shown in this chapter, but not all do. If I don't explain a certain feature in this chapter, chances are good that it's a feature specific to the application or printer that you're using and is explained in that program's or printer's documentation.

Printing a document

If everything has gone well so far, the actual act of printing a document is pretty simple. Just follow the steps here and in a few minutes, pages should start popping out of your printer like magic. (In the sections that follow, I talk about some print options that you'll probably need someday.)

1. **Open a document that you want to print.**

2. **Choose File⇨Print (or use the keyboard shortcut ⌘+P).**

   You see the basic Print sheet, as shown in Figure 12-4.

Figure 12-4:
Your basic
Print sheet.

3. **Change any settings that you like in the Print sheet and then click Print. Wait a few minutes and then walk over to your printer to get your document.**

Dictating perfection . . . sort of

The Print command appears in the File menu in the vast majority of the Mac programs that you'll use. Every so often, you may come across a program that doesn't follow these conventions, but I would say at least 98+ percent of commercial Mac programs put the Print command in the File menu and use ⌘+P for its keyboard shortcut.

One of the best things about the Mac is that Apple has published a set of guidelines that all Mac programs should use. Consistency among programs is one of the Mac's finest features. Notice how 98+ percent of all programs house the Open, Close, Save, Save As, Page Setup, and Print commands in their File menus and the Undo, Cut, Copy, and Paste commands in their Edit menus. That's the kind of convenience and consistency that the Macintosh Human Interface Guidelines recommend.

Macintosh Human Interface Guidelines also recommend that the keyboard shortcut ⌘+P should be reserved for the command "plain text" unless it is used for Print, in which case ⌘+T should be used for Plain Text (just like how

the keyboard shortcuts ⌘+B and ⌘+I are usually used to format bold and italic text, respectively). So ⌘+P is almost always the shortcut for the Print command in the File menu.

My point: Choosing File➪Print (⌘+P) *won't* work for you if any one of the following is true with the software you're using:

✔ The Print command is on a different menu.

✔ There *is* no Print command.

✔ The Print keyboard shortcut is anything but ⌘+P.

If any of the above is true for a program that you're using, you just have to wing it. Look in all the menus and check out the product's documentation to try to get a handle on the Print command for that program. You can also write the software company a brief note mentioning that it could make things easier on everyone by putting the Print command in the proper place and using the generally agreed-upon keyboard shortcut.

Choosing from different printers

Just as you can in the Page Setup sheet, you can choose which printer you want to use from the Printer pop-up menu of the Print sheet. Remember that you can only choose from the printers that you have added via the Print Center, as you read in the section earlier in this chapter, the one I lovingly refer to as "Setting up a printer for the first time."

Choosing custom settings

If you've created a custom group of settings previously, you can choose from them in the Presets pop-up menu of the Print sheet. I touch more on this feature in the "Save Custom Settings" section later in this chapter.

The Print sheet also features another pop-up menu called `Copies & Pages` (refer to Figure 12-4) that offers additional options.

I go through these options and their sub-options one at a time in the following sections.

Copies & Pages

When Copies & Pages is selected in the pop-up menu, you can choose how many copies to print and the page range that you want to print.

Click in any of the fields in this sheet and then press the Tab key. Your cursor jumps to each of the text fields in the sheet in rotation. Pressing Shift+Tab makes the active field jump backward.

- ✔ **Copies:** In this text field, set how many copies that you want to print. The Print sheet defaults to one copy (1) in most applications, so you'll probably see the numeral 1 in the Copies field when the Print sheet appears. Assuming that's the case, don't do anything if you want to print only one copy. If you want to print more than one copy of your document, highlight the 1 that appears in the Copies field and type the new number of copies that you want.

- ✔ **Pages:** Here you find two radio buttons to choose from: All or From. If you want to print your entire document, select the All option. If you want to print only a specific page or range of pages, mark the From radio button and then type the desired page numbers in the From and To text entry boxes.

  For example, suppose that you have a 10-page document. You print the whole thing and then notice a typo on page 2. After you correct your error, you don't have to reprint the whole document — only the one with the correction. Reprint only page 2 by typing a **2** in both the From and To fields. You can type any valid range of pages (um, you can't print out page 20 if your document is only 15 pages long) in the From and To fields.

Layout

Choose Layout from the pop-up menu to set the number of pages per printed sheet, the layout direction, and whether or not you prefer a border. (See Figure 12-5.)

- ✔ **Pages per Sheet:** Choose from preset numbers here in this pop-up menu to set the number of pages that you want to print on each sheet. (*Note:* Pages appear smaller than full-size if you use this option.)

- ✔ **Layout Direction:** Choose from one of four buttons that govern the way the small pages are laid out on the printed page.

  Click any of these buttons, and the *proxy* (the rectangle on the left displaying the numbers 1–16 in sequential order in Figure 12-5) will change to show you the effect of your choice.

- ✔ **Border:** Your choices from this pop-up menu are none, single hairline, single thin line, double hairline, and double thin line.

Figure 12-5:
The Layout
sheet.

Output Options

Choose Output Options from the pop-up menu to save your file as a PDF or PostScript. *PDF* stands for *Portable Document Format,* the file format made famous by Adobe and its Acrobat program. It's also a type of document that almost anyone with a computer can open and view (using Acrobat Reader or the OS X Preview application, which you'll find in the Applications folder).

Unless the program that you're using added something, Save as File is the only choice on this screen. If you mark that check box, you have a choice of PDF or (sometimes) PostScript. So why the heck is it called Output Options? I think it should be singular and say something more descriptive, such as *Save as File* and then just let you select the format for that file.

In Mac OS X version 10.2 Jaguar, this is even more redundant with the addition of a Save As PDF button at the bottom of every Print sheet.

If you're preparing a file for someone else to use on another computer, PDF is often the best format to use because it preserves both text and graphics exactly as they appear onscreen.

Summary

When you select Summary in the pop-up menu, you can see the printing details for your document, as shown in Figure 12-6. Look here for one final check to verify your print job settings: how many copies you want, whether you want them collated, the page range of your print job, your layout choice(s), and whether to save a file as a PDF, plus any settings specific to your particular printer or the application that you're printing from.

Figure 12-6:
Summary for the about-to-be-printed document.

Notice the entry for `Quality & Media` near the bottom of the text in Figure 12-6. This is an example of a printer-specific setting. Not every printer will offer a Quality & Media setting, and some call it by another name, but most inkjet printers do offer something like it.

Save custom settings

After you finalize the printer settings for Copies & Pages, Layout, Output Options, and any other options your printer driver provides, choose Save As from the Presets pop-up menu. Name the settings and from now on, that setting appears as an option in the Presets pop-up menu. Just choose your saved set before you print any document with which you want to use it.

Previewing Your Documents

When you click the Preview button, you see a version of the page or pages that you're about to print, displayed by the Preview utility at a size small enough to allow you to see the whole page at once, as shown in Figure 12-7.

If you have any doubt about the way that a document will look when you print it, check out Preview first. When you're happy with the document preview, just choose Print from the File menu (or press ⌘+P). Preview works with the Preview application that Apple includes with Mac OS X. With the Preview feature, you do cool things like

Figure 12-7:
A Print Preview of an Internet Explorer document.

- ✔ **See all the pages in your document one by one.**

- ✔ **Zoom in or out to get a different perspective on what you're about to send to the printer (pretty cool!).**

- ✔ **Rotate the picture 90 degrees to the left or right.**

- ✔ **Spot errors before you commit to printing something.** A little upfront inspection can save you a lot of paper and frustration.

- ✔ **Add headers and footers.** Many applications include, or allow you to include, header or footer fields to fill in. *Headers* include information or page numbers that run at the top of each page, like this book uses. *Footers* — you guessed it — are the same thing, but they display at the bottom of a page. They aren't visible while you're working on a document, but they do appear in the printed version (if you set them to). Use Preview to get a look at the header or footer before you print a document. Just zoom in on that area of the page to take a closer look and make any changes that you want within the application that created the file.

Check out the Preview program's View menu and its toolbar. Here you can zoom in or out, rotate your document, move forward or backward (through multi-page documents), and other stuff. So I urge you to pull down the View menu and check it out. If you have a multi-page document (or multiple documents) open, a drawer will pop out of the side of the window (visible in Figure 12-7 on the right side of the window) to let you move through the pages.

To hide and show the drawer, click the Thumbnails button, choose View⇨Thumbnails or use the keyboard shortcut ⌘+T.

Font Mania

Jazz up your documents — or make them a little more serious — with different fonts. To a computer user, *font* means typeface — what the characters look like. Although professional typographers will scream at my generalization, I'll go with that definition for now.

Tens of thousands of different fonts are available for the Macintosh. You don't want to use the same font that you'd use for a garage sale flyer as you would for a résumé, right? Lucky for you, Mac OS X comes with a bunch of fonts, as shown in Figure 12-8. Some are pretty predictable, such as Times New Roman (it's the font of this paragraph), but OS X gives you some artsy ones, too, such as Brush Script. If you get really get into fonts, you can buy single fonts and font collections anywhere that you can buy software. Plenty of shareware and public domain fonts are also available from online services and user groups. Some people have thousands of fonts.

The pre-installed fonts live in two different folders, both called Fonts. One is in the Library folder at root level on your hard disk; the other is in the Library subfolder within the System folder, as shown in Figure 12-8.

Figure 12-8:
Mac OS X
includes
these fonts
and plenty
more.

OS X actually has three different Font folders. The third one, also called Fonts, is in the Library in your home directory. The subtle distinction between the three is explained below.

Installing new fonts

To install any new font, drag its icon into one of the two Fonts folders that you have access to, as follows:

- **If you want other users to be able to access the new font,** drag the font's icon to the Fonts subfolder inside the Library folder, which is at the root level of your hard drive. This Fonts folder has universal access. (The two Library folders are covered in Chapter 10.)

- **If you want to limit access to the new font to solely yourself,** drag the font's icon to the Fonts subfolder located in the Library folder inside your home folder.

The Fonts folder on the right in Figure 12-8 — the one in the Library inside the System folder — is reserved for OS X and can't easily be modified. If you try to remove or add a font to it, you'll be told that's not possible, as shown in Figure 12-9.

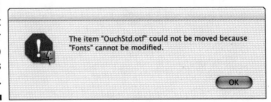

Figure 12-9:
Denied!
You can't
remove or
add a font to
this Fonts
folder.

If you've designated a Classic System Folder, OS X will also load any fonts in its Fonts folder, for a total of four different folders named Fonts.

Types of fonts

There are many font formats with names like OpenType, Mac TrueType, Windows TrueType, PostScript Type 1, bitmap, and dfont. No problem — Mac OS X supports them all. In fact, the only font format I know of that OS X doesn't support is PostScript Type 3.

That said, the two most common formats for Macs are TrueType and PostScript Type 1, but OpenType is making big strides to join the elite.

✔ **TrueType fonts:** These Apple standard-issue fonts come with Mac OS X. In common use on Macs as well as on Windows machines, these fonts are scaleable. *Scaleable fonts* use only a single outline for the font, and your Mac makes these fonts bigger or smaller when you choose a bigger or smaller font size in a program.

✔ **Type 1 fonts:** These fonts are often referred to as PostScript Type 1 fonts, and they are the standard for desktop publishing on the Mac (as well as Windows and UNIX). Tens of thousands of Type 1 fonts are available. (Not nearly as many TrueType fonts exist.)

Type 1 fonts come in two pieces: a bitmap font suitcase and a second piece (called a *printer font*). Some Type 1 fonts come with two, three, or four printer fonts, which usually have related names. Just toss all the parts in the appropriate library folder, and you'll have those fonts available in every program that you use.

✔ **OpenType fonts:** OpenType fonts are really PostScript Type 1 fonts where the printer fonts are combined into one file with a TrueType font. This gives you the greater typographic control that high-end typesetters require with the one-file convenience of TrueType.

Chapter 13

Applying Yourself to the Applications Folder

● ●

In This Chapter

▶ Checking out applications included with Mac OS X

▶ Tips for getting the most out of some of them

▶ A folder chock-full of useful utilities

● ●

Mac OS X comes with a whole folder full of applications — software that you can use to do everything from surfing the Internet to capturing an image of your Mac's screen to playing QuickTime movies to checking the time. In this chapter, I give you a thumbnail view of each — at least the ones I don't cover in other chapters — and tell you a bit about working with applications in Mac OS X.

Many software developers often get ideas for cool shareware and commercial applications from what they find in the Mac OS Applications or Utilities folders. They look at what Apple has provided for free and say, "Hey, I can add some cool features to that!" The next thing you know, you have new and improved versions of Mail, Terminal, Grab, TextEdit, and others. If you use an Apple-supplied application but find it lacking, check your favorite shareware archive (www.versiontracker.com, www.macupdate.com/, and www.tucows.com are a few good ones) for a better mousetrap.

Folder Full of Apps

The applications that you get with Mac OS X are all stored in (where else?) the Applications folder. Hang with me as I run 'em down!

First, though, you need to open the Applications folder, the contents of which you can see in Figure 13-1. You can get there in three ways:

✔ Click the Applications button on the toolbar in any Finder window

✔ Choose Go⇨Applications

✔ Press ⌘+Shift+A

Acrobat Reader 5.0

 Acrobat Reader, Adobe Systems' application to read, print, and browse PDF documents, was added to the Applications directory in OS X version 10.1. *Portable Document Format* (PDF) is Adobe's cross-platform standard for electronic documents. PDF is also the underlying document model used by *Quartz,* OS X's graphics engine. Of course, you can also read and print PDF documents by using Apple's Preview application; however, Acrobat Reader includes a number of good features, such as recognizing bookmarks and hypertext links within the document, allowing for much easier navigation.

Figure 13-1: Checking out Mac OS X applications.

I set Acrobat Reader as the default program to open all PDF files instead of Preview. (**Hint:** You start by clicking on a PDF document and choosing File⇨Get Info and then selecting the Open with Application check box from the Get Info window's Open With panel.)

Address Book

Just like it sounds, the *Address Book* is the place to store contact information for your family, friends, and anyone else whom you want to keep track of. It works with the Mail application, enabling you to quickly look up e-mail addresses when you're ready to send a message. Use it with iChat, too, to help you quickly chat with your online friends. It can also work with any other application whose programmers choose to make the connection.

For example, my Sony Ericsson wireless phone can obtain my contact information (wirelessly!) from Address Book (through the magic of Bluetooth). I talk more about the Address Book in Chapter 11. For more on Bluetooth, see the sidebar entitled "Whither Bluetooth?" elsewhere in this chapter.

AppleScript

AppleScript is like a tape recorder for your Mac. It can record and play back things that you do, such as opening an application or clicking a button. You can use it to record a script for tasks that you often perform and then have your Mac perform those tasks for you later. You can write your own AppleScripts, use those that come with your Mac, or download still others from the Web. The following sections should give you some indication as to how much — or how little — you care about AppleScript.

Discovering whether you give a hoot about AppleScript

Describing AppleScript to a Mac beginner is a bit like three blind men describing an elephant. One man may describe it as the Macintosh's built-in automation tool. Another may describe it as an interesting but often-overlooked piece of enabling technology. The third may liken it to a cassette recorder, recording and playing back your actions at the keyboard. A fourth (if there were a fourth in the story) would assure you that it looked like computer code written in a high-level language.

They would all be correct. *AppleScript,* the Mac's built-in automation tool, is a little known (at least up to now) enabling technology that works like a cassette recorder for programs that support AppleScript recording. And scripts do look like computer programs (which could be because they *are* computer programs).

If you're the kind of person who likes to automate as many things as possible, you may just love AppleScript because it's a simple programming language that you can use to create programs that give instructions to your Mac and the applications running on your Mac. For example, you can create an AppleScript that launches Mail, checks for new messages, and then quits Mail. The script could even transfer your mail to a folder of your choice.

I call AppleScript a time-and-effort enhancer. If you just spend the time and effort it takes to understand it, using AppleScript will save you oodles of time and effort.

Therein lies the rub. This stuff is far from simple. And it's far beyond the purview of a 384-page *For Dummies* book. Still, it's worth learning about if you'd like to script repetitive actions for future use.

You can put frequently used AppleScripts on the Dock or on your Desktop for easy access. Apple also provides a script menu extra, located in the Scripts folder within the Library folder at the top level of your startup disk. It comes with a number of free scripts to automate common tasks. I'd tell you what those scripts are, but the collection is large and always growing, so if you're interested in such things, you should check www.apple.com/applescript regularly. There are also a number of AppleScripts to place in your Finder toolbar, automating such common tasks as trimming filenames to 31 characters for compatibility with pre-OS X users.

Checking out AppleScript

The Applications folder contains an AppleScript folder, which in turn contains the Script Editor program plus an alias to a folder full of sample AppleScripts.

Script Editor is the application that you use to view and edit AppleScripts. Although more information on Script Editor is beyond the scope of this book, it's a lot of fun. And the cool thing is that you can create many AppleScripts without knowing a thing about programming. Just record a series of actions that you want to repeat and use Script Editor to save them as a script. If you choose to save your script as an application by selecting Application from the Format menu in the Save sheet, you can then run it by double-clicking its icon.

If the concept of scripting intrigues you, I suggest that you open the Example Scripts folder and rummage through it to check out the scripts available at www.apple.com/applescript. When you find a script that looks interesting, double-click it to launch the Script Editor program where you can examine it more closely.

Calculator

Need to do some quick math? The Calculator application gives you a simple calculator, with all the basic number-crunching functions that your pocket calculator has. To use it, you can either click the keys with the mouse or you can use your numeric keypad (on your keyboard) to type numbers and operators (math symbols such as +, –, and =). Check out the Calculator in Figure 13-2. Now, in MacOS X version 10.2 Jaguar, the Calculator has added an Advanced mode (turning it into a powerful scientific calculator) and a paper tape to track your computations (and if you want, provide a printed record). It can even speak numbers aloud. (Use the Speech menu to access that particular feature.)

I find it interesting that until the advent of MacOS X version 10.2 Jaguar, the only thing that had changed about the Calculator since the Mac was invented was the interface. In other words, no functionality had been added or removed in almost 20 years. How many computer programs can say that? (For the curious: Calculator was a Desk Accessory in early versions of the Mac OS and an Apple Menu Item in versions 8 and 9.)

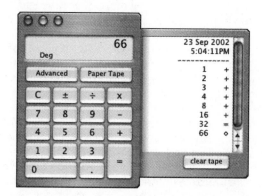

Figure 13-2:
The
Calculator,
simple
(top) and
advanced
(bottom).

Chess

This is a visual implementation of the GNU (stands for Gnu's Not Unix) chess-playing game. You can play against the computer at a variety of settings. Chess is a fairly strong player and should provide a good contest for any chess player who has less than a master ranking. You can see what it looks like in Figure 13-3. Notice that in the figure, the Dock is hovering over the window. You can auto-hide the Dock by choosing ⬛⇨Dock⇨Turn Hiding On (or by pressing ⌘+Option+D).

To play a game, launch Chess and then choose Game⇨New. If you're playing against the computer, you play as white, so click a white piece and move it. The computer responds by moving a black piece, making it your turn again. Because this is *Mac OS X For Dummies* rather than *Chess For Dummies*, I won't even attempt to tell you how to improve your chess game here.

You can tinker with a couple of preferences in the Chess program. To make the computer a more formidable opponent, choose Chess⇨Preferences and drag the Level slider toward the word Hard. You can also choose to play human versus human or change the name that the computer uses from the rather unimaginative Computer to something more evocative (maybe Kasparov). The last option in the Preferences dialog lets you turn Voice Recognition on or off. (The default is On, which is why you see the circular Speech Recognition window on the right in Figure 13-3.) If you choose to use it, you press the Esc key, and then speak your moves ("Knight G1 to F3," and so on). It works pretty well but, of course, requires that you have an appropriate microphone connected to your Mac.

If you need a hint (as I often do) as to a good next move, choose Move⇨Hint or press ⌘+Shift+H. The program will show you the move that it calculates to be your best choice by blinking both the piece that it thinks you should move and the square to which you should move it. You don't have to take the program's suggestion — just make a different move if you decide to decline the suggestion.

Clock

You don't need to use the Clock application unless you want to make changes to the time display on your Mac and you don't want to open System Preferences.

Clock is easily visible on the Dock; its icon displays the current time in analog or digital format, for your viewing pleasure. The Clock application can be set to launch when you start up Mac OS X.

Figure 13-3:
The super-
snazzy Mac
OS X 3-D
Chess
game.

All you can do in the Clock application (choose Clock⇨Preferences) is choose whether the clock appears in a floating window or on the Dock, and whether it shows an analog or digital display. Frankly, given the fact that you have a clock in the menu bar, this program is of little use.

To set your Mac's date and time, change the settings in the Date & Time pane of System Preferences, not the Clock application. You also use this System Preference to set menu bar clock options, including whether to display the menu bar clock.

DVD Player

This application will only be present on Macs that have a DVD player installed. Inserting a DVD in such a Mac automatically starts the DVD Player. You can then watch the movie on your Mac unless you've changed the default in the CDs & DVDs System Preferences, which is to Open DVD Player when you insert a video DVD.

The Apple System Profiler application (in the Utilities folder) can tell you whether you've got a DVD drive or AGP graphics in your Mac. Just launch it and read the first page of information.

If you choose About this Mac in the Finder, there's a new More Info button that you can click that also opens Apple System Profiler.

iCal

iCal is a wonderful utility that's a daily/weekly/monthly pocket and desktop calendar equivalent. You can publish your calendar(s) to a .Mac account or other compatible (WebDav) server as well as subscribe to calendars that others publish. Integrated with the Address Book, you can select people who you want to invite to a scheduled event. Figure 13-4 shows me inviting some friends to a small shindig.

iChat

Text-based chatting on the Internet is an old and popular pastime. Numerous protocols abound with names such as IRC (Internet Relay Chat), ICQ (a mnemonic play on *I Seek You*), AIM (AOL Instant Messenger), and many others. iChat supports AIM and lets you communicate with other Mac.com members as well as others on your local network via Rendezvous. You can even hook up online with anyone connected to AOL's massive AIM network, including joining AOL chat rooms, even if you aren't an AOL subscriber. (***Note:*** You do have to know the chat room's name.) Figure 13-5 shows me having a brief conversation with someone we both know and love.

Figure 13-4:
iCal uses Address Book and Mail to invite people to scheduled events.

OK, this is definitely weird... sending instant messages TO MYSELF!!!

I tell you what's even weirder...

And that's answering instant messages to myself!

Yup. I agree totally!

Figure 13-5:
Share files
while
chatting
with iChat.

You can even drag and drop files (like photos from iPhoto) onto the message area when chatting with someone, and the file will be sent right to her iChat window! This is way easier than creating an e-mail to send the file while you're chatting.

Image Capture

Use this program to transfer images from your Universal Serial Bus (USB) digital camera, various SmartMedia readers, or from many supported scanners. If you don't have such a device, don't worry about it. If you do have one and the software that came with it doesn't work with OS X (or even if it does), try Image Capture.

I discuss Image Capture in a bit more detail in Chapter 22.

iMovie

This is Apple's fantastic digital video editing program. You can use it to edit digital video files or to control compatible FireWire-equipped digital camcorders. You can also use it to create great slideshows for presentations, with both narration and background audio. Trying to cover this software could fill a book of its own, and it does — check out Todd Stauffer's *iMovie 2 For Dummies* (Hungry Minds, Inc.).

Internet Connect

This program replaces the old Point-to-Point Protocol (PPP) application in earlier versions of Mac OS.

Internet Explorer

Internet Explorer (IE) is Microsoft's Web browser for the Mac, and (lucky you!) it ships with OS X. Read a discussion of IE in Chapter 11. Depending upon your version of OS X, there may be an Internet Explorer folder here in the Applications folder, and within that the Internet Explorer icon from which you can start IE. But the quickest way to open Internet Explorer is still to click its e-shaped icon on the Dock.

iPhoto

If you have a digital camera — or even if you don't but have a large collection of photographs in digital form (maybe from Kodak PictureCDs or scans) — you'll love iPhoto. Use *iPhoto* to organize your pictures into albums (a single picture can be in as many albums as you want without having to create any duplicates); print them out; send them to Kodak for professional photo printing; or send them to Apple to be published in a coffee-table book, published as a Web page (or on your Mac.com Web page), exported as a slideshow, or for use as your Desktop picture.

iTunes

Another great piece of multimedia software from Apple, iTunes lets you play CDs, create your own audio or MP3 CDs (assuming that you have a CD burner), play MP3, AIFF, WAV, and Audible.com files, integrate with your iPod or other MP3 player, listen to Internet radio stations, and view some rather pretty visual displays.

Mail

Mail is the free e-mail program that comes with OS X. I cover Mail in Chapter 11.

Preview

You use Preview to open, view, and print PDFs as well as most graphics files (TIFF, JPEG, PICT, and so on). *PDF files* are formatted documents that include text and images. User manuals, books, and the like are often distributed as PDF files. You can't edit a PDF file with Preview, but you can leaf through its pages or print it. It's also the application that pops open when you click the Preview button in the Print dialog, as you discover in Chapter 12.

Any OS X program that prints offers PDF as a file format from which you can print your own documents (via the Output Settings pop-up menu choice or the Save As PDF button found in all OS X 10.2 [and later] print dialogs).

Adobe's Acrobat Reader application has many more features than Preview does. You can search for words in Reader, for example, but you can't in Preview. However, Preview is a good way to quickly check out or print a PDF file.

QuickTime Player

Use the QuickTime Player to view QuickTime movies or streaming audio and video. The quickest way to launch it is by clicking its icon on the Dock. It also opens automatically when you open any QuickTime movie document file.

Sherlock

I mention *Sherlock* — the cool search tool that you can use to find Web sites, people, software, stuff to buy, and lots more — in several chapters of this book. (The most comprehensive coverage is in Chapter 11.) To quickly open Sherlock, click its icon on the Dock (it looks like Sherlock Holmes' hat with a magnifying glass).

Stickies

Stickies are electronic Post-it Notes for your Mac. They're a convenient place to jot notes or phone numbers. Some Stickies are shown in Figure 13-6.

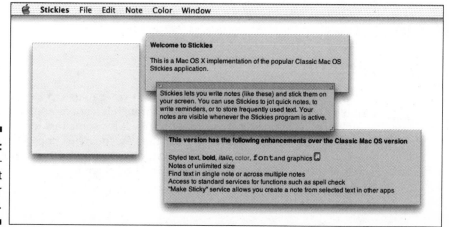

Figure 13-6:
Stickies —
Post-it
Notes for
your Mac.

Stickies are supremely flexible. Move them around onscreen (just drag 'em by their title bar) and change their text to any font and color that you desire by using the Note menu. Make your Stickies any color that you like by using the Color menu. You can collapse a Stickie by Option+clicking its grow box (top-right corner of the title bar). Also, you can print them and import and export text files from them.

Anything that you type on a Stickie is automatically saved as long as you keep that note open. But when you close a note (by clicking its close box, choosing File⇨Close, or using the keyboard shortcut ⌘+W), you lose its contents forever. Fortunately, Stickies give you a warning and a second chance to save the note in a separate file on your hard drive. You can also export Stickies (choose File⇨Export Text) and save Stickies as plain text, rich text format (RTF) files, or as rich text format with attachments (RTFD) files. The last two formats support fonts and other formatting that plain text format does not.

Stickies have grown up in Mac OS X. They work pretty much as they always have, but now you have more options available, such as a spell checker. You can also import pre-Mac OS X Stickies, in addition to plain text files. The old Stickies application supported colors, but not fonts, as Mac OS X Stickies do.

System Preferences

I mention System Preferences throughout this book. For complete details, though, check out Chapter 15.

You can open the System Preferences application in any of these three ways:

- ✔ Double-click its icon in the Applications folder.
- ✔ Click its icon on the Dock.
- ✔ Choose System Preferences from the menu.

TextEdit

TextEdit is a word processor/text editor that you can use to write letters, scribble notes, or open Read Me files. Although it's not as sophisticated as AppleWorks or Microsoft Word, you can use it for some text formatting and to check your spelling. TextEdit supports images, too. (Just copy an image in another program and paste it into a TextEdit document. Or, you can use drag-and-drop to drop an image into a TextEdit document from many applications.)

Here's a neat (but mostly useless) trick: Drag any icon from the Finder into a TextEdit document and drop it there. The icon then appears in the document. (It's not a real icon. You can't open it or anything — it's just a picture.)

Utilities

Here's another folder full of stuff. Most of the items in the Utilities folder work with other applications to do some useful thing. You may never even open a lot of these applications. The Utilities folder appears in Figure 13-7; stick with me for a brief tour of each application that you find there.

AirPort Admin Utility

You use AirPort Admin Utility to change individual Internet settings of an AirPort Base Station, such as your Internet Service Provider's (ISP) phone number.

AirPort Setup Assistant

The name is pretty self-explanatory. You run this program to configure your AirPort card for wireless networking.

Apple System Profiler

Apple System Profiler is a little program that gives you information about your Mac. What a concept! If you're curious about things such as what processor your Mac has or what devices are currently connected to it, give the Profiler a try. Poke around the Commands menu and check it out; this little puppy is benign and won't hurt anything.

Figure 13-7:
The Utilities folder.

If you ever have occasion to call for technical support for your Mac, software, or peripherals, you're probably going to be asked to provide information from Apple System Profiler. So don't get rid of it just because you don't care about this kind of stuff.

Asia Text Extras

This folder contains four items: Chinese Text Converter, IM Plugin Converter, Plugin_Text_Sample, and TrueType Font Editor. Because I speak no Asian languages, I have no idea what to do with them.

Audio MIDI Setup

This program is the control center for any MIDI devices built into or connected to your Mac.

Bluetooth File Exchange

If you have a Bluetooth device and your Mac has a Bluetooth adapter connected to a USB port (or has Bluetooth built in, although no Mac has it at the time of this writing), you can drag icons for Address Book items (vCard files), iCal items (vCal files), and pictures (.gif files) onto the Bluetooth File Exchange icon to copy the file from your Mac to the Bluetooth device wirelessly via Bluetooth.

Whither Bluetooth?

Bluetooth is an upcoming standard for wireless communication between intelligent devices over short distances. At least that's my definition. The first devices have just come on the market, and one of them is the Sony Ericsson T68i wireless phone that I've been using.

Bluetooth is a smart protocol. When two Bluetooth devices have been prepared (actually, paired), they recognize each other when they are within range — 20–30 feet — and then automatically perform whatever task they've been instructed to perform when they pair.

My phone can receive calendar items, contacts, and little pictures from my Mac. And I can back up the phone's memory to my Mac's hard disk as well. If I attach the Bluetooth adapter to my PowerBook, I can use the phone as a wireless modem and surf the Internet or check my e-mail from the beach if I want to, just like on TV.

What AirPort is to wireless networking, Bluetooth is to intelligent wireless peripheral connections.

Bluetooth isn't very fast and has a limited range (around 20–30 feet from your Mac). But it's swell for sending small amounts of data back and forth between devices. Watch for digital cameras, printers, and other devices that you currently use via USB to offer Bluetooth connectivity soon.

ColorSync Utility

This is a single-purpose program that verifies the contents of color-matching profiles installed on your Mac. If you don't use ColorSync (Apple's color-matching technology to ensure what you see onscreen is the same as what you print on any device), don't worry about it.

Console

Mac OS X is based on an operating system called *UNIX,* which is a powerful operating system with lots of incredibly geeky features and capabilities that most Mac users don't really want to know about (and that Apple hides from you unless you want to work with them). But for those who want to find out what's going on under the hood of Mac OS X (or even to tinker around with the engine), the Console application provides a window into the deep, dark world of UNIX. Console displays system messages that can help you to troubleshoot problems with Mac OS X — assuming that you know how to interpret them.

Don't let it scare you — most folks will never need Console.

CPU Monitor

Check here to see how your Mac's CPU (its processor) is performing.

DigitalColor Meter

This is a little program that displays what's on your screen as RGB (red-green-blue) or CIE (the abbreviation for a chromaticity coordinate system developed by the Commission Internationale de l'Eclairage, the international commission on illumination) values. If you're not a graphic artist or otherwise involved in high-end color document production, you'll almost certainly never need it.

Directory Access

This little program is meant for system administrators on large networks. If your computer is connected to a campus or corporate network, talk to your network administrator about these settings.

If you're a home user, just ignore it.

Disk Copy

In most cases, you install new software on your Mac from a CD-ROM or by downloading it from the Internet. Software vendors typically use an installer program that decompresses and copies files to their proper places on your hard drive. After you've installed the software, you're back in business.

Apple has a variation on this theme called the *disk image,* and more developers are adopting the disk image format for their downloadable installers and updaters. When mounted on your Desktop — more on what *mounting* means in a minute — a disk image looks and acts just like a real disk. You can open it and see its contents in a Finder window; you can copy files from its window to another disk; and you can drag it to the Trash to remove it from your Desktop. To make a disk image appear on your Desktop, you double-click the image file. At that point, the Disk Copy application takes over and puts an icon (which for all intents and purposes looks like a disk) on your Desktop.

Disk Copy not only mounts images when you double-click them, but it can also be used to create your own disk image files and to burn disk image files onto CD-ROM discs.

You can erase a CD-RW or DVD-RW disc from within Disk Copy. Choose File⇨Erase CE/DVD-RW Disc or use the keyboard shortcut ⌘+Control+E.

Because disk images can be transferred via the Internet and because they act just like disks, they're a great substitute for a CD-ROM or other disc-based software installer. A software maker can create both a CD version of an installer and a disk image that can be downloaded.

If you're a Mac OS 9 user, Disk Copy is pretty much the same. The difference is that this version is optimized for use with OS X, includes support for a new disk image format (.dmg), and sports the new, improved OS X interface.

Disk Utility

If you're having problems with your hard drive or need to make changes to it, Disk Utility is a good place to start. This application has four active components: First Aid, Erase, Partition, and RAID.

Once again, if you're a Mac OS 9 user, First Aid is pretty much the same as before but optimized for use with OS X and sporting the new Aqua interface.

First Aid

If you suspect that something's not quite right with your Mac, the First Aid portion of Disk Utility should be among your first stops. Use First Aid to verify and (if necessary) repair an ailing drive. To use it, click the First Aid button on the left side of the Disk Utility window. Click a volume's icon and then click Verify. You get information about any problems that the software finds. If First Aid doesn't find any problems, you can go on your merry way, secure in the knowledge that your Mac is A-OK. If verification turns up trouble, click Repair to have the problem fixed. You can also use First Aid to fix disk permission problems.

You won't be able to use the copy of Disk Utility in your Applications/Utilities folder to repair your OS X boot disk. To do that, you must reboot from the Mac OS X CD and run the copy of Disk Utility on that CD-ROM.

You can't use Disk Utility First Aid to fix a CD-ROM or DVD-ROM disk, nor can it fix most disk image files (see the discussion of Disk Copy just before this section). These disks are read-only and can't be altered.

You *can* fix Zip disks, SuperDisks, DVD-RAM discs, or any other writeable media that can be mounted by your Mac.

Erase

Use Erase to format (completely erase) a disk. You can't do this to the startup disc — the one with Mac OS X on it.

When you format a disk, you erase all information on it, permanently. Formatting can't be undone and shouldn't be attempted unless you are absolutely sure this is what you want to do. Unless you don't want or need whatever's currently on the disk, you need a complete backup of the disk before formatting. If the data is critical, you should have at least two (or even three) known-to-be-valid back-up copies of it before you reformat.

Of partitions and volumes

Partitioning a drive lets you create multiple volumes. A *volume* looks and acts just like a hard drive, but if it's a partition, it's not a drive at all. Rather, it's a section of the drive that's completely separate from all others. You can create any number of partitions, but it's a good idea to limit yourself to no more than a small handful. Lots of people, including me, use one partition for Mac OS X and another for Mac OS 9.

You can only create drive partitions on a newly formatted drive. So to partition a drive, first format it in Drive Setup and then create partitions. Before you do, give some thought as to how large of a partition that you want to create. You won't be able to change your mind later.

I think that partitions should be no smaller than 2GB. You can get away with 1GB if you have a 4GB or smaller drive, but you don't need to create a lot of little partitions just to store your stuff. Instead, use folders: They work just great for organizing things the way you like. The one exception to this rule is if you burn a lot of CDs with your CD-RW drive. In that case, a 650MB or 700MB (if you use that size CD) partition lets you "prototype" your CDs before you burn them to see just how much stuff will fit on a single 650MB or 700MB disk.

By the same token, I think you should limit the number of partitions that you create. A PowerMac G4 with a 20GB drive does just fine with two (or maybe three) partitions.

Partition

Use this tab to create disk partitions (multiple volumes on a single disk), each of which is treated as a separate disk by OS X.

RAID

By using Redundant Array of Individual Disks (RAID), you can treat multiple disks as a single volume, which is sort of the antithesis of partitioning.

Display Calibrator

 Use this little program to calibrate your display, adjusting the way it displays white and colors. It's easy and kind of fun, so give it a try. Just launch it and follow the simple instructions that you see in the Display Calibrator Assistant window, as shown in Figure 13-8.

Figure 13-8:
Use the
Display
Calibrator
Assistant to
adjust your
monitor.

I suggest you give it a try; it will probably make what you see on your screen look better.

Grab

 Want to take a picture of your screen? I used to do this a lot so that I could bring you the screen shots (what you see in the figures) in this book. You can use Grab to take a picture of all or part of the screen and then save that file for printing or sending around (like to everyone that you think may want to see your Desktop pattern or how you've organized your windows). The first edition of this book used Grab, but I used the superb Snapz Pro X utility (Ambrosia Software; www.ambrosiasw.com) for the figures in subsequent editions. It's definitely worth the shareware fee.

Grab's best feature is the ability to do a timed screen capture. Like those cameras that let you start the timer and then run to get into the shot, Grab gives you ten seconds to bring the window that you want to the front, pull down a menu, get the cursor out of the way, or whatever you need to do to get the screen just right.

Grab's default behavior is to display no cursor. If you want to show a cursor in your screen shots, choose Grab➪Preferences and then select a pointer from the ten choices in the Preference dialog box by clicking it. Or to have no cursor, click the topmost, leftmost item, which is an empty box (that indicates *no cursor*).

Installer

Here's an application that you'll never need to open yourself. But don't get rid of it because software developers, including Apple, write installer scripts that automate the process of putting software on your Mac. These scripts know where everything should go and in what order — and in order to run, those installer scripts need to find this little program. So just leave it alone, and everything will be hunky-dory.

Java

This folder contains three items:

- **Applet Launcher:** Used to run Java applets without launching your Web browser.

- **Java Plugin Settings:** A control panel for Java and plug-ins that you may run in your Web browser or Applet Launcher.

- **Java Web Start:** A nifty little tool that lets you launch full-featured applications written in the Java language with a single click from within your Web browser. One big advantage of an application written in Java is that you don't have to wait for the publisher to create a Mac OS X version. The same Java code that runs on Windows or Linux or Solaris (Sun's version of UNIX) will run on Mac OS X and inherit the Mac OS X interface.

Key Caps

Here you find the keys to use to make special characters, such as a trademark symbol (™), a bullet (•) or a Greek beta (ß) character (okay, so it's really the German *double-s*, but everyone I know uses it for beta). You can also use Key Caps to see what characters are available in the Symbol font, which is a special typeface with characters that aren't letters and numbers but *dingbats* (special printing symbols).

Take a look at the keyboard display in Key Caps; it looks like your standard Mac keyboard. Now hold down the Option key and look again. All the keys show the characters produced when you use them in combination with the Option key held down (see Figure 13-9).

Figure 13-9:
Key Caps displays the characters that appear when you press a modifier key.

You can see different characters by pressing different combinations of modifier keys. In Figure 13-9, you can see a standard keyboard when you press no modifier key (top left), when you press the Shift key (bottom left), when you press the Option key (top right), and when you press the Option and Shift keys together (bottom right).

The Font menu of Key Caps lists all the fonts installed on your Mac. When you select one and then type a character or characters into the Key Caps text field, you can see how the font will look and also what (if any) special characters that font has. Choose Symbol or Zapf Dingbats to get a look at the non-text characters that you can choose when using these fonts.

Copy and Paste functions work in the Key Caps program. If you type something in Key Caps, you can select (highlight) it, copy it (to the Clipboard), and then paste it into another document. You can also select what you type, drag it to an open document, and drop it there.

Keychain Access

A *keychain* is a way to consolidate all your passwords — the one you use to log into your Mac, your e-mail password, and passwords required by any Web sites. Here's how it works: You use a single password to unlock your keychain (which holds your various passwords) and then you don't have to remember all your other passwords. Rest assured that your passwords are secure because only a user who has your keychain password can reach the other password-protected applications.

To create a new keychain, choose File⇨New Keychain.

To add passwords to the keychain, you must first create a keychain and a password. Then you can add passwords to the chain.

After you set up a keychain, just open Mail or another application that supports the keychain and change your password. Respond *Yes* when prompted whether you want to add the password to the keychain.

How do you know which programs support the Keychain utility? You don't until you're prompted to save your password in a keychain in that Open dialog, connect window, or so forth. If a program supports Keychain, it offers a check box for it in the user ID/password dialog or window.

The Keychain utility is particularly cool if you have multiple e-mail accounts that each has a different password. Just add them all to your keychain, and you can get all your mail at once with one password.

To add a Web site password to a keychain, open the Keychain Access application and click the Add button. In the New Password Item window that opens, type the URL of the site in the Name text field, type your username in the Account text field, and then type your password in the Passphrase text field, as shown in Figure 13-10.

Figure 13-10:
Add a URL
to the
keychain in
Keychain
Access.

To use the new URL password, double-click the URL in the Keychain Access window. A small Get Info window will pop up. Click the Go There button to launch your browser (if it isn't already running) — you're taken and logged in to the Web site that you choose. This will work even with Internet Explorer, but if you type a URL into IE's Address field, it won't check your keychain.

NetInfo Manager

Here's another little program for system administrators on large networks or power user administrators of shared Macs. If you're a home user, just ignore it.

Network Utility

And here is yet another little program for system administrators on large networks. But unlike the others — the ones I've told you to ignore if you're a home user — this one can come in handy if you're a veteran Internet user. It offers common Internet utility functions such as ping, traceroute, whois, finger, and such. If you don't know what any of this means, don't worry. Just ignore this program and you'll be fine.

ODBC Administrator

If you have need to access corporate databases using Open Database Connectivity (ODBC), your database administrator will give you the values that you need to plug into this tool. If you're not going to be doing that, don't worry about this tool.

Print Center

Print Center is the program that you use to configure your Mac to use printers and to manage print jobs. I discuss Print Center in Chapter 12.

Process Viewer

Here's another behind-the-scenes tool. In *UNIX* (the operating system behind Mac OS X), applications and other things going on behind the scenes are called *processes*. Each application (and the operating system itself) can run a number of processes at once. In Figure 13-11, you see 44 processes running. Interestingly, only three applications are open (the Finder, Grab, and Process Viewer itself).

Geeks and troubleshooters can use Process Viewer to identify what processes are running, which user owns the process, and how much of the CPU and memory that the process is using. You can even stop a process if you think that it may be causing problems for you.

Messing around in Process Viewer is not a good idea for most users. If you're having problems with an application or with Mac OS X, try quitting open applications, force-quitting applications (press ⌘+Option+Esc), or logging out and then logging back in again before you start mucking around with processes.

StuffIt Expander

Nowadays, you encounter compressed files and archives of compressed and encoded files and folders everywhere you turn, especially if you get any files from the Internet. *StuffIt Expander* can decompress or decode StuffIt (.sit), PC Zip (.zip), UNIX gzip (.gz), UNIX compress (.z), BinHex (.hqx), and a whole host of other compression and encoding formats. I strongly recommend putting StuffIt Expander's icon on the Dock, which will allow you to just drag the compressed files onto the icon to decompress them.

Name	User	Status	% CPU	% Memory
Timbuktu Extension	root	Running	4.80	1.60
Window Manager	bobl	Running	1.30	4.30
check_afp	root	Running	0.00	0.20
Process Viewer	bobl	Running	0.00	1.20
StatusItem	root	Running	0.00	6.10
init	root	Running	0.00	0.00
loginwindow	bobl	Running	0.00	1.10
pbs	bobl	Running	0.00	0.20
Dock	bobl	Running	0.00	1.20
mach_init	root	Running	0.00	0.00
SystemUIServer	bobl	Running	0.00	0.90
Finder	bobl	Running	0.00	5.30
Snapz Pro X	bobl	Running	0.00	16.40
SecurityAgent	bobl	Running	0.00	0.60
Host Relauncher	root	Running	0.00	0.00
ATSServer	bobl	Running	0.00	0.60
ARD Agent	root	Running	0.00	0.30
ARD Helper	root	Running	0.00	0.00
coreservicesd	root	Running	0.00	2.00
slpd	root	Running	0.00	0.10
kextd	root	Running	0.00	0.10
nfsiod	root	Running	0.00	0.00
nfsiod	root	Running	0.00	0.00
nfsiod	root	Running	0.00	0.00
nfsiod	root	Running	0.00	0.00
update	root	Running	0.00	0.00
lookupd	root	Running	0.00	0.20
automount	root	Running	0.00	0.10

Figure 13-11:
The Process
Listing
window of
Process
Viewer.

Terminal

Mac OS X is based on UNIX. If you need proof, or if you actually want to
operate your Mac as the UNIX machine that it is, Terminal is the place
to start.

Because UNIX is a command-line based operating system, you need to use
Terminal to type commands. You can issue commands that show a directory
listing, copy and move files, search for filenames or contents, or establish
or change passwords. In short, if you know what you're doing, you can do
everything on the command line that you can in Mac OS X. For most folks,
that's not a desirable alternative to the windows and icons of the Finder
window. But take my word for it; true geeks who are also Mac lovers get all
misty-eyed about the combination of a command line and a graphical user
interface.

If you do decide to tinker with Terminal and the UNIX-y innards of Mac OS X, please take some time to bone up on UNIX itself. Everything that you learn about UNIX will work on your Mac OS X. A good book on the subject is *Learning the UNIX Operating System (Nutshell Handbook)* by Jerry Peek, Grace Todino, and John Strang. Or try *UNIX Visual QuickStart Guide* by Deborah S. Ray and Eric J. Ray, which is the UNIX book that I keep on my desk, just in case.

Chapter 14

The Classic Environment: Like Mac OS 9, Only Better

Mac OS X is capable of running two different operating systems. Mac OS X, of course, runs your machine, but Mac OS 9.2.2 — the Mac OS version just before Mac OS X — is available too, if you need it.

Why would Apple give you two operating systems, and what in the world do you do with more than one? I explain this in the following section, and later I explain how two operating systems on one computer work together, how you can use them, and why you would want to.

Mac OS X version 10.2 Jaguar requires version 9.2.2 of Mac OS to provide the Classic environment. But most (if not all) programs don't distinguish between Mac OS 9, 9.0.1, 9.0.2, 9.0.3, 9.0.4, 9.1, 9.2, 9.2.1, and 9.2.2. So when I call a program a *Mac OS 9 program,* what I mean is that it's not an OS X program and that it will run under any version of Mac OS 9.

In other words, when I talk about stuff that works with (or appears in) all versions of Mac OS 9, I say *Mac OS 9* or *Mac OS 9.x.* When I'm talking about Classic or another feature or program that requires OS 9 version 9.2.2, I say *Mac OS 9.2.2.*

If you're not sure whether to or how to install Classic on your system, see the Appendix of this book, where I discuss the different ways that you can install Classic.

Retail boxed copies of Mac OS X version 10.2 Jaguar don't include a Mac OS 9 install CD. Classic is supported fully, but you'll have to come up with your own copy of a Mac OS 9 install CD (or a copy of your Mac OS 9 System Folder) to use it. Also, Macs sold after January 1, 2003 won't be able to boot into Mac OS 9, although they will still be able to run Classic.

If you have an older Mac OS 9 install CD lying around, you might be able to install that version and then use the OS 9 Software Update control panel to update it to 9.2.2. It's worth trying if you don't have another way of getting an OS 9 System Folder on your Mac. And, of course, you must have an OS 9 (9.2.2) System Folder on a local disk or volume to use Classic.

You Can Call It Classic

Mac OS X is the software that controls your Mac (as I describe in Chapter 1) — it's the magic that starts your computer, displays the Desktop, and gives you access to all the tools that you use every day to work with your files and applications.

Mac OS 9.2.2, called *Classic* when running under Mac OS X, actually runs inside an operating system (OS) *emulator* — software that does most, but not all, of what an operating system does by pretending to be one. When you launch an older application, it's as if you've booted a computer within your computer; that is, Classic first emulates the startup process, loading all the stuff that it needs to mimic Mac OS 9.2.2 and run the application.

Running under Mac OS X, Classic is an application, just like AppleWorks, Internet Explorer, or TextEdit. With the Classic application running, you can use Mac OS 9.2.2's Apple menu (if at least one Classic program is running) and you can open Mac OS 9 applications. You also have access (by switching to any OS X window) to your Mac OS X Home, Desktop, and applications. Finally, you can switch to another program (when a Classic program is active) by choosing it from the Application menu, located on the far right of the Mac OS 9.2.2 (Classic) menu bar.

Most Macs sold after January 1, 2003 can't start up in Mac OS 9. Which means the *only* way to run older software on newer Macs is via Classic.

All currently open applications — including any Classic apps — appear in your Dock for easy access.

When emulation *isn't* the sincerest form of flattery

Emulators aren't just for Mac OS 9/Classic. Some, like Classic, do everything that an operating system does except boot up the computer. Some bridge the PC/Mac gap: With Pentium emulators (such as Virtual PC for Mac OS, for example, you run Windows software on your Mac in a window that looks like, well, Windows. Other kinds of emulators, such as those used in companies in which a Mac or PC needs to connect to a mainframe or other big computer, run the mainframe's software in a window on your desktop computer. Most emulators, including Classic, enable you to use the keyboard shortcuts and commands that the emulated system (Mac OS 9, in the case of Classic) uses.

What's so great about Classic?

If you're a Mac newbie or don't have applications or other tools that work with Mac OS 9, you may wonder why Apple would go to the trouble of including Classic in Mac OS X and why you'd want to use it. Well, I think Classic makes OS X a lot better by making available a panoply of older programs that would otherwise be relegated to the slagheap. And long-time Mac users love Classic because it provides access to programs that haven't been updated for Mac OS X. (The following section discusses this in much greater detail.)

Doin' the Classic dance and liking it

If you're a former Mac OS 9 user, you probably have lots of applications and documents that ran under Mac OS 9. For example, suppose that you have Adobe's Photoshop 6.5. You don't have the Mac OS X-native version of Photoshop (version 7) yet, but you do have your copy of Photoshop 6.5, which worked perfectly with Mac OS 9. Classic lets you use version 6.5 until you decide to upgrade to the OS X version of Photoshop. Are you with me? Old software, old files, new operating system.

Although you certainly will want programs written for OS X (often called *OS X native* applications) rather than programs that run as Classic applications, sometimes you have no choice: The program that you want isn't available as a native OS X app — it either runs in Classic or not at all.

To make software work with Mac OS X, the folks who write it *(developers)* have to rewrite *(port)* OS 9 programs for Mac OS X. Or they have to create them from scratch by using special programming tools designed to create native OS X applications. Not all developers have done this yet because lots of people still use older Macs with older versions of Mac OS and because rewriting programs costs money and takes time.

But Apple has encouraged them, and they have responded. These days, very few OS 9 (Classic) apps are being released; almost all software for the Mac today is OS X native.

Working with Classic

Frankly, there's not much to working with Classic. If you launch an old program, it launches itself and just works. But, in the inimitable *For Dummies* tradition, I'm going to tell you all about it anyway. First I talk about launching Classic. Then I talk about opening Classic applications. Last but not least, I show you how to boot up with OS 9.2.2 for those occasions where Classic just won't do.

Launching Classic (or letting it launch itself)

You don't really launch Classic, per se. It launches itself whenever you open any Mac OS 9 application (or a document that belongs to that application). When you do, your Mac figures out that the program or document is a *classic*, and the Classic environment launches automatically.

That's not exactly true. Although you can't launch it in the traditional sense (by opening its icon), you can make it launch from the Classic System Preferences pane. In the upcoming "Setting Classic Preferences" section, I'll show you how.

The first time that you launch Classic, a dialog appears asking you to allow Mac OS X to install some files in the Mac OS 9.2.2 System Folder — the folder that runs the Mac OS 9.2.2 environment that you'll be working with. These files are needed to bridge the gap between Mac OS X and Mac OS 9.2.2, so click OK when you see the dialog.

After you launch Classic, you first see a small status window (shown in Figure 14-1) with a progress bar and a Stop button . . . just in case you change your mind and don't want Classic to launch.

After you start Classic, you can watch the emulator load by clicking the right-pointing triangle below the progress bar (just to the left of Show Mac OS 9 Desktop Window in Figure 14-1). Clicking this triangle expands the window to show you the progress of the startup process (as shown in Figure 14-2). If you're a Mac OS 9 user, you'll recognize the welcome screen.

Figure 14-1:
Opening
Classic
launches
the
Mac OS 9.2
emulator.

Figure 14-1:
Opening
Classic
launches
the
Mac OS 9.2
emulator.

Figure 14-2:
Expand the
window and
view the
familiar OS 9
welcome
screen.

If you don't choose to view the startup process by expanding the Classic
window, just wait a bit and watch the progress bar inch its way along until
Mac OS 9.2.2 launches and is ready to use. At that point, the Classic window
disappears, your Classic application becomes active, and you see the
Mac OS 9.2.2 menu bar. Check it all out in Figure 14-3.

Opening a Classic app

With Classic running, you can launch any pre-Mac OS X application by
double-clicking its icon. If Classic isn't already running, double-clicking a
Classic application automatically launches both Classic and the application.

When you double-click a MacWrite (or other document) file associated with a Classic app, for example, the Classic application launches and so does MacWrite (or whatever Classic application created the file).

You can tell when you're using a Classic program because when it's active (front-most on your screen), you see the old OS 9-style menu bar, complete with a multi-colored Apple menu in the upper-left corner of your screen. Figure 14-4 shows the old striped Apple menu and its blue OS X counterpart.

The OS X Apple icon will be gray instead of the default blue if you select the Graphite Appearance in the General System Preferences pane. In any event, it's always a solid color in the OS X menu bar and always rainbow-colored in Classic menu bar.

Figure 14-3:
The Classic text cleaning program, textSOAP, is active; the OS X Desktop and Finder window (my Home) are inactive but can still be seen in the background.

Figure 14-4:
The Classic Apple menu (left) and the OS X Apple menu (right).

Getting oriented ("Toto, we're not in OS X, anymore . . .")

Classic is a strange bird, combining things that are familiar from each of the two operating systems on your Mac. In the following sections, I walk you through what to expect when Classic is active.

Menu bar

The menu bar that you see when working in a Classic application is the Mac OS 9.2.2 version. You'll know it by the multi-hued Apple logo in the top-left corner. Compare that with the Mac OS X Apple, which is a solid color (either blue or gray depending on your choice in the General System Preference Pane).

The Mac OS 9.2.2 menu bar appears when you have a Mac OS 9 application open and active. If Classic has been launched but no Classic application is running, you'll see the Mac OS X menu bar.

Because space here won't allow me to go over all the features that you can access from the Classic menu bar, I'll point out a few and encourage you to explore them on your own. Although most of the menus on the menu bar belong to the Classic application that's open (textSOAP in Figure 14-3), a couple — sometimes more — are part of Mac OS 9.2.2.

The first feature of the Mac OS 9.2.2 menu bar is the Apple menu (topped by that rainbow Apple logo, as shown in Figure 14-5). The old customizable Apple menu is among the coolest of all Mac OS 9 features and one that lots of Mac OS X users miss. This menu contains all sorts of things: It houses tools for working with parts of Mac OS 9 (control panels, the calculator, and so forth), as well as aliases to folders (or files, if you've put them there). The beauty of the Apple menu is that it's available in all Classic Mac applications.

Another menu that I want to tell you about is the Application menu, located at the top far-right corner of the OS 9.2.2 menu bar. You'll know it by the application's name and icon — textSOAP (Classic) in Figure 14-5. The Application menu displays a listing of all applications that are currently running, including both Classic and Mac OS X applications.

Dock and icons

Just like in Mac OS X, the Finder's Desktop and windows are visible when you're working in the Classic environment. That includes the Dock and any icons that you have on the Desktop. The Dock is pretty smart about Classic: When you open a Classic application, the application's icon appears on the Dock; the icon disappears when you quit the application. In Figure 14-6, you can see the Dock with two Classic and a bunch of Mac OS X applications running. Telling them apart is tricky — the Classic application icons are, well, sometimes a little *uglier* than the Mac OS X ones. Where OS X icons have clean lines, OS 9 icons can look jaggy and . . . well . . . ugly. (That's because they're old, lower-resolution icons.) Check out Figure 14-6 to see for yourself.

Finder windows

Whether a Classic application or the Mac OS X Finder is active, you might see Mac OS X Finder windows (assuming that any are open and that your Classic application isn't blocking your view of them). You can use them to open or move files as you normally would with Mac OS X alone. If you double-click a file that belongs to a Mac OS 9 application, that program opens when you launch the Classic application.

Figure 14-5:
Access the Apple menu when a Classic application is open.

Mac OS 9 icons

Figure 14-6:
Pretty and not-so-pretty icons on the Dock.

Getting back to OS X

To get out of Classic and back to OS X, just click the Desktop, any OS X icon in the Dock, any OS X application in the Application menu, or any Finder window, and you're back to good ol' Mac OS X as quick as a bunny.

To quit the Classic application, you'll need to use the Classic System Preference Pane as described in the next section.

Setting Classic preferences

In Chapter 15, I talk about System Preferences panes, but because the preferences for Classic are important to this discussion, I cover them here and now.

If you have multiple hard drives or partitions with Mac OS 9.2.2 installed on them, you can choose which one to use as the operating system for the Classic environment. You make that choice in the Classic pane of System Preferences. (See Chapter 15 for more on System Preferences in general.) Just select the drive or partition (mine is Macintosh HD in Figure 14-7), and the next time that you launch Classic, it uses that volume's copy of Mac OS 9.2.2. Volumes that don't include Mac OS 9.2.2 appear dimmed in the preferences window.

Figure 14-7:
Classic
System
Preferences.

By selecting the Start Classic When You Log In check box, you tell Mac OS X to do just that. The advantage is that you won't have to wait a minute or two for Classic to launch the first time that you launch a Classic application. The disadvantage is that Classic uses a hefty amount of RAM and other system resources.

If you select the Warn Before Starting Classic check box, when you open a Classic application or a document owned by a Classic application, OS X will present a dialog warning you that Classic is about to start up and offers the choice of starting or not starting it, as shown in Figure 14-8.

Figure 14-8:
OS X tells
you that
Classic is
starting and
asks what
you'd like
to do.

Classic is Starting

You have the preference set to warn before starting
Classic. Click Start Classic to continue starting.
Starting continues automatically after 30 seconds.

[Don't Start]   [Start Classic]

Running Classic when you don't need it slows OS X's performance, so I prefer to keep Start Classic When You Log In disabled and Warn Before Starting Classic enabled. Classic then only runs when I'm sure that I want and need it — and never when I don't.

Note the three buttons at the bottom of the System Preferences Classic pane's Start/Stop tab. (The last two are used mostly when the Classic environment crashes, freezes, or otherwise acts improperly.)

- **Start:** Launches Classic without first launching a Classic program. (If Classic is already running, this button toggles to Stop.)

  In the earlier section "Launching Classic (or letting it launch itself)," I offer this tip: *Although you can't launch it (Classic) in the traditional sense (by opening its icon), you can make it launch using the Classic System Preferences pane.* The Start/Stop button is what I was talking about.

- **Restart:** Restarts Classic (big surprise), which is like rebooting OS 9.2.2 without having to reboot OS X.

  You can continue to work in OS X — listen to iTunes, edit movies in iMovie, surf the Web, get your mail, and so on — while Classic starts or restarts. Which is just another reason OS X is better.

- **Force Quit:** Forces the Classic environment to quit, even if it's crashed or frozen.

Getting more info on Classic

To get the most from Classic, take a look at the version of this book that was written especially for Mac OS 9: *Mac OS 9 For Dummies* (well, duh!). I'm very proud of it. Read the chapters on the Apple menu and those that cover the contents of the System Folder. You'll discover a lot more about the wonders available to you in the Classic environment.

Booting from Mac OS 9.2.2

Before I finish with Classic, here's one more thing you may want to know — how to boot your Mac so it runs OS 9.2.2 instead of OS X.

As I mention earlier in the chapter, if you bought a Mac after January 1, 2003, it may not be capable of booting OS 9 at all. If that's the case, Classic is the only way that you can run OS 9 software.

And as I mention earlier in the chapter, some programs — mostly games — just won't work when you try to run them in the Classic environment under OS X. When that happens, you'll have to start up your Mac with OS 9.2.2 if you want to use that program.

No problem; it's a snap. Here's how:

1. **Open System Preferences by clicking its icon in the Dock or choosing System Preferences from the menu.**

2. **Click the Startup Disk icon to open the Startup Disk pane.**

3. **Click a Mac OS 9.2.2 icon to select it, as shown in Figure 14-9.**

   If you've installed OS 9.2.2 on two or more volumes, you'll see two or more OS 9 System Folders; select the one that you want to boot from.

Figure 14-9: Choose Mac OS 9.2.2 to start up your Mac (while running Mac OS X).

4. **Restart your Mac by choosing Restart from the menu or by clicking the Restart button.**

   That's all there is to it. When your Mac comes back to life, you'll be running Mac OS 9.2.2.

If you have both OS 9.2.2 and OS X on the same volume or disk, be careful not to rename any of OS X's folders or throw any of OS X's folders in the Trash (while you're running OS 9.2.2). The results could be catastrophic — you could easily render OS X inoperable.

When your Mac runs OS 9.2.2 and you want to run OS X again, you can't open the Startup Disk System Preferences pane because it's part of Mac OS X and it isn't available while running OS 9.2.2. Now what?

Again, no problem. You do it the old-fashioned way — by using the Startup Disk control panel.

1. **Open the Startup Disk control panel by choosing Control Panels⇨Startup Disk from the menu.**

2. **Click the folder representing Mac OS X, as shown in Figure 14-10.**

3. **Click the Restart button in the Startup Disk window.**

   That's it. In a few moments, you'll be back up and running with Mac OS X.

Figure 14-10: Choose Mac OS X to start up your Mac (while running Mac OS 9.2.2).

Chapter 15

What Your Mac Prefers

In This Chapter

▶ Getting to know System Preferences

▶ Changing your Desktop appearance

▶ Adopting an international flair

▶ Setting dates and time

▶ Sounding off — or on

*E*veryone works a bit differently, and we all like to use our Macs in a certain way. System Preferences is the place in Mac OS X where you can set options that are just right for you. You can set everything from the appearance of your screen to the kind of network or Internet connection that you have — and a whole lot more. In this chapter, I take you on a tour of all the Mac OS X System Preferences panes. Hang on; it's gonna be a long, but informative, ride.

Introducing System Preferences

You find System Preferences on the Apple (⌘) menu and in the Dock. Choose System Preferences from the ⌘ menu or click it in the Dock to get a look at all the options that I discuss in this chapter. Check out all the features that you can change from the System Preferences window, as shown in Figure 15-1.

What you see in Figure 15-1 is the System Preferences window. But when you click any of the icons here, the bottom part of the window changes to reflect the options for the icon that you click. When this happens, I call the bottom part of the window a *pane*. So, for example, when you click the Date & Time icon in the System Preferences window, the bottom part of the window becomes the Date & Time System Preference pane.

Figure 15-1:
The System
Preferences
window:
Change
your world.

System Preferences is Apple's new name for Control Panels, which is a set of tools that's been around since the earliest versions of Mac OS. The biggest difference between System Preferences and Control Panels is that Control Panels (mostly) loaded at start up, displaying an icon on the screen when they loaded. System Preference panes don't. They don't load at start up; they're just there.

Just where? The actual files for Preference Panes are stored in the Preference Panes folder, in the Library folder in the System folder. (*Note:* This is the OS X System folder, not the OS 9 System Folder-with-a-capital-F.) If you choose to install third-party preference panes, they can go either in that folder (if you want them to be available to all users) or in the Preference Panes folder in the Library in your Home folder (if you want to keep them to yourself).

Some System Preferences relate to topics that I cover in other chapters. The most notable of these are the Network and Internet preferences, which I discuss in Chapter 11. I let you know in this chapter any time that I skip a preference that you can read about in another chapter.

Look back at the System Preferences window in Figure 15-1. By default, four System Preference icons — Displays, Sound, Network, and Startup Disk — appear in the toolbar. Apple kindly put them up top so that you can find them more easily and because these are probably the ones that you'll use most frequently. Also on the toolbar (far left) is the Show All button. I tell you more about this in the upcoming section "Using System Preferences." Below that, Apple has divided System Preferences into four groups: Personal, Hardware, Internet & Network, and System.

Who is Apple to decide which System Preferences you'll be using most? If you want to change this configuration, add your own favorites to the toolbar by simply dragging any icon you like from the bottom of the window onto the toolbar. Your new custom design is waiting for you each time that you open System Preferences. To remove an item, just drag it off the toolbar — it'll disappear with a poof.

As a nice touch, you can change these frequently accessed items from name-and-icon to just icon or to just name (in two sizes each, no less) and back again by ⌘+clicking the Hide Toolbar button (the gumdrop in the upper-right corner) as shown in Figure 15-2.

Figure 15-2:
⌘+click
the gray
gumdrop to
change your
toolbar.

Using System Preferences

Before I examine the items in the System Preferences window, I need to explain a couple of things about using them. This info applies to all System Preferences, so listen up.

To use a System Preference, just click it once to open its pane. You can double-click if that habit is ingrained in your mouse finger, but there's no need.

Okay, so you've finished working with a System Preferences pane, but you want to open another one. You could simply close the one that you've been working on, or you could cut to the chase by clicking the Show All button, located at the far left of the top row of icons on the System Preferences window (as shown in Figure 15-1). Clicking the Show All button returns the icons for all available System Preferences to view on the screen.

Here's an even more convenient way: Choose the System Preferences that you want from the View menu. All the icons that you see in Figure 15-1 also have an entry on this menu; choose one, and its System Preference pane appears immediately.

Here's another nifty tip: You can get rid of the categories all together and display the icons in alphabetical order. As a bonus, it makes the System Preferences window roughly 25 percent smaller onscreen.

When you choose View➪Show All Alphabetically, the categories disappear, the window shrinks, and the icons are alphabetized, as shown in Figure 15-3.

To switch from alphabetical view back to category view, choose View➪Show All In Categories or use the keyboard shortcut ⌘+L.

Figure 15-3:
Alphabet-
ical or
categorical
— however
you prefer
your Pref-
erences.

Unlocking a preference

Many System Preferences need to be unlocked before you can use them because some of these settings are applicable for all users and thus require an Administrator password. After all, you can't have just any user of your Mac change the Network configuration and break it for everyone. See Figure 15-4 to see what a locked preference looks like. Notice the locked lock icon in the lower-left corner and that everything is grayed out and unavailable. Now compare that with Figure 15-5, where the lock has been unlocked (by supplying an administrator user name and password) and all items are enabled.

You don't have to unlock all System Preferences to change them, just some of them. When I come to a System Preference that must be unlocked before you can use it, I'll let you know up front. Deal? Good.

Figure 15-4:
A locked
System
Preferences
pane.

Only users with Administrator privileges can unlock some System Preferences. See Chapter 16 for more info on administrators and permissions.

To unlock a preference, do the following:

1. **Click the lock icon in the lower-left corner of the System Preferences pane (shown in the margin).**

   Mac OS X responds with an Authenticate dialog in which you enter your user name and password.

   The user name and password that you use here must be a user with administrator privileges on this Mac. If your user account isn't set up with administrator privileges, you can't unlock locked panes or change them. You'll need to supply an administrator's user name and password or learn to live with it the way it is.

   The first user that you create with OS X (when you first install it) is always an administrator.

2. **Enter this user information and then click OK.**

   Mac OS X unlocks the System Preference that you're working with.

In Figure 15-5, you see the Network System Preferences pane after being unlocked. Notice that you can now make changes to it; before you unlocked it, all the options were grayed out and impossible to change.

Figure 15-5:
An unlocked
System
Preference
displays its
options.

Locking a preference

To relock a System Preferences pane (after you unlock it), merely click the
lock icon again. It will lock itself instantly.

Setting Preferences

Ready to dig into each of the System Preferences? Great. I start with the first
category (Personal, as shown in Figure 15-1) and work from left to right.

Personal preferences

The following preference panes are displayed in the Personal category.

Desktop

Open the Desktop System Preferences pane to set your Desktop color or
picture. Apple provides a number of collections from which you can choose
via the Collection pop-up menu, or you can choose a different folder of
images if you want. You can also drag an image file into the *well* (that
indented box in the upper left of the pane).

Dock

 I cover the Dock and its preferences in great detail in Chapter 3. Rather than waste any more trees, I'll just move along to. . . .

General

 General Systems Preferences give you control over the color scheme that you see in Mac OS X as well as what happens when you click a scroll bar (see Figure 15-6).

Don't get too excited. It only controls two color settings: the color that text becomes highlighted when you select it and what color buttons pulsate (throb) to get your attention.

Throbbing buttons are always the default button. If you press Return or Enter, the default button is pressed. In earlier versions of Mac OS, the default button had a thick border to indicate that it was the default. So throbbing buttons in OS X are the same as buttons with a thick border in Mac OS 9 (and earlier).

Appearance options

In the General System Preferences pane, you can choose specific aspects of how your Mac looks and feels.

- **Appearance pop-up menu:** Use choices from this menu to choose from different appearances, changing the overall look of buttons and window controls (the jellybeans in the scroll bars).

  Apple, however, in its infinite wisdom, provides only two choices — Blue and Graphite. Other appearances might be available (try the Internet) but thus far are not sanctioned by Apple.

- **Highlight Color pop-up menu:** From here, you can choose the color that text becomes surrounded by when you select it in a document or in an icon's name in the Finder window. This time Apple isn't so restrictive. You have seven highlight colors to choose from, plus Other, which brings up a color picker from which you can choose almost any color.

Scroll bar behavior

The Place Scroll Arrows radio buttons let you choose whether you have the traditional single arrow at either end or the default (introduced in OS 8) of both arrows together at the bottom or right of the scroll bars.

Select from two radio buttons next to the Click in the Scroll Bar To heading to move your view of a window either up or down by a page (the default behavior for OS 9) or to the point in the document roughly proportionate to where you clicked in the scroll bar.

Figure 15-6:
The General
System
Preferences
pane.

Select the Scroll to Here radio button if you often work with long (multi-page) documents. You'll find it quite handy for navigating long documents. And don't forget — the Page Down key on your keyboard does the same thing as selecting the Jump to the Next Page choice, so you'll lose nothing by selecting Scroll to Here.

The Number of Recent Items pop-up menus control how many applications and documents are remembered in your ⌘⇨Recent Items submenu.

The Font Smoothing Style pop-up menu offers four settings for anti-aliasing (smoothing) fonts on screen. The categories are

- ✔ **Standard - Best for CRT:** You know, your standard, clunky tube-type monitor.

- ✔ **Light:** Just a hint of the essence of smoothing for your text.

- ✔ **Medium - Best for Flat-Panel:** For those sleek, flat-panel monitors and notebooks, too.

- ✔ **Strong:** Mondo-smoothing. I happen to like it on my flat-panel display, but you might not.

Ignore Apple's editorial comments and try all four. Then choose the one that looks best to your eyes.

The Turn off Text Smoothing for Font Sizes *x* and Smaller pop-up menu (where *x* is the pop-up menu setting) does just what it says. Fonts that size and smaller are no longer *anti-aliased* (smoothed) when displayed.

I have no idea why Apple limits you to only the four choices in the menu.

International

If you're in the U.S., you might assume that you don't need to set anything in the International System Preferences pane. After all, you chose to see your Mac's menus and commands in U.S. English when you first installed Mac OS X. But wait — the International System Preferences pane has more in it than just a choice of language. Here's where you can set date and time formats — probably the most useful feature for U.S. folks — and yes, you can choose a new language here, too.

The International System Preferences pane has five tabs: Language, Date, Time, Numbers, and Input Menu. I describe each in the following sections.

Language

Click the first (leftmost) tab — the Language tab — of the International pane. Here you find options that you can choose to set your Mac's order of preference for languages used in applications. Make your choices in the top half of this screen; to organize your choices, drag an entry up or down in the list. If an application uses the first language that you indicate in this list, you see the application's commands and menus in that chosen language. If your first language choice isn't available, the next option is used, and so on.

The lower portion of the Language tab lets you select a script to attach to the language that you chose in the top part of this pane. The script that you choose affects sort order, case conversion, and word definitions.

Date

Set the format for date and time display in applications on the second tab (Date) of the International System Preferences pane. These settings are accessible by applications for formatting purposes, as are those for Time. This is where you specify settings — such as a 24- versus a 12-hour clock or month-day-year ordering — so that all your applications can format the values appropriately, both those from the clock and those you enter from the keyboard or programmatically.

Note that when you change an option in the Date tab, you can see the results displayed at the bottom of this tab. Change the look of your date settings from the choices in the Region pop-up menu, located near the top of the Date tab window.

You can also choose non-U.S. date settings from the Region pop-up menu. If you change other settings in the Date tab, *Custom* appears in the Region pop-up menu, indicating that you've fiddled with its preset date options — you wild thing, you!

Under the Long Date heading (on the left side of this window), you can choose four items to display: Weekday, Month, Day, and Year. Each has its own pop-up menu. Each time you make a change, the results appear at the bottom of this window. Use these menus to change the order of display, which is a lot of what the regional settings are about. In Europe, for example, the day of the month typically appears before the name of the month (8 May 2000), but U.S. folks usually like their months to show up first (May 8, 2000).

You can also add a text prefix (any text you want) to appear before the long date. Just type it in the Prefix text box.

Finally, if you select the Leading Zero for Day check box, dates before the 10th of the month (the 1st through the 9th) appear with a zero before them (01, 02, and so on).

Check out the options under the Short Date heading that you find on the right side of the Date tab window. Options that you can set here include a pop-up menu to set Month/Day/Year format and a text box to specify what type of separator symbol you want to use, such as a front slash (/) or a dash (-). From the three check boxes beneath Short Date, you can also choose to use a leading zero in your dates for a day (11-*01*) or a month (*01*-12) and whether to show the century in your date format (12-12-*00*).

Time

The Time tab is the third (middle) tab of the International System Preferences pane (as shown in Figure 15-7). Like what you find on the Date tab, the Time tab offers you options from the Region pop-up menu. Choices within this menu (located at the top of the Time tab window) correspond with the way that time is written in various parts of the world. Use the radio buttons (on the left side of the window) to choose whether to use a 12- or 24-hour clock and whether to set noon and midnight as 0:00 or 12:00. You can also set how you want to set time before and after noon (AM or p.m., for example), what type of separating punctuation to use between hour and minute (such as the colon in 12:13 p.m.), and a check box for setting the use of a leading zero for the hour (4:56 or 04:56). Again, like the Date tab, when you change an option in the Time tab, you can see the results displayed at the bottom of this tab.

Numbers

Set options on the Numbers tab (the fourth one) of the International System Preferences pane to choose which characters to use when displaying decimal numbers (a period is common in the U.S., but a comma is more common in Europe), as well as which separators to use to set off thousands (1,000 or 1000, for example). Like what you find on the Date and Time tabs, the Numbers tab offers you options from the Region pop-up menu. You can also pick a currency symbol, such as $ or £.

Figure 15-7:
Choose the
items and
order to
display
in the
Time tab.

Input Menu

The Input Menu tab is the final (rightmost) tab of the International System Preferences pane. Select from a variety of check boxes here to choose a new keyboard mapping — you can pick from a variety of countries. When you do, a new menu appears in the Finder's menu bar, as shown in Figure 15-8.

Or, if you're so inclined, choose a *Dvorak map:* That's the one with keys mapped in an alternative layout that places the most commonly used keys on the home row. You can choose this from the Input Type list.

Do not under any circumstances click the Options button on the Input Menu tab unless you have good reason to use foreign keyboard layouts on occasion. The ⌘+Option+spacebar keyboard shortcut, when turned on, can cause unpredictable behavior if you later forget that you turned it on. Use this thingy with caution, especially if you use Photoshop (which uses ⌘+Option+spacebar as the shortcut for Zoom Out).

Login Items

When you start up your Mac or if you use it after someone else has, you must log in before you can get to your files and begin working. You also need to enter your name and password to get to some options, as I describe in the "Using System Preferences" section earlier in this chapter.

Figure 15-8:
The Input Menu menu (left) and the Input Menu tab in the International pane (right).

The Login Items System Preferences pane enables you to choose programs that you'd like to launch automatically when you log in (it works like Startup Items in OS 9).

This is where you select applications, documents, or even folders to open automatically every time that you start up, restart, or log into your Mac.

To add a new login item, click the Add button at the bottom of this window and then locate the program that you want. (For help on how to locate a file, read through Chapter 8.) When you find the program that you want (via a standard Open File dialog) and click the Add button, it appears in the Login Items tab as shown in Figure 15-9. If you want the program's windows hidden (but still want the program running), select the Hide check box to the left of its name.

Here's an even easier way to add a new log-in item — just drag it onto the Login Items window as I demonstrate in Figure 15-9.

You can also change the order in which items in this list open by dragging them up or down in the list. Last, but not least, to remove an application, just click it to select it and then click the Remove button at the bottom of this window.

Figure 15-9:
Add appli-
cations to
Login Items.

My Account

This is where you manage information about you and your user account on this Mac. It's a three-trick pony, shown in Figure 15-10:

1. **To change your password, click the Change button next to My Password.**

   A sheet will appear asking for your current password, new password (twice, for verification), and an optional password hint.

2. **To change your picture, click any picture in the row below the Choose Another button.**

   This is the picture that you'll see at login for your user account.

   If none of those suit you, click the Choose Another button to select any graphic file on any mounted disk. Here's an even easier way — just drag a picture file from the Finder onto the picture well. (The picture well contains that cute Jaguar-Apple icon in Figure 15-10.)

3. **To open Address Book to edit your card, click the Edit button, and Address Book will open to your card.**

Figure 15-10:
I'm repre-
sented by a
cute fur-
covered
Apple now.

Screen Effects

Most computer experts will tell you that you don't really need a screen saver to protect your monitor from screen burn-in these days, and I guess Apple agrees. This pane was called Screen Saver until Jaguar's release; today it's known as Screen Effects, which is a more appropriate moniker, I must say.

If you want a screen saver . . . um . . . a screen *effect* — some folks do like to see pictures floating around the screen when they're not working — you can use the Screen Effects preference pane to set one. Mac OS X comes with several screen saver modules; to see what the selected module looks like in action, click the Test button. Press any key to end the test.

To set up the screen saver, first choose a screen saver from the list in the Screen Saver tab of the Screen Saver preference pane. Next, click the Activation tab and drag the Time until Screen Saver Starts slider to the number of minutes that you want the Mac to wait before activating the screen saver. You can also choose to require a password to wake up the screen saver in this tab.

Finally, click the Hot Corners tab to choose which corner(s) of your screen activates the screen saver and which deactivates it. Now when you move your mouse to a selected corner, you activate or deactivate the screen saver.

You can choose to have Screen Effects require a password to wake it by marking the Use My User Account Password radio button in the Activation tab. This is a great (albeit not bulletproof) way to keep curious onlookers from seeing your stuff.

That's it. You're done!

TIP

If you like Screen Savers/Effects, find plenty more available at your favorite downloadable software repository (mine's www.versiontracker.com). Many are free, and some cost a few bucks. Some of those, like Marine Aquarium in Figure 15-11 (from www.order-n-dev.com), are even worth paying for.

Figure 15-11:
Search the Web for other cool screen savers.

I paid my $21.95, and it was worth every penny. It's so lifelike I sometimes believe those are real fish in my monitor. Plus, unlike other fish I've owned, these never float (or explode from overfeeding). I love this saver/effect; it's the only one I use anymore.

Hardware preferences

The following preference panes are displayed in the Hardware category.

CDs & DVDs

Introduced with Mac OS X version 10.2 Jaguar, this preference pane lets you decide what your Mac should do when you insert a blank or pre-recorded CD or DVD. Choose here from five pop-up menus; you can also set your Mac to launch certain applications, run AppleScripts, or nothing at all.

ColorSync

The ColorSync System Preferences pane offers you color-matching technology that ensures color consistency between screen representation and color output.

Don't mess with this preference unless you know what you're doing and you know you have to. This preference's settings are irrelevant to the average user: Nothing good whatsoever will happen if you change them. Unless you are also using the ColorSync color-matching system on your printing devices and scanners and you also understand how color-matching works, you're likely to do more harm than good if you fool with this.

Displays

Click the Displays icon in the System Preferences window for options to set your Mac's monitor. When you open this window, you see the Mac's current monitor settings on the Display tab (see Figure 15-12). My monitor happens to be a Color LCD display, so that's what you see in the title bar.

To change the monitor's settings, select the number of colors that you want your monitor to use from the Colors pop-up menu. Most monitors and video cards support multiple resolutions, and some also allow you to choose a refresh rate.

By default, OS X selects the Show Modes Recommended by Display check box, enabling you to pick only those options that OS X thinks are best for your video card and display. If you deselect this check box, you have more choices, but they aren't necessarily the best ones.

The list of resolutions governs how much stuff you see on your monitor. The smaller the numbers, the less you'll see and the bigger you'll see it. Bigger numbers mean you see more, but it's smaller. Got it?

Figure 15-12:
The Display tab shows the Mac's current display settings.

Most monitors have settings to adjust their brightness and some also enable you to adjust their gamma settings. If your monitor supports these features, you see the Brightness and Gamma Control slide bars at the bottom of the Display preferences window. If you have these features, adjust them the way that looks best to your eyes.

The Show Displays in Menu Bar check box gives you the little menu that you see at the upper-right of most of the figures in this book, where you can change the resolution and color depth without bringing up System Preferences or bring up System Preferences already open to the Displays pane.

Finally, from the Color tab, you can choose a pre-configured profile for your monitor (if it's an Apple brand monitor) or calibrate your display yourself. To do this, click the Calibrate button, and an assistant will walk you through the process.

If you have a laptop, you will see the Detect Displays button shown in Figure 15-12; if you have a desktop Mac, you won't have it. It does just what its name implies: When you connect an external display, if it isn't recognized automatically (which it usually is), click this button and the display is instantly recognized without restarting!

This OS X-only detail is good to remember if you use several different external displays or projection systems in different locations. It saves you from shutting down/restarting and makes the whole process a little sweeter. Just click and you're done.

Finally, if you have two video cards or are using a PowerBook and external monitor together, you'll see a third tab called Arrangement. Drag the little pictures representing your monitors around in the window to arrange your screens. Make it match the physical set up of your monitors as closely as possible. If you want to place the menu bar on the other screen, drag the little picture of the menu bar from one little screen to the other.

The Arrangement tab only appears on PowerBooks and on desktop Macs if you have more than one graphics card installed in your computer and if your computer is capable of displaying an extended Desktop.

Energy Saver

All recent Mac models are Energy Star compliant, allowing you to preset your machine to turn itself off at a specific time or after a specified idle period. Here's how.

1. **Click the Energy Saver icon in the System Preferences window.**

   On the Sleep tab, you can choose to have your computer go to sleep (a low-power mode) automatically after so many minutes of idle time (kind of like a killer screen saver).

2. **To turn this feature on, move the slider beneath the Put the Computer to Sleep When It Is Inactive For heading until the desired time appears beneath it.**

   You can choose as little as 1 minute or go to the other extreme and turn it off by moving the slider to Never. Check it out in Figure 15-13.

Figure 15-13:
Set how long your Mac waits before taking a snooze (15 minutes for me).

You can also set separate sleep times for your Mac's display and choose whether to let your hard disk go to sleep if it supports sleep mode. Setting the display to sleep might come in handy if you want your Mac to keep doing what it's doing and you don't need to use the monitor. The hard drive sleep option is less useful unless you've got a PowerBook or an iBook. Checking this option will force your hard drive to sleep after a few minutes of inactivity, which will save your battery.

To activate display sleep, select the Use Separate Time to Put the Display to Sleep check box and then drag the slider to the idle time that you want.

To wake up your Mac from its sleep, merely move your mouse or press any key on the keyboard.

Drag the slider to 30 or 45 minutes for sleep; then remember to turn off your Mac manually when you're not going to need it for a day or more.

The Options tab is home to a small collection of useful settings. On this tab, you'll find check boxes telling the Mac to restart automatically after a power failure, to automatically wake up when the modem detects an incoming call (useful for fax software), and to automatically wake for network administrative access (handy in a corporate setting where an IT person maintains system configurations).

PowerBook and iBook users get additional Energy Saver options including the ability to display a battery status indicator in the menu bar near the clock as well as two pop-up menus:

- ✔ **Optimize Energy Settings:** Lets you fine-tune Energy Saver settings even further, with choices for Highest Performance, Longest Battery Life, DVD Playback, Presentations, and Custom (your own settings).

- ✔ **Energy Saver settings:** The second laptop-only menu lets you configure two different sets of Energy Saver settings: one for when your computer is plugged into a power source, and the other for when you're running on battery power.

Keyboard

Open the Keyboard System Preferences pane for options to modify how your keyboard responds to your keystrokes.

On the Settings tab, slide the Delay Until Repeat slide bar to set how long you have to hold down a key before it starts repeating.

Drag the Key Repeat Rate slider to set how fast a key repeats when you hold it down. This feature comes into play, for example, when you hold down the dash (-) key to make a line or the asterisk (*) key to make a divider.

You can type in the box at the bottom of the window to test your settings before closing this panel.

New in version 10.1 of OS X is the Full Keyboard Access tab, shown in Figure 15-14. By using the settings here, you can use the keyboard to access just text input fields and lists (which is what you're used to by default) or you can set it to access all the controls in a window or dialog, which lets you tab to buttons and check boxes and avoid using the mouse (if that's your preference).

In Figure 15-14 where the dialog reads "Press Control (ctrl) + the key shown to highlight the area," Apple means that when you press one of the magic key combinations, you can use the tab or arrow keys to move among items in the menu bar, Dock, a window's toolbar, or palettes (floating windows). If you really hate to use your mouse or if your mouse is broken, these keyboard shortcuts can come in really handy. I like to use them on my PowerBook when I'm traveling and don't have room to hook up a mouse because I really don't like using the built-in mouse-thing (technically called a *trackpad*).

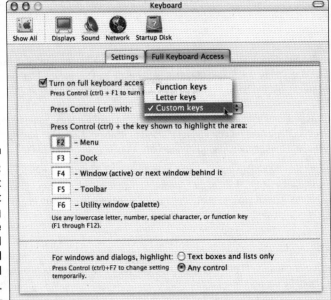

Figure 15-14:
Access just
about
anything
from the
keyboard
with Full
Keyboard
Access.

Mouse

Adjust the settings in the Mouse System Preferences pane, as shown in Figure 15-15, to set your mouse speed and double-click delays. Move the Tracking Speed slider to change the relationship between hand movement of the mouse and cursor movement on the screen. A faster tracking speed settings (moving the slider to the right) sends your cursor squirting across the screen with a mere flick of the wrist; slower mouse speed settings (moving the slider to the left) make the cursor crawl across in seemingly slow motion, even when your hand is flying. Set this setting as fast as you can stand it — I like the fastest speed. Try it: You might like it.

If you have a portable Mac with a trackpad, such as a PowerBook or iBook, you'll see an additional tab — Trackpad — where you can set the tracking speed and double-clicking behavior of your trackpad.

The Double-Click Speed setting determines how close together two clicks must be for the Mac to interpret them as a double-click and not as two separate clicks. Move the slider arrow to the leftmost setting (Very Slow) for the slowest. With this setting, you can double-click at an almost leisurely pace. The rightmost position (Fast) is the fastest setting, which I prefer. The middle area of the slider represents a double-click speed somewhere in the middle.

Changes in the Mouse System Preferences pane take place immediately, so you should definitely play around a little and see what settings feel best for you. You can test the effect of your changes to the Double-Click Speed setting in the Double-Click Here to Test text box at the bottom of the window before you close this preference pane.

Note: If you have a PowerBook or iBook, there will also be a tab for trackpad settings with the same two settings and options to specify just what tasks the trackpad can be used for, such as tapping it rather than pressing the button when you want to click something. You also get a separate Scroll Speed slider. You can even tell OS X to ignore the trackpad while you're typing. But all these goodies are only for laptop Macs with trackpads.

Figure 15-15: Set how fast your mouse moves and double-clicks.

Sound

 Use options in the Sound System Preferences pane (as shown in Figure 15-16) to control the way the Mac plays and records sound.

To make your Mac's volume louder or softer, use the Output Volume slider at the bottom of the window. Select the Mute check box to turn off your all sound. Use the Balance slider in the Output tab to make one stereo speaker louder than the other.

On the Sound Effects tab, you can choose an alert (beep) sound and set the alert volume. The Alert Volume slider controls Alert (that is, beep) volume. You can also specify through which output device they play, if you have more than one, by selecting from the Play Alerts and Sound Effects Through pop-up menu.

 You can find new sounds on the Internet at your favorite shareware archive (www.versiontracker.com, www.macupdate.com/, and www.tucows.com are a few that I like and recommend).

To install new sounds, move them into the Sounds folder inside the Library folder at root level on your hard drive if you want them to be available to all users of this Mac. Or put them in the Sounds folder inside the Library folder in your home folder if you want to be the only one that can use them. (See Chapter 10 for more info on these two Library folders.)

Figure 15-16:
The Sound
System
Preferences
pane with
the Sound
Effects tab
showing.

Use the Output tab shown in Figure 15-17 to specify what speakers are used for sound output.

Two that won't show (unless . . .)

Two more preference panes might appear in the Hardware section, but only if your Mac has the appropriate hardware connected to it.

Bluetooth

Bluetooth is wireless networking for low-bandwidth peripherals introduced in Mac OS X version 10.2 Jaguar. If your Mac is equipped with a Bluetooth adapter, you can synchronize wirelessly with phones and Palm devices, print wirelessly to Bluetooth printers, and who knows what else (it's very new technology). The pane is shown in Figure 15-18.

Bluetooth is designed to work with *iSync,* Apple's new synchronizing technology. As I write this, iSync has not yet been made available. It should be neat, but I reserve judgment until I actually use it.

Ink

Ink is Mac OS X's built-in handwriting recognition engine, also introduced in version 10.2 Jaguar. If you have a stylus and tablet connected to your Mac, just turn it on in this pane and you can write anywhere you can type with the keyboard.

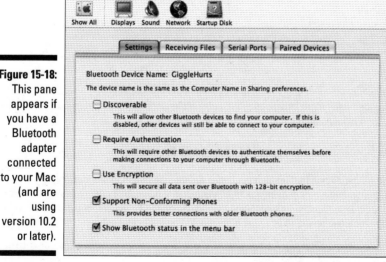

Figure 15-17: Control your different output choices here.

The Ink pane (with the Gestures tab selected) is shown in Figure 15-19, but alas, you'll only see it if you have one of the handful of tablets that Ink supports connected to your Mac.

Figure 15-18: This pane appears if you have a Bluetooth adapter connected to your Mac (and are using version 10.2 or later).

Figure 15-19:
You see the
Ink pane
only when
you have
the proper
hardware
connected
(and are
using
version 10.2
or later).

All currently supported tablets are come from Wacom (www.wacom.com) with prices as low as $100 for a small wireless stylus and tablet.

Internet & Network preferences

The following preference panes are displayed in the Internet & Network category.

Internet

The Internet System Preferences pane is where you configure Mac OS X for Internet access — your home page, preferred search engine, default Web browser, and so on.

There are four tabs in this pane; here's what they do:

✔ **.Mac (formerly iTools):** If you have a .Mac account, you can type your name and password here so that you don't have to type them every time that you use your iDisk or Mail. (See Chapter 11's section on .Mac if you want to know what this is all about.)

Click the Free Sign Up button, and your Web browser will open and take you to the Apple .Mac Sign Up page.

✔ **iDisk:** This shows how much of your iDisk (your remote disk maintained on Apple's servers for .Mac members) is used and how much is available. It also allows you to make your Public Folder Read-Only and add password protection.

✔ **Email:** On this tab, you specify your chosen Email reader — Mail is pre-selected, but if you use another program, this is where to select it. Here also are fields for your e-mail address, incoming mail server, account type, account ID, password, and mail server.

If you're not sure what goes in these fields, ask your Internet Service Provider (ISP).

If you use .Mac as your e-mail provider, you can select the Use .Mac Email Account check box. When you do, many of the fields are filled out (correctly) for you.

✔ **Web:** This tab is where you choose your default Web browser program. Internet Explorer is pre-selected, but if you prefer a different browser, select it from the Default Web Browser pop-up menu.

Under the Default Web Browser pop-up menu are fields where you can specify your home page, default search engine, and the folder where you want downloaded files to go into.

The default folder for downloaded items is your Desktop, which I think is pretty convenient, but it can get really full and messy if you do a lot of downloading. You'll never have to hunt for that file you just downloaded; it'll be right there on the Desktop where you can easily find it. That said, you can then move it to any folder you have access to if you so desire. If you do a lot of downloading, you might want to create a Downloads folder inside your Home or Documents directory to house them.

Network

Set options in the Network System Preferences pane to connect your Mac to the Internet or to a network. Although I talk a little about this pane in Chapter 11, I promised you more detail here. So here's some detail.

If you're part of a large office network, check with your System Administrator before you change anything in this pane. If you ignore this advice, you run the risk of losing your network connection completely.

At the top of this pane is the Location pop-up menu. If you use your Mac in more than one place, you can set up a separate configuration for each location and then choose it from this menu. A *location*, in this context, consists of all the settings in all the tabs in the Network System Preferences pane. After you have this entire pane configured the way that you like, pull down this menu and choose New Location. Type in a name for the new location and then click OK. Then you can change all the settings in this pane at once by choosing that location from the pop-up menu.

If your Mac has a single network or Internet connection, like most home users have, just choose Automatic from the Location menu and be done with it.

Below the Location menu is the Show pop-up menu. Here you choose your Internet connection. If you use a modem to connect to the Internet, choose Internal Modem. If you have another type of Internet access, such as ISDN, cable modem, or Digital Subscriber Line (DSL), choose either Ethernet or Built-in Ethernet.

Below this menu you see four tabs. Unfortunately, you'll need to talk to your ISP or network administrator to find out how to configure them; I can't tell you how in this book because there are just so many configurations that depend upon your particular ISP and service. I will, though, give you a brief rundown on what each one does:

- **TCP/IP:** *TCP/IP* is the language of the Internet. On this tab, you specify things such as your IP Address, Domain Name Servers, and Search Domains.

- **PPP or PPPoE:** These acronyms stand for Point-To-Point Protocol and Point-To-Point Protocol over Ethernet. Which one you see depends on what you've selected from the Show menu. All modems use PPP; some cable and DSL modems use PPPoE. Your ISP will tell you whether you need to do anything with this tab.

- **AppleTalk:** *AppleTalk* is a homegrown network protocol invented by Apple. Some (but not all) networked printers require it to be turned on for them to function. For more information about AppleTalk in general, this tab in particular, and printers, see Chapter 12.

- **Proxies:** If you're on a large network or your Mac is behind a firewall, you might need to specify one or more proxy servers. If so, your network administrator can help you with this tab's settings. If you're a home user, you'll probably never need to touch this tab. Finally, some ISPs require you to specify proxy servers; if you need to do this, ask your ISP what to do.

QuickTime

 QuickTime is Apple's multimedia technology for both Mac and Windows. When you watch a movie on your Mac (unless you're watching a DVD, of course), chances are good that it's a QuickTime file.

QuickTime is probably already configured properly. When you click the QuickTime preference icon, you see five tabs: Plug-In, Connection, Music, Media Keys, and Update. Just check to make sure that QuickTime is set as follows and then leave this preference alone.

The Plug-In tab deals with the way your Internet browser handles multimedia files; it contains three check boxes:

✔ Select the **Play Movies Automatically** check box if it's not already checked if you want your browser to play movies when it encounters them.

✔ Select the **Save Movies in Disk Cache** check box to save QuickTime movies in the browser's cache folder (in your Home/Library/Preferences folder; if you use Internet Explorer, they're in Explorer/Temporary Items.)

Don't rely on this feature. Some movies don't download at all when you view them in your browser; others only download the first frame. If you need to harvest QuickTime movies from the Web, you'll be better off buying the $30 QuickTime Pro upgrade, which, among other things, lets you save QuickTime movies from within your browser, as shown in Figure 15-20.

✔ Select the **Enable Kiosk Mode** check box to hide the QuickTime controller (Play/Pause/Volume/and so on) within your browser.

Figure 15-20:
Control-
click to save
a movie
(left) with
QuickTime
Pro; if you
don't pay for
the Pro
upgrade,
Save As is
disabled
(right).

Click the Connection tab and select the speed of your Internet connection by choosing the appropriate option from the Connection Speed pop-up menu. If you're not sure what your connection speed is, ask your ISP. (If you're not sure what an ISP is, I suggest that you read Chapter 11.)

The MIME settings button at the bottom of this pane offers advanced options for receiving files over the Internet. I suggest you leave these alone unless you're instructed to change it by someone knowledgeable, such as your ISP.

Ignore the Music and Media Keys tabs. I still haven't figured out what they're for even though they've been in QuickTime for years. If you want to use a music synthesizer other than the built-in QuickTime Music Synthesizer or if someone sends you a secured media file (or you download one), you'll have to figure it out then. So far I have never had to touch these two settings.

Change settings in the Update tab to update your QuickTime software automatically (if you have an Internet connection). Because each successive version of QuickTime has added cool and useful features, I suggest that you select the Check for Updates Automatically check box. After you do, your Mac will check for new versions of QuickTime whenever you connect to the Internet. As Martha Stewart says, "It's a good thing."

Sharing

This is another option that you'll use when networking your Mac. There are two facets of Sharing — sharing a single Mac with other users and sharing files via an office network or the Internet. Read all the gory details in Chapter 16.

System System preferences (kind of redundant)

The following preference panes are displayed in the System category.

Accounts (formerly Users)

This pane, which is only useful to users with Administrator access, is where you create and administer user accounts on your Mac. I cover this in greater detail in Chapter 16, but I promised earlier to show you how to get rid of logging in entirely if you don't like it. Here's what to do.

If you don't have any reason to worry about someone else logging on and making mischief (or if you don't share your Mac), you can disable the log-in screen in the Login Options tab.

When you disable logging in, you also affect the preferences set by anyone else who shares your Mac. So, if your Desktop pattern, keyboard settings, and so forth are different from those of someone else who uses your machine, those preferences won't be properly reflected if each of you don't have your own log-in account. Even if you're not worried about security, consider keeping logging in enabled if any other users have accounts on your machine.

To disable the logging in requirement, you may first need to unlock the Accounts System Preference. (For more on unlocking a preference, see the "Using System Preferences" section earlier in this chapter.)

To disable log in, select yourself in the list of users and mark the Log In Automatically as Your Name Here check box.

Note that only one account is allowed to use auto-login. If another user wants to use this Mac, you need to choose Log Out from the menu or press ⌘+Shift+Q.

For non-automatic logins, the Login Options tab has additional choices. You can choose to have your login window display just two fields — user name and password — or the flashier list of users of this Mac, complete with those cute little pictures.

The Disable Restart and Shut Down buttons and Show Password Hint after 3 Attempts to Enter a Password check boxes do just what their names imply.

Classic

Open the Classic System Preferences pane to choose the drive or drive partition that contains a Mac OS 9.2.2 System Folder to use when working in the Classic environment. I dig deep into the Classic environment in Chapter 14. Suffice it to say that if you have Mac OS 9 applications or if you're nostalgic for the way things were in Mac OS 9, you need to use the Classic System Preferences pane.

I'll repeat what I said in Chapter 14 about version numbers to avoid any confusion:

Mac OS X (10.2) requires version 9.2.2 of Mac OS, commonly referred to as Mac OS 9.2.2, to provide the Classic environment. But most (if not all) programs don't distinguish between different versions of Mac OS 9. So when I call a program a *Mac OS 9 program,* what I mean is that it's *not* an OS X program and that it will run under any version of Mac OS 9. In other words, when I talk about stuff that works with (or appears in) all versions of Mac OS 9, I say *Mac OS 9.* When I'm talking about Classic or another feature or program that *requires* OS 9.2.2, I say *Mac OS 9.2.2.*

Date & Time

Within the Date & Time System Preferences pane, you can configure your Mac's internal clock (which many programs use) and the clock that you see in the menu bar. Four tabs appear — Date & Time, Time Zone, Network Time, and Menu Bar Clock — which you use to set all things temporal.

Setting the date

Set the correct date on your Mac from the Date & Time tab of the Date & Time System Preferences pane. First, set the options beneath the Today's Date heading. Either click a day in the current month's calendar or use the navigation arrows to choose a month or year in the past (left) or in the future (right). Then click the calendar day that you want. You can see the Date & Time tab (of the Date & Time System Preferences pane, if you want to be fussy about it) in Figure 15-21.

You won't be able to set the date or time if you've already set up your Mac to receive the correct time from a network time server. (I discuss time servers in the section later in this chapter called "Setting network time.") If you don't see the arrows to change the month, year, or time, click the Network Time tab (fourth tab) and then click the Stop button there to disable automatic time checks. Return to the Date & Time tab, and you're able to make the changes you want.

Setting the time

You can also set your machine's time from the Date & Time tab. In the Current Time field that appears above the clock face, click the number that you want to change. That number should be highlighted, a pair of up- and down-arrows appears to the right of this field, and there will also be a little gray arrowhead below the field subject to change. Increase the selected number by clicking the up-arrow; decrease it by clicking the down-arrow. You can also use the arrow keys on the keyboard to increase or decrease the number. Or you can type a new number right over the selected number.

Figure 15-21:
Set date
and time
preferences
here.

When you have the time how you want it, click the Save button. Or, if you mess up, click the Revert button to return to the way it was before you began.

Use the Tab key to move from number to number. The settings for the hour, minute, and second are selected in sequence when you press the Tab key. If you want to move backward through the sequence, press Shift+Tab. As long as you hold the Shift key down, you cycle through the numbers in reverse order when you press Tab.

Note that the time expressed runs on a 24-hour (military) clock. The Date & Time System Preferences doesn't include any a.m. or p.m. options, although it does show you an analog 12-hour clock with an AM or PM next to it if you're military-time-challenged.

Setting the time zone

Click the Time Zone tab to set your machine according to what time zone you're in. Click your part of the world on the map that appears or choose a time zone from the pop-up menu. The map is updated to show your time zone when you do.

Setting network time

Network time servers are very cool, enabling you to synchronize your Mac's clock to a super-accurate time server on the Internet. To use a time server, however, you must be connected to the Internet when your Mac checks the time.

Follow these steps to set up access to a time server:

1. **Click the Network Time tab of the Date & Time System Preferences pane (shown in Figure 15-22).**

2. **Select the Use a Network Time Server check box and then either type** time.apple.com **in the NTP Server text field or select it from the pop-up menu.**

3. **Click the Set Time Now button.**

Apple's Network Time Server is time.apple.com. You're allowed to use it, of course.

I love this new-ish feature (it was added in OS 9). I'm anal about this type of thing and love having my clocks 100 percent accurate. I used to use SetClock (freeware for modems) or Vremya (freeware for TCP/IP connections) to do the same thing, but now I don't have to thanks to Apple's foresight.

Figure 15-22:
Set up
automatic
synchroni-
zation with
a network
time server.

If you have trouble with the network time server feature, Apple posts a technical note that lists dozens of alternative network time servers. You can find this tech note (and several other tech notes you may find useful) by going to the Apple Knowledge Base (`http://kbase.info.apple.com`) and searching for *network time server*.

The Menu Bar Clock tab

This tab controls the display of the clock in the right corner of your menu bar. The five options in this tab are accompanied by a check box to turn each on or off. Those options are

- **Show the Date and Time in the Menu Bar check box:** As you might expect, if you select this check box, you'll see a clock on the right side of the menu bar. Left unselected, you don't.

- **View As pop-up menu:** From the View As pop-up menu, you can choose Text (in which case you get the standard text display), or you can choose Icon (in which case you get a little analog clock icon that updates to display the time). If you choose to display an icon, the following options are unavailable (disabled).

  - **Display the time with seconds:** Select this check box to display the time with seconds (04:20:*45*).

  - **Show AM/PM:** If you select this check box, you see AM or PM after the time (4:20 *PM*).

- **Show the day of the week:** See the day of the week before the time (*Monday* 4:20 PM) when you select this check box. If this check box is not marked, all you see is the time (4:20 PM).

- **Flash the time separators:** Select this check box to have the separating colons (:) between the hours and minutes (and seconds if you select the Display the Time with Seconds check box) blink on and off. If you deselect this check box, you still see the colons but they don't blink.

- **Use a 24-hour clock:** If you're military or have lived abroad, you may prefer the 24-hour clock, where 1 p.m. is expressed at 1300 hours and so on. If so, mark this check box.

Software Update

Occasionally, Apple releases a new version of some of the software that's part of a Mac system. Such releases may be a patch for the system software, a bug fix for a utility program, or even a new version of Internet Explorer. You can set Software Update (see Figure 15-23) to check for new software, as well as to notify you of changes and download the fresh, hot files to your Mac. *Note:* You must have an Internet connection to use this feature.

You can choose to update your software automatically by marking the lone check box on the Update Software tab in this preference pane. If you do, you can choose how often your Mac checks for updates from the pop-up menu.

Click the Check Now button at the bottom of the window to manually check for updates any time you like, even if you've selected the Automatically radio button.

Figure 15-23:
Use
Software
Update to
check for
new system
software.

The Installed Updates tab shows which updates, if any, that you've already installed. Click the Open as Log File button, and the installed update log will open in the Console application for you to review or save.

Speech

 Choose your desired Speech settings from the Speech System Preferences pane. Click the Default Voice tab to set the voice your Mac uses to communicate with you, as shown in Figure 15-24. Choose from the list of voices on the left side of the pane to select the voice your Mac uses when it reads to you. After you make a selection, a sample of the voice that you selected will play aloud.

Each voice's characteristics (the language, gender, age, and description) appear on the right when that voice is selected. Use the Rate slider (bottom-right of the window) to speed up or slow down the voice. Then click the Play button to hear this voice at its new speed.

I like Fred, who says, "I sure like being inside this fancy computer."

Click the Speech Recognition tab to set up *speech recognition* — the ability to talk to your Mac and have it understand you. Alas, I'm going to have to use another weasel-out here — I just don't have a chapter's worth of space left to explain all the other Speech goodies. Sigh. Well, okay, here are a few more tips, hints, and rants.

Figure 15-24:
Set speech
preferences
here.

You'll need a decent microphone to use this feature. Unfortunately, Macs don't come with one, and the mike that's built into iMacs isn't quite good enough. Even worse, many new Mac models, including the Titanium PowerBooks, don't even have a microphone port, so you have to use a microphone that connects via your Universal Serial Bus (USB) port. Luckily, both USB microphones and converters for connecting standard microphone connectors to USB are fairly common these days.

Dr. Bott is a great little Mac-only company that specializes in little items like USB microphones and analog-to-USB converters. Its Web address is `www.drbott.com`, or you can call 877-611-2688. Eric Prentice is the CEO; tell him that Bob sent you.

You can't use this feature to dictate text to your Mac — you'll need IBM's ViaVoice or MacSpeech's iListen to do that. But you can use it to launch programs ("Computer, open Microsoft Word") and other stuff, like emptying the Trash, when you say to. Frankly, I haven't used it for more than a few minutes — it just doesn't work well enough yet. Still, it's kind of neat and worth playing with if you have the time and a decent Mac microphone.

Just for kicks, check out the Spoken User Interface tab, shown in Figure 15-25. You can have your Mac speak what shows in alert boxes and dialogs: "The application Microsoft Word has quit unexpectedly" or "The Finder requires your attention."

Figure 15-25:
This tab makes your Mac talk to you . . . a lot!

Two additional (and quite useful) settings on the Spoken User Interface tab are the Text under the Mouse and the Selected Text when the *x* Key is Pressed check boxes (where *x* is the name of the key that you've assigned).

Startup Disk

From choices within the Startup Disk System Preferences pane, you select which hard drive, server volume, or hard drive volume (if you've partitioned your hard drive or have more than one hard disk) should act as the startup disk when more than one drive with system software is connected to the Mac. To use it, first unlock the Startup Disk preference if you have to (for more on unlocking a preference, see the "Using System Preferences" section earlier in this chapter) and then click the icon for the drive that you want to start up the Mac the next time that you restart.

This feature is very useful if you have both a Mac OS X start-up disk and a start-up disk with another version of Mac OS on it, such as Mac OS 9 or Mac OS 8.6. If you want to start up with the older operating system, just click that disk's icon in the Startup Disk System Preferences pane and restart your Mac; it now starts up with OS 8.6.

If you have OS 9.2.2 installed on the same volume as OS X, you can set this preference to choose which OS you boot from. You see two System Folder icons at the top of the pane — one with OS 9.2.2 and the other with OS X. Click the one that you want to boot from and then restart.

When you've selected the OS with which you want to restart, click the Restart button in the window.

For more information on using the Startup Disk System Preference pane, skip to the end of my discussion of the Classic environment in Chapter 14.

As I mention elsewhere in this book, Macs sold after January 1, 2003 may not be able to boot into OS 9. They will still run Classic but won't be capable of booting into 9.

Universal Access

Many years ago, Apple pioneered Easy Access to assist computer users who had disabilities or difficulty in handling the keyboard and mouse. Universal Access is the OS X implementation of that assistance. As shown in Figure 15-26, this pane has three check boxes and four tabs.

Mark the Allow Universal Access Shortcuts check box if you want the keyboard shortcuts listed throughout this pane on the various tabs to be enabled.

Mark the Enable Access for Assistive Devices check box to use special equipment to control your computer.

Mark the Enable Text-to-Speech for Universal Access Preferences check box to have this pane's text read to you.

The Seeing tab lets you turn on a terrific feature: hardware zoom. Turn it on and off with the shortcut ⌘+Option+* (asterisk). Zoom in and out using the shortcuts ⌘+Option++ (plus key) and ⌘+Option+– (minus key), respectively. Try this feature even if you're not disabled or challenged in any way; it's a great feature for everyone.

You can also display the screen as white on black (like a photographic negative), as shown in Figure 15-27. The shortcut is ⌘+Option+Control+*; use the same keyboard shortcut to toggle back to normal.

Finally, the Zoom Options button lets you specify minimum and maximum zoom levels, display a preview rectangle when zoomed out, and toggle image smoothing on or off.

Figure 15-26:
Universal
Access
assists
users with
mouse or
keyboard
use issues.

Figure 15-27:
White-on-
black is
easier for
some
people to
read than
black-on-
white.

The Hearing tab lets you choose to flash the screen whenever an alert sound occurs.

This feature, created for those with impaired hearing, is quite useful if you have a PowerBook or iBook and want to use it where ambient noise levels are high.

The Keyboard tab offers two types of assistance: Sticky Keys and Slow Keys. *Sticky Keys* treat a sequence of modifier keys as a key combination. In other words, you don't have to simultaneously hold down ⌘ while pressing another key. For example, with Sticky Keys enabled, a standard keyboard shortcut is accomplished by pressing ⌘, releasing it, and then pressing the other key. There are check boxes to inform you with a beep and/or on-screen display what modifier keys have been pressed.

Slow Keys lets you adjust the delay between when a key is pressed and when that key press is accepted.

Finally, the Mouse tab lets you specify that you want to use the keys on the numeric keypad in place of the mouse. In this situation, everything centers around the numeric keypad's 5 key (which means clicking the mouse): 8 is up; 2 is down; 4 is left; 6 is right; and 1, 3, 7, and 9 are diagonal movements. Pressing 0 (zero) means that the mouse is held down so that the other numeric keys now drag in the indicated directions.

Part IV
U 2 Can B a Guru

In this part . . .

Here I get into the nitty-gritty underbelly of Mac OS X. In this part, I cover semi-advanced topics including sharing (files, that is), automating your Mac by using AppleScript, complete with some easy-to-follow info that's guaranteed to get you scripting. Don't skip the chapter on backing up your files, followed by the all-important troubleshooting chapter, which takes you on a quick tour of Dr. Mac's (okay, Dr. Bob's) top troubleshooting tips for those times when good software goes bad.

Chapter 16

"Mine! Miiiiine!" Sharing Your Mac and Liking It

*H*ave you ever wanted to grab a file from your Mac while you were halfway around the world or even around the corner? If so, I've got good news for you — it's not difficult with OS X, believe it or not, even though computer networking in general has a well-deserved reputation for being complicated and nerve-wracking. The truth is, you won't encounter anything scary or complicated about sharing files, folders, and disks (and printers, for that matter) among computers as long as the computers are Macintoshes. And, if some of the computers are running Windows, Mac OS X version 10.2 Jaguar even makes that (almost) painless. Your Macintosh includes everything that you need to share files and printers. Everything, that is, except the printers and the cables (and maybe a hub). So here's the deal: You supply the printers and cables, and this chapter will supply the rest.

Mac OS X is a multi-user operating system. After you create a user account for someone to share your Mac, that user can log on to your Mac two different ways with the same username and password. They can log *on* while sitting at your Mac or they can log *into* your Mac from a remote location via the Internet or a local area network (LAN).

The first sections of this chapter provide an overview and tell you everything that you need to know to set up new user accounts and share files successfully. I won't show you how to actually share a file, folder, or disk until the

"Consummating the Act of Sharing" section later in this chapter. Trust me, there's a method to my madness. If you try to share files without doing all the required prep work, the whole mess becomes confusing and complicated — kind of like networking a pair of PC clones.

One last thing: If you're the only one who uses your Mac and you don't intend to share it or its files with anyone else, you can safely skip this whole chapter if you like.

Introducing File Sharing

Macintosh file sharing enables you to use files, folders, and disks from other Macs on a network — any network, including the Internet — as easily as if they were on your own local hard drive. If you have more than one computer, file sharing is a must. It's fun, it's easy, and it's way better than SneakerNet. (*SneakerNet* is the moving of files from one computer to another via floppy disk or other media, such as Zip, Jaz, Orb, CD-R, CD-RW, DVD-RAM, and so on, according to the unpublished epic, "The Dr. Macintosh Unabridged Dictionary.")

Before diving in and actually sharing, first check out a few necessary terms:

- **Network:** For our purposes, a network of two or more Macs connected by Ethernet cables or AirPort wireless networking.

- **Ethernet:** A network protocol and cabling scheme that lets you connect two or more computers so they can share files, disks, printers, or whatever.

- **Ethernet ports:** Where you plug an Ethernet cable into your Mac.

  Be careful. On your Mac and printer, the Ethernet ports look a lot like phone jacks, and the connectors on each end of an Ethernet cable look a lot like phone cable connectors. But they aren't the same. Ethernet cables are typically thicker, and the connectors (RJ-45 connectors) are a bit larger than the RJ-11 connectors that you use with telephones. (See examples of both types of connector ends in the margin.) When you connect an Ethernet cable to your Mac, you won't be able to put it into your RJ-11-friendly modem port (and you shouldn't try). Standard phone cables fit into Ethernet ports, but you shouldn't try that either because they'll probably fall out with the slightest vibration. It's unlikely that either mistake will cause any permanent damage, but it won't work and will frustrate you to no end.

- **Local devices:** Devices that are connected directly to your computers, such as hard drives or CD-ROM drives. Your internal hard drive, for example, is a local device.

✔ **Remote devices:** Devices that you access (share) over the network. The hard disk of a computer in the next room, for example, is a remote device.

✔ **Protocols:** Kinds of languages that networks speak. When you read or hear about networks, you're likely to hear the words AppleTalk, EtherTalk (or Ethernet), and TCP/IP bandied about with great regularity. These are all protocols. Macs can speak several different protocols, but every device (Mac or printer) on a network needs to speak the same protocol at the same time in order to communicate.

Support for the AppleTalk protocol is built into every Mac. Your Mac includes all the software that you need to set up an AppleTalk network; the hardware that you need to provide comprises Ethernet cables and a hub (unless you use crossover cables) or an AirPort base station. I'm using *hub* here generically — its more powerful cousins, switches and routers, will also work.

Although you can use Transfer Control Protocol/Internet Protocol (TCP/IP) to do a lot of the same things that you can with AppleTalk, I concentrate on Apple's protocol, AppleTalk. By learning how to activate and use it, you'll master the basics that you need to dig into the language of the Internet.

AppleTalk is particularly useful when you have all Macs on your network. It's the easiest to configure and doesn't require additional information such as IP addresses. If you want to use the Internet to connect to another computer (or have it connect to yours), however, you need to use TCP/IP.

New with Mac OS X version 10.2 Jaguar is support for a protocol called Bluetooth. This is wireless connectivity with devices such as cell phones in addition to other computers; however, it works over very short ranges and at lower speeds than Ethernet or AirPort. Further, it requires an adapter, called a *dongle*, on Macs employing Bluetooth.

Portrait of home office networking

A typical Mac home office network consists of two Macintoshes, an Ethernet hub, and a network printer (usually a laser printer, although networked inkjet printers are becoming more common). Check out Figure 16-1 to see the configuration of a simple network. In the figure, the black lines between the devices are Ethernet cables; the rectangular device with those cables going into it is a hub. (I tell you more about cables and hubs in the section "Three ways to build a network" later in this chapter.) You need enough Ethernet cable to run among all your devices.

With the setup that you see in Figure 16-1, either Mac can use the other Mac's files, and both Macs can print to the same printer.

Figure 16-1:
Two Macs
and a
printer make
up a simple
Mac
network.

Mac   Mac   Printer

Hub

A network can and often does have, however, dozens or hundreds of users. Regardless of whether your network has 2 nodes (machines) or 2,000, the principles and techniques in this chapter apply.

Three ways to build a network

Back when you could connect a whole bunch of Macs and printers by simply running cables among them, most small Mac networks were pretty much the same. You attached a small device (a LocalTalk connector) to the first Mac and then ran plain old telephone cable to the next Mac, which also had a LocalTalk connector. By stringing more phone cable and more LocalTalk connectors, you had yourself a little network.

To cross over, or not?

The type of Ethernet cable required to connect two Macs without a hub or other middle-device has changed over time. In the old days, you absolutely had to have a crossover cable or the Macs wouldn't be able to see each other.

The basic rule had always been that to connect two Macs, you had to use a crossover cable. And if you had a hub or router or other intermediary device, you had to use regular Ethernet cables.

It's less true today because many Macs built in the past year or two — and every Mac sold today — has new and improved Ethernet that

can determine what type of cable (regular or crossover) that you're using and then automatically adjust itself so that cable works properly.

These days, you may encounter three possibilities: If you want to connect two older Macs, you need a crossover cable. If you want to connect an older Mac to a newer Mac, you may or may not need a crossover cable. And, if you want to connect two late-model Macs, you can use either a regular Ethernet cable or a crossover cable.

When in doubt, check Mac OS Help in the Help menu (press ⌘+Shift+?).

Today, building a Mac network is a little more complicated. Most Macs that support Mac OS X don't include LocalTalk ports, and Ethernet and wireless networks require a little more setup.

In this chapter, I assume that you're working on a small network, the kind typically found in a home or small business. If you're part of a mega-monstrous corporate network and you have questions about your particular network, talk to the PIC (*person in charge,* also known as your *network administrator*). If you're trying to build one of these mega-networks, you'll need a book a lot thicker than this one.

The following list gives you three common ways to build a modern network:

- ✔ **AirPort:** If all your Macs are equipped with AirPort wireless cards and if you have the AirPort Base Station, you don't need cables at all. Just plug in the base station, and Macs with AirPort cards can communicate with each other. If you use an Ethernet printer (connected to your Mac by Ethernet cable), you need to connect it to the base station before you can print from your wireless Macs. Both the Base Station and printer have Ethernet ports, so you can use a crossover cable to make the connection.

  Although this setup is more expensive than Ethernet cables and a hub, it's also more flexible because you can move your devices anywhere. (Well, almost anywhere; you're limited to 150 feet per AirPort.)

  For more information about wireless networking, check out the Apple AirPort Web page at `www.apple.com/airport/`.

- ✔ **Small Ethernet:** If you have only two devices to network (two Macs, or a Mac and an Ethernet printer, in most cases), you can use an Ethernet crossover cable to connect them directly to one another via the Ethernet ports. You can purchase a crossover cable (which looks just like a standard Ethernet cable) at your local electronics store. *Note:* Be sure to ask for a crossover cable, or your network won't work. Plug one end of the crossover cable into one of your two devices and the other end into the other.

  An Ethernet crossover cable won't work with a hub; a regular Ethernet cable won't work without one (in many Macs, as explained in the sidebar "To cross over, or not?"). Therefore, it makes sense to label your crossover cable(s) as such because they look exactly like regular Ethernet cables, and it's easy to become confused if you have a bunch of similar-looking cables.

- ✔ **Traditional Ethernet:** All modern Macs have an Ethernet port. To connect your Mac to a network, you need Ethernet cables for each Mac and a little device called a *hub.* (A hub is like the middle of a wagon wheel, with spokes representing the wires coming out of it.) A typical Ethernet hub includes two to eight Ethernet ports. You plug the hub in to an electrical outlet and then connect Ethernet cables from each of your Macs and printers (from their Ethernet ports) to the hub. Voilà! — instant network. Hubs are pretty cheap, starting as low as $10; cables start at a few bucks, increasing in price as the length (and quality and shielding) of the cable increases.

If you have a cable modem or Digital Subscriber Line (DSL) as your Internet connection, you may need a router or switch instead of a hub. They're similar but cost a bit more and have additional features that you may or may not need. Your ISP can tell you whether you're going to need one. For what it's worth, I have a cable modem, but it works fine with a cheap hub; I didn't need a more expensive router until I wanted to have more than one of the Macs talking to the Internet at the same time.

Setting Up File Sharing

Before I get into the nitty-gritty of sharing files, you must complete a few housekeeping tasks, such as turning on file sharing, turning on AppleTalk (if you want to share files with an AppleTalk-enabled file server or print to an AppleTalk printer), and enabling sharing over TCP/IP (that is, over the Internet) if you plan to share that way.

Turning on file sharing

Before you can share files, you have to turn on Mac OS X's built-in File Sharing feature. Follow these steps to do so:

1. **From the menu on the Finder menu bar, choose System Preferences (or click the System Preferences icon on the Dock) and then click the Sharing icon.**

   The System Preferences Sharing pane appears.

2. **At the top of the Sharing pane, type a name in the Computer Name text field if you haven't already done so and then type a name (the same one as the computer name will work, if you want) in the Rendezvous Name field.**

   In Figure 16-2, you can see that I named mine BobsTiBook for both the computer name and the Rendezvous name. You can name yours anything you like.

3. **On the Services tab, mark the sharing services that you want to use (such as Personal File Sharing) and then click the Start button (beneath the heading Personal File Sharing Off) to activate file sharing (see Figure 16-2).**

Figure 16-2:
Turning
personal file
sharing on
and off.

Why does it say `Personal File Sharing Off` above the button? Because it *is* off. After you click the Start button, the button name changes from *Start* to *Stop,* and the text above the button changes to `Personal File Sharing On`, indicating that file sharing is on.

Starting AppleTalk

If you want to share files with an Apple file server or print to a networked printer that requires AppleTalk, as many do, you have to enable AppleTalk. (See the "Introducing File Sharing" section earlier in this chapter for a definition of AppleTalk.) Here's how:

1. **From the menu on the Finder menu bar, choose System Preferences (or click the System Preferences icon on the Dock).**

   The System Preferences window appears.

2. **In the System Preferences window, click the Network icon (located in the toolbar and also in the main part of the window).**

   The Network System Preferences pane appears.

   You can get here in one step by choosing Location⇨Network Preferences.

3. **If the pane is locked, click the lock icon (bottom-left corner) to unlock the Network System Preference, type your name and password, and then click OK.**

   If your Mac is set up for multiple users, only users with administrative privileges can unlock these locks. Those with such privileges are the first user (created when you installed OS X) and any other user who you've given administrative privileges to in the Accounts System Preference pane, which I discuss in the "Access and Privileges: Who Can Do What" section later in this chapter.

4. **Choose Built-in Ethernet or AirPort (whichever you use) from the Show pop-up menu (if it isn't already chosen) and then click the AppleTalk tab.**

   The AppleTalk tab of the Network System Preferences pane appears.

   Now you see the AppleTalk tab of the Network System Preferences pane in all its glory — onscreen and in Figure 16-3.

5. **Mark the Make AppleTalk Active check box.**

6. **Click the Apply Now button in the lower-right corner of the AppleTalk tab to confirm your action.**

   That's it. You can quit the System Preferences application now.

Figure 16-3:
The AppleTalk tab of the System Preferences Network pane.

Sharing with TCP/IP

TCP/IP is the network protocol used on the Internet. It's also the protocol used by OS X for sharing files. It enables Macs, PCs, and other computers to communicate with each other (sometimes, but not always, via the Internet), even if they're running different operating systems. TCP/IP is always on, so you don't have to do anything further about it.

If you want remote users to be able to use an File Transfer Protocol (FTP) client program (instead of using File Sharing on another Mac) to upload and download files to and from this computer, mark the FTP Access check box in the Sharing System Preferences pane's Services tab. If you want to enable Windows or Linux — or to allow other users of other operating systems to share files with you — this check box needs to be marked. (I talk more about FTP and FTP clients in Chapter 22.) Windows users can also share files if you turn on Windows File Sharing in the Sharing pane's Services tab. This new feature in Mac OS X version 10.2 Jaguar takes most of the pain out of working with people using Microsoft Windows systems.

Mac users could use an FTP client to access your Mac, but they'll probably want to use File Sharing instead because it's easier.

Security risks are involved in allowing FTP access. I strongly suggest that you go to Apple's Web site (`www.apple.com`) and read about them before you enable this feature.

Computers connect to one another by using a number-based addressing system *(an IP address)* that's standard all over the world. You can (and most big companies do) use this system to communicate in offices and over the Internet. If you need to know more about using TCP/IP to connect to computers on your network than I've told you here, talk to the system administrator or the network geek in charge of these things where you work.

I touch more on TCP/IP in the "Connecting to a shared disk or folder" section later in this chapter where you can read how to use it to connect to a Mac or other server that's running it.

Rendezvous, the new zero-configuration network protocol included in Mac OS X version 10.2 Jaguar (and later versions, of course) makes networking simple. If two devices (and this includes all Macs running version 10.2 Jaguar or later) speak Rendezvous, you don't have to do any configuration (besides turning the sharing on). Rendezvous queries the other available networked devices to see what services they offer and support and then configures the connections for you automatically.

Access and Privileges: Who Can Do What

Before you can share your Mac with other users or share files over a network, you need to tell your Mac whom is allowed to do what. Lucky for you, this process just happens to be what I cover in this section.

Users and groups and guests

Macintosh file sharing (and indeed, Mac OS X as well) is based on the concept of users. Shared items — drives or folders — can be shared with no users, one user, or many users, depending on your needs.

✔ **Users:** People who share folders and drives (or your Mac) are *users*. A user's access to items on your local hard drive is entirely at your discretion. You can configure your Mac so that only you can access its folders and drives or so that only one other person (or everyone) can share its folders and drives.

When you first set up your Mac, you created your first user. This user automatically has administrative powers, such as adding more users, changing preferences, and having the clearance to see all folders on the hard drive.

For the purposes of this book, I assume that some users for whom you create identities won't be folks who actually sit at your Mac but rather those who only connect to it from a remote location when they need to give or get files. But they *could* use the same name and password to log on while sitting at your desk.

For all intents and purposes, a remote user and a local user are the same. In other words, after you create an account for a user, that user can log on to this Mac while sitting in your chair in your office or log on to this Mac from a remote location via AppleTalk/Ethernet or the Internet.

✔ **Administrative users:** Although a complete discussion of the special privileges that a user with administrator privileges has on a Mac running OS X is far beyond the scope of this book, note two important things:

  • The first user created (usually when you install OS X for the first time) is automatically granted administrator (admin) powers.

  • Only an administrator can create new users, delete some (but not all) files from folders that aren't in his or her Home folder, lock and unlock System Preference panes, and a bunch of other stuff. If you try something and it doesn't work, make sure that you're logged in as a user with admin privileges.

You can give any user administrator privileges by selecting that user's account, clicking the Edit User button, and then selecting the Allow User to Administer This Machine check box in the sheet that drops down. You'll find this check box when you create a new user or edit an existing user in the Accounts System Preference pane.

✔ **Groups:** *Groups* are UNIX-level designations for privilege consolidation. For example, there are groups named staff and wheel (as well as a bunch of others). Your main account is, for example, is in the wheel group.

If you're wondering whether you can create *your own* groups, as you could under OS 9 and earlier Mac operating systems, the answer is, well, yes and no. If you want to delve into the intricacies of the NetInfo Manager application to do it yourself, then "Yes;" but if you don't, then the answer is "No, please don't." UNIX-related tasks such as this are far beyond the scope of this book. Very far beyond. . . .

✔ **Guests:** Those who access public folders on your Mac via file sharing are *guests*. They don't need a username or password. If they're on your network, they can see and use your public folder(s). If they're on the Internet and know your IP address, they can see and use your Public folder(s). Public folders are all that guests can access, luckily.

Creating users

Before users can share folders and drives (or share your computer for that matter), you need to create user identities for them. You perform this little task in the Accounts System Preferences pane.

Guests can use your public folder(s) — but no other folders — without having a user account.

To create users for the purposes of file sharing, you need to add the user as a user of your computer, too. In other words, giving a user access to certain folders on your system means that that user also has folders of his or her own on the Mac. When you add (create) a user, you need to tell your Mac who this person is. This is also the time to set passwords and administrative powers of this new user. Here's the drill:

1. **From the menu on the Finder menu bar, choose System Preferences (or click the System Preferences icon on the Dock), click the Accounts icon, and then make sure that the Users tab is selected.**

   The Accounts System Preferences pane appears. In this pane (shown in Figure 16-4), you can see the name of the first user (boblevitus; look under the Name heading) and the administrative control that this user has (look under the Type heading).

Figure 16-4:
The
Accounts
System
Preferences
pane shows
who can
use this
Mac.

As I mention previously, the first user created (usually at the same time you installed OS X) always has administrator privileges.

2. **In the Users tab, click the aptly named New User button (upper right).**

   A New User sheet opens.

   If the New User button is dimmed, you'll need to first click the lock (lower-left), supply your user name and password in the resulting dialog, and then click OK.

3. **In the Name text box, type the full name of a user whom you want to add.**

   In the Short Name text box, your Mac inserts a suggested abbreviated name (or *short name,* as it's called). Check out Figure 16-5 to see both.

   In Figure 16-5, I added **Steve Jobs** as a user, typing the full name in the Name field. You don't really need to type the user's full name, but I do so in this example to show you the difference between a name and a short name.

   The name of each user's folder (in the Users folder) is taken from the short name that you enter when you create a user.

4. **Press the Tab key to move to the next field.**

   Mac OS X suggests an abbreviated version of the name in the Short Name field (as shown in Figure 16-5). Because he's the only Steve that matters around here, I'll change the suggested *stevejo* to just plain *steve,* which is shorter than the short name recommended by OS X. (In other words, I type **steve** into the Short Name field, replacing the suggested *stevejo*.)

Figure 16-5:
Name the
new user;
your Mac
suggests a
short name.

A short name can't be longer than eight characters and can't contain spaces.

Users can connect to your Mac (or log on to their own Macs, for that matter) by using the short name, rather than having to type their full names. The short name is also used in environments in which usernames can't have spaces and are limited to eight or fewer characters.

5. **Tab to the New Password field and enter an initial password for this user.**

6. **Press the Tab key on your keyboard to move your cursor to the Verify text field.**

7. **In the Verify text box, type the password again to verify it.**

8. **(Optional) To help remember a password, type something to jog the user's memory in the Password Hint text box.**

If a user forgets his or her password and asks for a hint, the text that you type in the Password Hint field will pop up, hopefully causing the user to exclaim, "Oh yeah . . . *now* I remember!" A password hint should be something simple enough to jog the user's memory but not so simple that an unauthorized person may guess. The hint that I typed in Figure 16-5 for Steve is not a very good nor secure hint. Perhaps something like, "Your first teddy bear's name backwards" would be a better hint.

9. **(Optional) Assign a picture to the user.**

OS X will suggest one from its default collection, but you can select a different one from the scrolling row or drag one in from the Finder (or iPhoto).

10. If you want this user to administer the Mac (that is, have access to preferences, be able to create users, and so forth), select the Allow User to Administer This Computer check box.

11. If you want the user to be able to log into the Mac from a Windows machine, select the Allow User to Log in from Windows check box.

If you don't want to give the user either of these last two capabilities, just click the Save button in the lower-right corner of the sheet without marking either check box. (For more on capabilities, see the upcoming section "Limiting a user's capabilities.")

The new user now appears in the Accounts System Preferences pane's Users tab.

Changing a user

Circumstances might dictate that you need to change a user's identity, password, or accessibility, or perhaps delete a user. Follow these steps to change a user's name, password, or administration privileges:

1. From the menu on the Finder menu bar, choose System Preferences (or click the System Preferences icon on the Dock).

The System Preferences window appears.

2. In the System Preferences window, click the Accounts icon.

The Accounts System Preferences pane appears. Make sure that the Users tab is selected.

3. Either double-click the user's name or click it once to select it and then click the Edit User button.

The User sheet for that person appears.

4. Make your changes by selecting the existing username, short name, password, picture, and/or capabilities and then replacing the old with new text or a different setting.

In order to change a user, you must be logged in using an account that has administrator powers.

5. Click the OK button.

Removing a user

To delete a user — in effect, to deny that user access to your Mac — select the user who you want to delete and then click the Delete User button. You will be asked to confirm that you really want to delete the user. Click OK.

To remove a user from your Mac, you must be logged in using an account that has administrator privileges. When you delete the user, the files and folders that user owned will now belong to you (they aren't deleted).

Limiting a user's capabilities

Sometimes, especially with younger children or computer-phobic family members, you want to limit what they can access. For example, you might want to make certain programs off-limits. With Mac OS X version 10.2 Jaguar, you do this via the Capabilities button on the Accounts System Preferences pane's Users tab.

1. **From the menu on the Finder menu bar, choose System Preferences (or click the System Preferences icon on the Dock).**

   The System Preferences window appears.

2. **In the System Preferences window, click the Accounts icon.**

   The Accounts System Preferences pane appears. Make sure that the Users tab is selected.

3. **Click the user's name once to select it and then click the Capabilities button.**

   The Capabilities sheet for that person appears, as shown in Figure 16-6.

4. **Mark the desired check boxes to determine what the user can do on this computer.**

   - **Use Simple Finder:** Mark this check box to replace the normal Finder interface with one where many menu choices have disappeared as have a number of icons.

   - **This User Can:** Under this heading are four pretty self-explanatory check boxes (Remove Items from the Dock, Change Password, Open all System Preferences, and Burn CDs or DVDs). If you clear Open all System Preferences, those System Preference panes that require Administrator access to do anything will be dimmed and unavailable.

   - **Use Only These Applications:** Marking this check box enables the items in the list box below it. Then, by using the disclosure triangles and marking the Allow check boxes, you can specify programs which programs are available, making those not marked off-limits to this user.

In order to change a user's capabilities, you must be logged in using an account that has Administrator powers.

5. **Click the OK button.**

Figure 16-6:
Limiting a
user's
capabilities
and
program
access
is easy.

Mac OS X knows best: Folders shared by default

When you add users in the Accounts System Preferences pane as I describe earlier in this chapter, Mac OS X automatically does two things behind the scenes to facilitate file sharing: It creates a set of folders, and it makes some of them available for sharing.

When you add a user, Mac OS X creates a folder hierarchy for each user on the Mac, as I describe in Chapter 10. The user can create more folders (if necessary) and also add, remove, or move anything inside of these folders. Even if you open a user account solely to allow him or her to exchange files with you, your Mac automatically creates a folder for that user. Unless you, as the owner of your Mac, give permission, the user can't see or use folders outside the Home folder (which has the user's name) except for the Shared folder in the Users folder and the Public folders in every other user's folder, as described below.

✔ **Public:** A Public folder is located inside each user's folder. That folder is set up to be accessible (shared) by any user who can log onto the Mac. Furthermore, any user can log on (as a guest) and copy things out of this folder as long as he knows your Mac's IP address, even if he doesn't have an account on this Mac at all. Files put into the Public folder can be opened or copied freely.

Inside each user's Public folder is a Drop Box folder. Just like the name implies, this folder is where others can drop a file or folder for you. Only the owner can open the Drop Box to see what's inside or to move or copy the files that are in it. Imagine a street corner mailbox — after you drop your letter in, it's gone, and you can't get it back out.

✔ **Shared:** In addition to a Public folder for each user, Mac OS X creates one Shared folder on every Mac for all users of this Mac. The Shared folder *isn't* available to guests, but it's available to every person who has an account on this machine. You find the Shared folder within the Users folder (the same folder where you find folders for each user). The Shared folder is the right place to put stuff that everyone with an account might want to use. In Figure 16-7, you can see the Users folder for Bob's Mac, where Bob (bob1), Mr. Clean (clean), Simple Simon (simple), and Steve Jobs (steve) each have user folders. You can also see the Shared folder that all three use.

Here's an example of how all this works. If Bob has a user account called bob1 on his Mac, he can log in and work with any item in his user directory — the bob1 Home folder. He can also put files in his Shared folder that he wants to share with others users who sit at this particular Mac. Or he can put them in the Public folder if he wants them available to everyone with an account as well as guests logged on remotely via a LAN or the Internet. If bob1 wants to share a file with just clean, he can put it in the Public folder under the clean user account; or, if he wants to be sure that no one but clean sees it, he can put it into the Drop Box folder inside the Public folder for clean. The privileges to do all of this are set up when the user account is created — you don't have to lift a finger.

Figure 16-7:
Each user has a folder and can open or copy items from the Shared folder.

Name	Date Modified	Size	Kind
▼ bob1	Today, 5:39 PM	--	Folder
▶ Desktop	Today, 5:44 PM	--	Folder
▶ Documents	9/4/02, 10:48 AM	--	Folder
▶ Library	Yesterday, 7:30 PM	--	Folder
▶ Movies	8/24/02, 12:34 PM	--	Folder
▶ Music	8/24/02, 2:11 PM	--	Folder
▶ Pictures	9/22/02, 7:35 PM	--	Folder
▶ Public	8/24/02, 12:34 PM	--	Folder
▶ Sites	8/24/02, 12:34 PM	--	Folder
▶ clean	8/29/02, 10:36 AM	--	Folder
▶ Shared	7/14/02, 1:20 AM	--	Folder
▶ simple	8/24/02, 12:39 PM	--	Folder
▼ steve	Today, 5:25 PM	--	Folder
▶ Desktop	Today, 5:25 PM	--	Folder
▶ Documents	Today, 5:25 PM	--	Folder
▶ Library	Today, 5:25 PM	--	Folder
▶ Movies	Today, 5:25 PM	--	Folder
▶ Music	Today, 5:25 PM	--	Folder
▶ Pictures	Today, 5:25 PM	--	Folder
▶ Public	Today, 5:25 PM	--	Folder
▶ Sites	Today, 5:25 PM	--	Folder

Users — 22 items, 34.86 GB available

Sharing a folder or disk by setting privileges

As you might expect, access privileges control who can use a given folder or any disk (or partition) other than the startup disk.

Why can't you share the startup disk? Because OS X won't let you. Why not? Because it contains the operating system and other stuff that nobody else should have access to.

Throughout the rest of this chapter, whenever I talk about sharing a folder, I also mean disks and disk partitions other than your startup disk (which, when you think of it, are nothing more than big folders anyway). Why am I telling you this? Because it's awkward to keep typing "a folder or any disk (or partition) other than your startup disk." So anything that I say about sharing a folder also applies to sharing any disk (or partition) other than your startup disk. Got it?

You can set access privileges for the folder's owner, for all the people who have accounts on the Mac (a group), or for everyone who has the Mac's address whether they have an account or not (guests). To help you better understand, I'll talk a little first about owners and groups.

Contemplating privileges

When you consider who can use which folders, there are three distinct kinds of users on the network. I describe each of them in this section. Then, in the "Useful settings for access privileges" section later in this chapter, I show you how to share folders with each of them.

- **Owner:** The owner of a folder or drive can change the access privileges to that folder or drive at any time. The name that you enter when you log onto your Mac — or the name of your Home folder — is the default owner of shared folders and drives on that machine. Ownership can be given away (more on that in the "Useful settings for access privileges" section later in this chapter). Even if you own the Mac, you can't change access privileges for a folder on it that belongs to another user (unless you get UNIX-y and do so as `root`). The owner must be logged in to change privileges on his or her folders.

  OS X is the owner of many folders outside the Users folder. If OS X owns it, you'll see that System is its owner, as shown in Figure 16-8. Folders that aren't in the User directories generally belong to System.

You *can* change those access privileges without resorting to third-party utilities or using the Terminal (which I describe briefly in Chapter 13), as was necessary in OS X versions before Jaguar. Be careful. It's not a good idea to change them unless you know exactly what you're doing and why. Unfortunately, that discussion is far beyond the purview of this book.

✔ **Group member:** In UNIX systems, all users belong to one or more *groups*. The group that includes everyone who has an account with administrator privileges on your Mac is called `admin`. Everyone in the `admin` group has access to Shared and Public folders over the network as well as to any folder that the `admin` group has been granted access to by the folder's owner.

✔ **Everyone:** This category is an easy way to set access privileges for everyone with an account on your Mac at once. Unlike the `admin` group, which includes only users with administrative privileges, `everyone` includes, well, everyone (everyone with an account on this Mac, that is).

If you want people without an account on this Mac to have access to a file or folder, it needs to go in your Public folder, where they can log on as a guest.

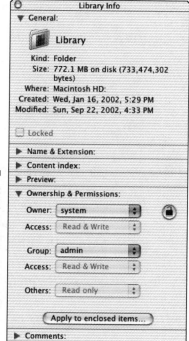

Figure 16-8: Mac OS X (System) owns this folder, and you can't easily change its access privileges.

Sharing a folder

Suppose that you have a folder that you want to share but with slightly different rules than those set up for the Public folder, the Drop Box folder within, or for your personal folders. These rules are *privileges,* and they tell you how much access someone has to your stuff.

Actually, the rules governing Shared and Public folders are privileges, too, but they're set up for you when Mac OS X is installed.

I suggest that you only share folders that are located within your Home folder or a folder within it. Because of the way UNIX works, the UNIX permissions of the enclosing folder can prevent access to a folder for which you *do* have permissions. Trust me, if you only share folders in your Home folder, you'll never go wrong. If you don't take this advice, you could wind up having folders that other users can't access, even though you gave them the appropriate permission.

You can set access privileges for folders within your Public folder (like the Drop Box folder) that are different from those for the rest of the folder.

I said this before, but it bears repeating: Whenever I talk about sharing a folder, I also mean disks and disk partitions other than your startup disk (which you just can't share, period). So don't forget that anything I say about sharing a folder also applies to sharing any disk (or partition) other than your startup disk.

To share a folder with another user, follow these steps:

1. **Select (single-click) the folder or drive icon and then choose File⇨Get Info (or use the keyboard shortcut ⌘+I).**

   The Info window for the selected item opens.

2. **Click the triangle to the left of the Ownership & Permissions panel near the bottom of the window.**

   The sharing options appear, as you see in Figure 16-9.

3. **Set access privileges for this folder by using the access privileges pop-up menus to control how much access each type of user has to the shared folder or drive.**

   When you click one of these pop-up menus, you see the privilege description that corresponds to the icon.

   You can choose from three types of access for each user or group, as shown in Table 16-1.

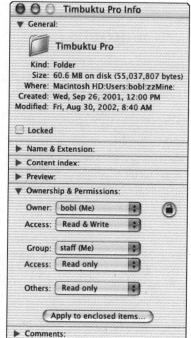

Figure 16-9:
Set file
sharing
here.

If you are the folder's owner (or have Administrator access), you can click the padlock icon and change the owner and/or group for the file or folder.

Table 16-1	Access Privileges
Access Privilege	*What It Allows*
Read & Write	A user with read and write access can see, add, delete, move, and edit files just as if they were stored on his or her own computer.
Read Only	A read-only user can see and use files that are stored in a shared folder but can't add, delete, move, or edit them.
Write Only (Drop Box)	Users can add files to this folder but can't see what's in it. The user must have read access to the folder containing a Write Only folder.
No Access	With no privileges, a user can neither see nor use your shared folders or drives.

Wherefore users and groups?

Mac OS X users who have used Mac OS 9 might wonder what's happened to the Users and Groups feature, which enabled you to create any number of user groups on a Mac. Because Mac OS X is based on the UNIX operating system, which deals very differently with permissions and access privileges than older versions of Mac OS did, it can't support old-style users and groups.

If you're brave or knowledgeable enough to dig into UNIX, you can make your own groups in Mac OS X. Creating a UNIX group confers identical access privileges and powers on its members. Although the process of creating a group is beyond the scope of this book, the process basically involves either gaining root access to the UNIX system and working from the Terminal command line or tinkering with the groups directory by using NetInfo Manager (requires Administrator access).

If you feel adventurous and know a little UNIX, try this: Open the Terminal program (in the Utilities folder inside the Applications folder) and type **man group**. Terminal will display the manual pages for the topic *group*. Press Space as many times as needed to scroll through the entire document. It probably won't help you create a group, but reading it won't hurt anything.

The `admin` group includes every user of a given Mac who has administrative privileges. Although it's not as good as the old Users and Groups feature (in OS 9 and earlier), it's a little better than no groups at all.

Useful settings for access privileges

The following sections show you just some of the more common ways that you can combine access privileges for a folder. You'll probably find one option that fits the way you work and the people you want to share with.

Allow everyone access

In Figure 16-10, I configure settings that allow access for everyone on a network. Everyone can open, read, and change the contents of this shared folder. Do this by choosing Read & Write from the Others pop-up menu in the Ownership & Permissions section of the folder's Get Info window.

Allow nobody but yourself access

The settings shown in Figure 16-11 reflect appropriate settings that allow owner-only access. No one but me can see or use the contents of this shared folder. Choose No Access in both the Group Access and the Others pop-up menus to do it yourself.

You need to change the Others pop-up menu to No Access first because Group member privileges must be at least as broad as Others privileges.

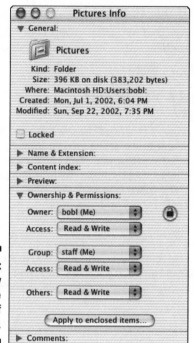

Figure 16-10:
Allow
everyone
access if
you want.

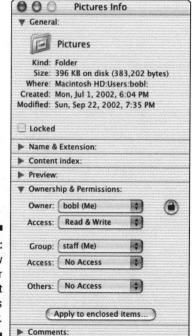

Figure 16-11:
Allow
access for
no one but
the folder's
owner.

Allow all administrative users of this Mac access

Check out Figure 16-12 to see settings that allow the group `wheel` (in addition to the owner) access to see, use, or change the contents of the shared folder. Choose Read & Write in the Group Access pop-up menu.

Allow others to deposit files and folders without giving them access (a Drop Box)

The settings in Figure 16-13 enable users to drop their own files or folders without being able to see or use the contents of the shared folder. After a file or folder is deposited in a drop folder, the dropper can't retrieve it because he or she doesn't have access privileges to see the items in the drop folder. To let everyone use this folder as a Drop Box, choose Write Only (Drop Box) from both the Group Access and the Others pop-up menus.

Read-only bulletin boards

If you want everyone to be able to open and read the files and folders in this shared folder, choose Read Only from the Group Access and the Others pop-up menus. If you do this, however, only the owner can make changes to files in this folder.

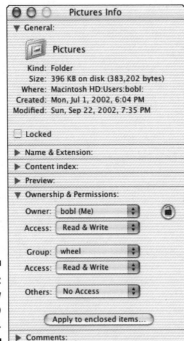

Figure 16-12:
Allow
access to
one group.

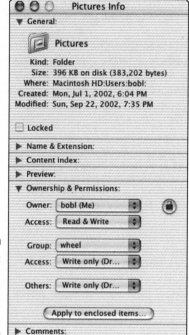

Figure 16-13:
Everyone
can drop
files in this
folder.

One more privilege

The Apply to Enclosed Items button, at the bottom of the access privileges section, does exactly what its name implies. This feature is a fast way to assign the same privileges to many subfolders at once. After you set privileges for the enclosing folder the way you like them, click this button to give these same privileges to all the folders inside it.

Be careful — there is no Undo for this action.

Consummating the Act of Sharing

After you set up sharing and assign access privileges, you can access folders remotely from another computer. (Just make sure first that you have access privileges to it.)

File sharing only has to be activated on the Mac where the shared files/folders reside, not on the Mac accessing them. When file sharing is turned off, you can still use it to access a remote shared folder on another machine as long as its owner has granted you enough access privileges and has file sharing enabled on his or her Mac.

If file sharing is turned off on *your* Mac, though, others won't be able to access your folders, even if you've assigned access privileges to them previously.

If you're going to share files and you leave your Mac on and unattended for a long time, logging out before you leave it is a very good idea. This prevents anyone just walking up to your Mac from seeing your files, e-mail, applications, or anything else that's yours unless you have given them a user account and granted them access privileges for your files.

Connecting to a shared disk or folder

On to how to access your Home folder from a remote Mac, which is a super-cool feature that's only bound to get more popular as the Internet continues to mature.

The following steps assume that you've got an account on the remote Mac, which means that you have your own Home folder on that Mac.

To connect to a shared folder on a Mac other than the one you're currently on, follow these steps:

1. **Make sure that you are already set up as a user on the computer that you want to log in to (GiggleHurts in this example).**

   If you need to know how to create a new user, see the "Creating users" section earlier in the chapter.

2. **On the computer that you're logging in from (call this one BobsTiBook), choose Go⇨Connect to Server.**

   The Connect to Server screen appears

3. **Click the remote Mac's name (GiggleHurts) in the column on the left and then click the Connect button (lower-right corner), as shown in Figure 16-14.**

   TCP/IP must be active on BobsTiBook (the Mac I'm using in the example). If it's not, you won't see any other machines on the network, nor will you be able to use any remote shared folders. In other words, file sharing doesn't have to be turned on (on the computer you're using), but TCP/IP does.

   The Connect dialog box appears. The person logged in on BobsTiBook's name automatically appears in the Name field (bob1 in Figure 16-15). If that's not you, type your username in the Name field.

Figure 16-14:
Set up a
remote
connection
here.

4. **Type your password into the Password field and then click the Connect button.**

You would mark the Guest radio button if you didn't have an account on GiggleHurts. Pressing ⌘+G is the same as marking the Guest radio button, and pressing ⌘+R is the same as marking the Registered User radio button. All you would get to see then are the Public folders of every user with an account on GiggleHurts. A registered user (like me in this example) also gets to see his Home folder plus everyone else's Public folder.

The Volume Selection dialog appears.

Figure 16-15:
Connecting
to access
folders on
a remote
Mac.

Volume is the Mac OS X term for all the shared folders on a single disk or volume that belong to that user. You can see what a volume looks like in Figure 16-16.

Figure 16-16:
Choose a
shared
folder to
connect to
on the
remote
Mac.

When you log onto a Mac on which you have a user account, you will always see a volume with your name. You will also see other volumes with usernames of every other user who has an account on this computer. If those users have not given you access privileges for specific folders, the only thing you'll see when you open their volume is their Public folder (and the Drop Box folder within it). If they've given you privileges for other folders, you'll see those as well.

If multiple items appear in the volume selection dialog (as shown in Figure 16-16), you can select more than one. Click the first item, hold down the ⌘ key, and then click each item once that you want to add to the selection. After you select all the items that you want to use, click OK, and they're all mounted on your Desktop.

5. **Select the volume that you want to use (bob1 in Figure 16-16) and then click OK.**

An icon appears on your Desktop (the Desktop of BobsTiBook), as shown in Figure 16-17. This icon represents a volume named bob1, which resides on the computer GiggleHurts. Notice that the icon for bob1 doesn't look like a drive or folder icon. This icon is what you see whenever a remote volume is mounted on your Desktop. You'll also see it if you add a server to your Favorites folder (more on that later) or view a server in the Finder window.

Open the volume icon, and its folder window appears (also called bob1), as shown in Figure 16-17.

Figure 16-17:
Mounted
volume
icons
appear on
the Desktop.

Unsharing a folder

To unshare a folder that you own, change the Group Access and Others privileges to None. After you do, nobody but you will have access to that folder anymore.

If you're not sure how to do this, see the "Sharing a folder" and "Useful settings for access privileges" sections earlier in this chapter.

Disconnecting from a shared volume

When you finish using the shared volume, disconnect by using one of these methods:

✔ Drag the shared folder icon to the Eject icon in the dock.

   When a disk or volume is selected (highlighted), the Trash icon turns into a little arrow, which represents *eject.* Nice touch, eh?

✔ Hold down the Control key, click the volume, and then choose Eject from the contextual menu that appears.

✔ Select the icon and choose File⇨Eject.

✔ Select the icon and press ⌘+E.

✔ If you've finished working for the day, choose Shut Down or Log Out from the menu. Shutting down or logging out automatically disconnects you from shared disks or folders. (Shut Down also turns off your Mac.)

Changing your password

You can change your password at any time. Changing your password is a good idea if you're concerned about security — if there's a chance your password has been discovered by someone else, for example.

You can change the password for your Mac, or you can change the password that you use to connect to your account on a remote user's Mac. I show you how to do both in the following sections.

Changing your Mac's password

To change the password on your Mac, just follow these steps:

1. **Choose System Preferences from the menu on the Finder's menu bar (or click the System Preferences icon in the Dock) and then click the My Account icon.**

   The My Account System Preference pane appears.

2. **Click the Change button next to My Password.**

   A Password sheet drops down.

3. **Type your current password into Current Password field to demonstrate that you are who you're supposed to be and not someone who just walked up to your unattended Mac.**

4. **Type your new password into the New Password field on the Password sheet.**

5. **Retype your password in the Verify field.**

6. **Click OK to save your changes.**

7. **Close the System Preferences window.**

Changing the password for your account on someone else's Mac

When you log into a remote Mac, you can change your own password if you like. Follow these steps to do so:

1. **Log into the remote computer on which you want to change your password (see the "Connecting to a shared disk or folder" section earlier in this chapter if you don't know how to log in to a remote computer).**

   The Connect dialog appears.

2. **Type your username into the Connect dialog if it's not already there.**

3. **Click the Options button in the Connect dialog.**

   The Options dialog appears, as shown in Figure 16-18.

Figure 16-18:
Change and encrypt your remote password here.

The Options dialog includes several options for encrypting your password as it is sent over the network. Mark the Add Password to Keychain check box to store your passwords in a single place on the Mac, meaning that you don't have to retype them each time you access a Mac or other remote resource. Read more about the keychain in Chapter 13.

4. **Click the Change Password button.**

   The Change Password dialog window appears, as shown in Figure 16-19.

5. **Type your current password in the Old Password field.**

6. **Type your new password in the New Password and Confirm Password fields.**

Figure 16-19:
Enter your old and new passwords.

7. Click OK.

Your password is changed, and you return to the Connect dialog.

8. (Optional) Type your new password and then click Connect to log onto the other Mac.

You can skip this step by clicking the Cancel button in the Connect dialog if you don't need to use anything on the remote Mac at this time. Your password is still changed, and you'll need to use the new password the next time that you log onto this Mac.

Setting up shortcuts to remote volumes (and folders)

Here are three ways that you can make using remote volumes and folders easier. The first is to use aliases, the second is to use OS X's Favorites, and the third uses aliases and the Dock. The following sections describe each of these methods.

Setting up a shortcut using aliases

After you've mounted a volume for the first time, you can make it easier to use in the future by creating an alias for it. The next time that you want to use that volume, just opens the alias, and the Connect dialog appears. You type your password, and the volume appears (is mounted) on the Desktop. No Connect to Server; no other dialogs; no muss and no fuss.

You can do this to any folder within the volume, too. It works just the same with one minor difference: The alias opens that folder, but it also mounts the volume that contains the folder and opens it, too. If you find this bothersome, just close the Home folder's window. The folder within — the one you made the alias of and want to work with — remains open, and you can continue working with it.

Setting up a shortcut using favorites

Here's another easy way to mount a volume: Just click the remote volume's icon (or any folder icon within that volume), and then while it's selected (highlighted), choose File⇨Add to Favorites (or press ⌘+T) from the Finder's menu bar. An alias to the remote volume or folder appears in the Favorites folder and on the Favorites submenu of the Go menu.

Setting up shortcuts in the Dock (and on the Desktop)

If you use remote folders often, follow these steps to create a folder that sits on your Dock, ready to call remote computers at your very whim:

1. **Log onto each remote volume (or folder) that you want to be included in the shortcut folder on your Desktop.**

2. **Create an alias for each remote volume or folder that you want easy access to.**

3. **Move the aliases that you created in Step 2 to a new folder on your Desktop (call it Remote Folders or something equally obvious).**

4. **Drag the Remote Folders folder onto the Dock.**

   Here are two easy ways to open any of the volumes or folders in the Remote Folders folder.

   - You can open the Remote Folders folder and double-click any of the aliases in it.

   - You can click and hold (or Control+click) the Remote Folders icon in the Dock, which causes a menu to pop up that shows all the aliases in the Remote Folders folder.

   Either way, that volume or folder will appear on your Desktop almost instantly.

Connecting to your own computer from a remote computer

In this section, I show you several file-sharing tricks that you can use on the road. The first explains how to log onto your home Mac easily from anywhere in the world by plugging into someone else's network. The second is a trick that I call *office-on-a-disk,* which is a way to take your shortcuts (see the previous section) with you, even when you use someone else's Mac. Finally, I'll take a look at how to access your files remotely via modem connection.

These techniques are especially useful for iBook or PowerBook users or if you need to connect to your Mac from someplace other than your home or office network.

Assume for the moment that you're on a network, perhaps at a client's office. In this section, I show how you would make the connection with a modem. For example, say you take a plane trip. You bring your PowerBook so that you can work on the plane. When you get to your destination, you want to copy the files that you've been working on to your home Mac to back them up. Well, you can do that with file sharing, which is easy if you've read about file sharing in the earlier sections of this chapter and understand how to connect to a remote Mac. (If you aren't sure how to do that, please reread the previous sections of this chapter now. If you don't, the following technique will only confuse you.)

Because you are the owner of your home Mac, you have full access privileges to both your Home folder and also to the rest of your Mac, just as you would if you were working from home. Also, because you own your Mac, you don't need to make any changes to file sharing privileges in order to log on and use your stuff.

You can connect to your home Mac via an Ethernet network or a modem. I'll talk about Ethernet first, then the nifty office-on-a-disk, and finally I'll talk about using a modem.

Logging on remotely via Ethernet

Okay, so you've arrived at your destination. The first thing to do is plug your PowerBook's Ethernet cable into the network and find out what TCP/IP address info that you need to use this network (by asking the PIC, or *person in charge;* also sometimes known as the network administrator or resident geek). With those tasks completed, you're ready to do some sharing.

To connect to your home Mac from a remote computer, follow these steps:

1. **Choose Go⇨Connect to Server (on your PowerBook or other remote Mac, of course).**

2. **Type in the TCP/IP address of your Mac at home in the Address field and then click the Connect button.**

   The Connect to Server dialog appears.

3. **Type your username (it might be the same on the PowerBook as on your home Mac) and password and then click the Connect button.**

   The Volume Selection dialog appears. You see your Home folder, your startup hard drive, and any other disks or partitions that appear on the Desktop of your home machine.

4. **Choose a volume and then click OK.**

   The volume mounts on your PowerBook Desktop, and you're in business!

Logging on remotely via office-on-a-disk

Here's a great tip of an even easier way to use your hard drive while working at someone else's Mac. Before leaving your computer, make an alias of your hard drive and copy it to a Zip disk, an iPod, burn it onto a CD-R, or copy it to your PowerBook's hard drive. At a remote computer, open the alias of your hard drive. The Connect dialog appears, and as long as you type the correct password, your hard drive mounts on that Mac's Desktop. Neat!

This technique is often called *office-on-a-disk*. If you work in a largish office and find yourself trying to connect to your hard drive from someone else's computer, carry one of these office-on-a-disk disks with you at all times. And if you're using a PowerBook, keep the aliases to your Mac (and any others you use on the road) on the Desktop for quick access. You could also put them in a folder and drag the folder to the Dock. Then all the aliases are available in a pop up menu when you click and hold (or Control+click) on the folder's Dock icon.

If you have no Zip or other removable media disk, don't despair. Just because your Mac has no removable-media drive doesn't mean that you can't use a disk alias. The first time that you mount your hard drive on a remote Mac, make an alias of the mounted drive. Leave it on the Desktop or some other convenient location, and you can use it to quickly mount the drive.

Logging on remotely via a modem

Mac OS X includes Point-to-Point Protocol (PPP) software — Internet Connect — that enables you to connect to another computer or the Internet by modem.

With Internet Connect, you can access your home hard drive from a remote Mac when you're at another location. You do need a modem, and you also need to configure this modem for remote access, which luckily is a pretty simple process. Because remote access uses the same Accounts and File Sharing tools as network file sharing, you should probably bone up on file sharing in the sections earlier in this chapter if you haven't already.

To use a modem to log on remotely, follow these steps:

1. **Choose System Preferences from the menu or click the System Preferences icon in the Dock.**

2. **Click the Network icon.**

   The Network pane appears.

   You can consolidate Steps 1 and 2 by choosing ⌘⇨Location⇨Network Preferences.

3. **Choose Internal Modem from the Show pop-up menu, unless you have an external modem; in that case, choose that option.**

   If you've been using Ethernet rather than a modem, notice that two new tabs appear after you choose Internal Modem from the menu: the PPP tab and the Modem tab.

4. **Click the PPP tab.**

   PPP options appear, as shown in Figure 16-20.

5. **(Optional) Type a name for this connection in the Service Provider field.**

Figure 16-20:
The PPP tab of the Network pane is where you set up for remote access via a modem.

This gives a name to the connection information that you're now creating so you can easily reuse it in the future. Doing this will make life easier if you need to use this modem connection again.

6. **Type the phone number that you want to dial (including any dialing prefix and area code) into the Telephone Number field.**

7. **(Optional) Type an alternate phone number, if there is one, in the Alternate Number field.**

8. **Type your account name (Internet username) in the Account Name field.**

9. **Type your password in the Password field.**

10. **(Optional) If you want to log on without having to enter your password each time, select the Save Password check box.**

Selecting this check box means that someone with access to your Mac can log on to your account, so be careful, especially if you're working on an iBook or PowerBook.

11. **Click the PPP Options button to set preferences for how your connection is made and maintained.**

The PPP Options sheet appears, as shown in Figure 16-21. Of the many options you find here, I'll point out a few of the most useful in the following list:

- Select the Connect Automatically when Needed check box if you want your modem to connect to the Internet when you launch your browser, connect to a remote server, or retrieve e-mail. This check box must be marked, or your Mac won't connect to the Internet automatically when you choose Go⇨Connect to Server.

- Leave the Prompt Every *x* Minutes to Maintain Connection check box selected if you're paying long distance charges or Internet access charges. If you don't set this auto-disconnect timer, you could rack up a lot of toll charges if you forget that you're connected and online. If you choose this option, set the number of idle minutes by clicking within the number box and typing the number that you want.

- Select the Redial if Busy check box to do just that. You can choose the number of attempts that your modem will make and how long it should wait between attempts if it gets a busy signal instead of connecting.

12. **When you're done setting PPP options, click OK to close the PPP Options sheet.**

Figure 16-21:
Using PPP options to set PPP connects and stays connected.

13. (Optional) Click the Modem tab in the Network pane.

Your modem should be selected in the Modem pop-up menu. If you're having problems connecting, use the menu to find your particular modem and select it.

You won't need to do much with these settings unless you're having a problem connecting with the modem, but you can set little options here, too. Some options of note are

- Some modems, such as the Apple 56K modems included in most Macs, are capable of performing some error checking and data compression. It's not industrial-strength compression, but it can speed up data transfer.

- You can tell the modem to wait until it detects a dial tone before dialing. In less friendly environs, you have to know to insert commas into the phone number to pause.

- Choose whether to turn your speaker sound off (to rid yourself of that horrid screeching noise that modems make).

- Choose from tone or pulse dialing, if you need the latter for some strange reason.

And that retires the side. Just choose Go⇨Connect to Server and log onto the remote machine. (If you still don't know how, reread the "Connecting to a shared disk or folder" section earlier in the chapter.)

Chapter 17

Back Up Now or Regret It Later

Although Macs are generally reliable beasts (especially Macs running OS X), someday your hard drive will die. I promise. They *all* do. And if you don't back up your hard drive (or at least those files that you can't afford to lose) before that day comes, chances are good that you'll never see your files again. And if you do see them again, it will only be after paying Scott of DriveSavers Data Recovery Service a king's ransom, with no guarantee of success.

DriveSavers, the premier recoverer of lost data on hard drives, does good work and can often recover stuff that nobody else could. (Ask the producers of *The Simpsons* about the almost-lost episodes.) Understandably, DriveSavers charges accordingly. Here's the phone number for DriveSavers: 415-883-4232. Now pray that you never need it — and if you back up often, you won't. But if, somehow, none of this sinks in, tell Scott that I said, "Hi."

In other words, you absolutely, positively, without question *must back up* your files if you don't want to risk losing them. Just as you adopt the Shut Down command and make it a habit before turning off your machine, you must remember to back up important files on your hard drive and back them up often.

How often is often? That depends on you. How much work can you afford to lose? If your answer is that losing everything you did yesterday would put you out of business, you need to back up daily or possibly twice a day. If you would only lose a few unimportant letters, you can back up less frequently.

Backing Up Is (Not) Hard to Do

You can back up your hard drive in basically two ways — the brute-force method, or the easy way. Read on to discover both. . . .

Backing up by using the manual, brute-force method

The most rudimentary way to back up your files is to do it manually. Accomplish this by dragging your files a few at a time to removable disks, such as to a Zip, SuperDisk, or Jaz drive. Or, if you have a CD-R, CD-RW, DVD-R, or DVD-RW drive, burn a disc with the files that you want to back up. In effect, you're making a copy of each file that you want to protect. (See Chapter 9 for more info on removable storage.)

Yuck! If doing a manual backup sounds pretty awful, trust me — it is. This method takes forever; you can't really tell whether you copy every file; and you can't copy only the files that have been modified since your last backup. Almost nobody sticks with this method for long.

Of course, if you're careful to only save files in your Documents folder, as I suggest several times in this book, you can probably get away with backing up only that. Or, if you save files in other folders within your Home folder, back up the Home folder. As you'll read in a moment, it's even easier with back-up software.

Backing up by using commercial back-up software

If you ask me, a good back-up program is the best investment that you can make. Frankly, I like the security of knowing that every document that I modify today is being backed up automatically. And that's what back-up software is all about.

Back-up software automates the task of backing up, remembering what is on each back-up disk (if your backup uses more than one disk) and backing up only those files that have been modified since the last backup.

Furthermore, you can instruct your back-up software to only back up a certain folder (Home or Documents) and to ignore the hundreds of megabytes of stuff that make up OS X, all of which can be easily reinstalled from the Mac OS X CD-ROM.

Your first backup with commercial software should take anywhere from a few minutes to many hours and use one or more pieces of removable media — Zip, Jaz, CD-R, CD-RW, DVD-R, DVD-RW, magneto-optical disks, or any kind of tape backup. Subsequent backups, called *incremental backups* in back-up-software parlance, should take only a few minutes.

Be sure to label all the disks that you use for your backups during incremental backups because the back-up software may prompt you with a message like `Please insert backup disk 7`. If you haven't labeled your media clearly, you could have a problem figuring out which disk *is* disk 7.

For some unfathomable reason, Apple has almost never seen fit to provide back-up software with new Macs or include it with Mac OS. I know that some early-90s Macintosh Performas had a crummy back-up program, and if you pay the 99 bucks for .Mac, you get Apple's Backup program, but other than those two pathetic attempts, Apple has left millions of Mac owners clueless, giving them nothing more than a brief passage regarding backing up in the Macintosh *User's Guide*. Information on backing up should be in big red letters, in the first chapter of the guide, and include a warning from the Surgeon General or something. And it wouldn't kill Apple to provide a back-up utility, either. Sheesh, even Windows has a back-up command, albeit a lousy one. C'mon, Apple, give Mac owners a fair shake. At least include the lame Apple Backup program that some Performa owners got.

Fortunately, plenty of very good back-up programs are available for well under $150, including the excellent Retrospect (around $150) and Retrospect Express (around $50) from Dantz Development (www.dantz.com); TriBackup 3 (around $50) from Tri-Edre (www.tri-edre.com); and more modest synchronizer programs such as ChronoSync ($20) from Econ Technologies (www.econtechnologies.com), or ExecutiveSync ($20) from Jason Weber Products (www.jasonweber.com).

If you want the most flexible, top-of-the-line back-up software, spend a little more and pop for Retrospect. It can do everything the others can do and more. It's the only backup software that you'll ever need.

Why You Need Two Sets of Back-Up Disks

You're a good soldier. You back up regularly. You think that you're immune to file loss or damage.

Now picture yourself in the following scenario:

1. One day you take a SuperDisk or Zip disk to QuicKopyLazerPrintz to print your resume on the laser printer there. You make a few changes while at QuicKopyLazerPrintz and then take the disk home and stick it into your Mac. Unbeknownst to you, the disk became infected with a computer virus at QuicKopyLazerPrintz. (I discuss viruses in the sidebar "Virus trivia," elsewhere in this chapter.)

2. When you insert the disk into your Mac, the infection spreads to your hard drive like wildfire.

3. Then you do a backup. Your back-up software, believing that all the infected files have been recently modified (well, they have been — they were infected with a virus!), proceeds to back them up. You notice that the backup takes a little longer than usual, but otherwise, things seem to be okay.

4. A few days later, your Mac starts acting strangely. You borrow a copy of an excellent virus-detection software, such as Virex or Norton AntiVirus (formerly Symantec Anti-Virus), and discover that your hard drive is infected. "A-ha!" you exclaim. "I've been a good little Mac user, backing up regularly. I'll just restore everything from my back-up disks."

Not so fast, Buck-o. The files on your back-up disks are also infected!

This scenario demonstrates why you need multiple backups. If you have several sets of back-up disks, chances are pretty good that one of the sets is clean.

I always keep at least three current sets of back-up disks going at any one time. I use one set on even-numbered days, one on odd-numbered days, and update the third set once a week and store it somewhere other than my office (such as a neighbor's house or a safe deposit box). This scheme ensures that no matter what happens — even if my office burns, is flooded, is destroyed by a tornado or a hurricane, or is robbed — I won't lose more than a few days' worth of work. I can live with that.

Virus trivia

A computer *virus,* in case you missed it in *Time* or *Newsweek,* is a nasty little piece of computer code that replicates and spreads from disk to disk. Most viruses cause your Mac to misbehave; some viruses can destroy files or erase disks with no warning.

If you use disks that have been inserted in other computers, you need some form of virus-detection software. If you download and use files from Web and File Transfer Protocol (FTP) sites on the Internet, you need some form of virus detection as well.

You don't have too much to worry about if

- You download files only from commercial online services, such as America Online, which is very conscientious about viral infections.

- You use only commercial software and don't download files from Web sites with strange names.

You should definitely worry about virus infection if

- An unsavory friend told you about a Web site called `Dan'sDenOfPiratedIllegal StolenBootlegSoftware.com`.

- You swap disks with friends regularly.

- You shuttle disks back and forth to other Macs.

- You use your disks at service bureaus or copy shops.

- You download files from various and sundry places on the Internet, even ones that don't sound as slimy as `Dan'sDenOf PiratedIllegalStolenBootleg Software.com`.

- You receive e-mail with attachments (and open them).

If you're at risk, do yourself a favor and buy a commercial antivirus program. Although you can choose from many shareware and freeware antivirus solutions, none that I know of are as trustworthy as Virex or Norton. The big advantage of buying a commercial antivirus program is that the publisher contacts you each time that a virus is discovered and provides you with a software update to protect you against the new strain. Or, for a fee, the publisher can send you a new version of the software every time that a new virus is found.

On the commercial front, two leading virus-detection utilities are Virex and Norton AntiVirus (NAV; formerly Symantec Anti-Virus). Each has its advocates. I've used NAV for years and I have never been infected with a virus. My editor uses Virex and has also been virus-free.

Note: Most of the virus scares that you hear and read about won't affect you because they are specific to users of Windows systems. Most viruses are specific to an operating system — Mac viruses won't affect Windows users, Windows viruses won't affect Mac users, and so forth. The one real exception here is a "gift" from the wonderful world of Microsoft Office (Word, Excel, for example) users: the dreaded *macro viruses* that are spread with Word and Excel documents containing macros written in Microsoft's VBA (Visual BASIC for Applications) language. But you're even safe from those if you practice safe computing as I describe.

As it happens, so far almost all the viral activity affecting OS X involved various Windows macro virii. In fact, at the time of this writing, I know of no OS X-specific viruses nor of any that attack Mac OS X exclusively. And, so far, none that cause damage. Still, the advice in this chapter is sound — one never knows when the little boys out there will decide to attack the Mac. OS X viruses aren't impossible or non-existent; they just don't exist at this moment in time. But they could someday, so be safe rather than sorry.

Chapter 18

Troubleshooting Mac OS X

* *

In This Chapter

▶ Facing the dreaded Sad Mac

▶ Dealing with the flashing question mark

▶ Recovering from start-up crashes

* *

As a bleeding-edge Mac enthusiast with 15 years of Mac under my belt, I've had more than my share of Mac troubles. Over those years, I've developed an arsenal of tips and tricks that I believe can resolve more than 90 percent of Mac OS X problems without a trip to the repair shop.

If your hardware is dead, then, sadly, neither you nor I can do anything about it because this is now a job for your friendly Mac repairman and your fat checkbook. But if your hardware is okay, you have a fighting chance of using the suggestions in this chapter to get your machine up and running.

Dem Ol' Sad Mac Chimes of Doom Blues

 Although you usually see a happy, smiling Mac face when you turn your computer on, once in a blue moon you might see the dreaded Sad Mac icon (shown in the left margin) and hear that melancholy arpeggio in G minor (better known as the *Chimes of Doom*), or the sound of breaking glass or a car wreck, or any of the other horrible sounds that Macs make when they're dying.

The Sad Mac usually indicates that something very bad has happened to your Mac; often some hardware component has bitten the dust. But Sad Macs are rather uncommon — many Mac users go their entire lifetime without seeing one. If you ever have a Sad Mac experience, don't despair immediately. Before you diagnose your Mac as terminally ill, try booting from CD-ROM to bring it back to life. If you have your OS X installation CD-ROM ready, you can skip to the section "Booting from CD-ROM" later in this chapter. If you're not sure about your OS X installation CD-ROM, see the next section.

The ultimate start-up discs: The OS X installation CD

I bet you have a copy of the ultimate start-up disc right there on your computer table — the installation CD that came with your computer. You can recognize it by the large X on it.

In previous releases the X was shiny and aqua; in the Mac OS X version 10.2 Jaguar release, the X is spotted and furry. Just look for a CD with a big X.

In addition to the system software that you need to make your Mac work, all OS X installation discs include a working copy of Disk Utility, which I discuss in the section "Step 1: Run First Aid" section later in this chapter. If you see a flashing question mark when you start up your Mac, you may need to use the Disk Utility program's First Aid feature to repair hidden damage to your hard drive. Another of Disk Utility's features lets you verify and repair disk permissions, which is a handy thing to do if your Mac is telling you that you don't have enough permission to do things that you used to be able to do, such as move a file or folder, or move an icon to the Trash.

Read more about using these utilities throughout the rest of this chapter.

If you don't have a bootable CD-ROM, preferably a Mac OS X Install CD-ROM, you can't do most of the rest of the stuff in this chapter. So if you don't have it handy, go find it now. If you really can't find one, consider calling Apple or your Apple dealer to arrange for a replacement — you really shouldn't be without it.

If you get the flashing question mark when you try to start up your Mac, open the CD-ROM drive and pop the installation CD into it. Then, hold down the C key on your keyboard, and your Mac should boot just like magic. If that doesn't work, try holding down these four keys in the infamous four-finger salute: Delete+Option+⌘+Shift.

A good way to remember this keyboard combination — which is generally used to force your Mac to start up from a disc other than your internal hard drive, including a bootable CD-ROM — is to think of the mnemonic acronym *DOCS*: *D*elete+*O*ption+*C*ommand (⌘)+*S*hift.

Keep holding the four keys down until your Mac either boots from the CD or doesn't. If it doesn't, try another CD or other bootable disk (Jaz, Zip, SuperDisk, FireWire hard disk, and so on). If that doesn't work, you might need to take your Mac in for repairs.

If your Mac is new enough to support the built-in Startup Manager (most OS X-capable Macs are, but not all of them), you can also hold down the Option key while booting to display the built-in Startup Manager, which will show icons for any bootable discs that it sees and allow you to select one. This is useful if your usual boot disk is damaged or having issues during startup.

Better safe than Mac-less

The bootable Mac OS X CD-ROM is soooo important — try to have more than one copy around. That way, if one gets misplaced, damaged, eaten by the dog, scuffed, scratched, or otherwise rendered useless, you won't be out of luck. I keep the Mac OS X CD in my middle desk drawer and several other bootable CDs on the bookshelf. An older version of Mac OS and the CD that came with your computer are examples of extra bootable CDs that you might have hanging around. The Mac OS X installation CD is bootable as well. All these will boot your Mac in an emergency, which is why they're so important to have handy.

One thing that I would do if I only had one of these valuable CDs is to use Apple's Disk Copy (in Applications/Utilities) to create a disk image of the CD and then burn a copy or two as spares. Don't forget to test the burned discs to ensure that they work and are bootable.

Booting from CD-ROM

To boot your Mac from a CD-ROM installation disc, follow these steps:

1. **Insert a bootable CD-ROM (the Mac OS X CD is a good choice).**

   If your Mac uses a tray to hold the CD, make sure that it retracts and that the disk is in.

   If you're not sure about this bootable CD-ROM business, see the previous section.

2. **Shut down or restart your Mac.**

   If you shut it down, wait a few seconds and then start it up the usual way.

3. **Press and hold down the C key immediately and keep it pressed until your Mac either boots from the CD (you see a Welcome screen) or doesn't (you see a flashing question mark, a spinning wheel-of-death, or anything but a login window or the Finder).**

If you can boot from CD-ROM . . .

If you see the Mac OS startup (Welcome) screen when you boot (start up) from your CD-ROM, hope flickers for your Mac. The fact that you can boot from another disc (a CD-ROM in this case) indicates that the problem lies in one of two places: your hard drive and/or Mac OS X itself. Whatever the tangle, it will probably respond to one of the techniques that I discuss throughout the rest of this chapter.

So your Mac boots from the installation CD-ROM, but you still have this little problem: You prefer that your Mac boot from your (much faster) hard drive than the system software CD-ROM. Not to worry. All you need to do is reinstall Mac OS X (see the Appendix at the end of this book).

If you can't boot from CD-ROM . . .

If the techniques in this chapter don't correct your Mac problem or you still see the Sad Mac icon when you start up with the CD, your Mac is toast and needs to go in for repairs (usually to an Apple dealer).

Before you drag it down to the shop, however, try calling 1-800-SOS-APPL, the Apple Tech Support hotline. The service representatives there may be able to suggest something else that you can try. If your Mac is still under warranty, it's even free.

If you get the Sad Mac immediately after installing random access memory (RAM) — and this is quite common — double-check that the RAM is properly seated in its sockets. Don't forget to power down your Mac first.

Follow the installation instructions that came with the RAM chips or the ones in the booklet that came with your Mac. But even if they don't say to, you should either use an anti-static strap (available from most RAM sellers) or discharge static electricity by touching an appropriate surface (such as the power supply case inside your Mac) before you handle RAM chips.

If problems occur immediately after installing RAM (or any new hardware, for that matter), remove and reinsert the RAM chips to make sure that they're seated properly. If you still have problems, remove the RAM temporarily and see whether the problem still exists.

Question Mark and the Mysterians

When you turn on your Mac, the first thing that it does (after the hardware tests) is to check for a start-up disc with Mac OS 9 or X on it. If your system doesn't find such a disc on your internal hard drive, it begins looking elsewhere — on a FireWire or Universal Serial Bus (USB) disk or on a CD or DVD.

If you have more than one start-up disc attached to your Mac, as many users do, you can choose which one your Mac boots from in the Startup Disk System Preference pane. (See Chapter 15 for details.)

At this point, your Mac *usually* finds your hard drive, which contains your operating system, and the start-up process continues on its merry way with the happy Mac and all the rest. If your Mac can't find your hard drive or doesn't find on it what it needs to boot OS X, you'll encounter a flashing question-mark icon (as shown in the left margin).

Don't go cryin' *96 Tears*. This icon means that your Mac can't find a start-up disc, hard drive, or CD-ROM containing valid system software (either Mac OS X or a previous version supported by your particular Mac).

Think of the flashing question mark as your Mac's way of saying, "Please provide me with a start-up disk."

If Apple can figure out a way to put a flashing question mark on the screen, why the heck can't the software engineers find a way to put the words Please insert a startup disk on the screen as well? The curtness of the flashing question mark is one of my pet peeves about the Macintosh. I know — you're clever and smart (you're reading *Mac OS X For Dummies*, aren't you?), so you know that a flashing question mark means that you should insert a start-up disk. But what about everyone else?

If you encounter either of these warning icons, go through the steps that I outline in this section. I give you some different options to try, such as rebuilding your Desktop, using Disk Tools and First Aid, or zapping the parameter RAM (PRAM). If one doesn't work, move on to the next.

In the meantime, here are some less severe potential remedies for you.

Step 1: Run First Aid

In most cases, after you've booted successfully from the OS X CD, the first logical troubleshooting step is to use the First Aid option in the Disk Utility application.

Every drive has several strangely named components such as B-trees, extent files, catalog files, and other creatively named invisible files. They are all involved in managing the data on your drives. Disk Utility's First Aid feature checks all those files and repairs the damaged ones.

Here's how to make First Aid do its thing:

1. **Boot from your Mac OS X CD by inserting the CD and restarting your Mac while holding down the C key.**

   The OS X Installer appears on your screen.

2. **Choose Installer➪Open Disk Utility to launch the Disk Utility application that's on the CD.**

3. **When the Disk Utility window appears, click the First Aid tab to select that function of Disk Utility.**

4. **Click the icon for your boot hard drive at the left of the Disk Utility window (*OSX* in Figure 18-1).**

   Your boot drive is the one with OS X and your Home folder on it. I call this one *OSX*.

5. **Click the Repair Disk button.**

Your Mac whirs and hums for a few minutes, and the results window tells you what's going on. Ultimately, First Aid tells you (you hope) that the drive has been repaired and is now okay, as shown in Figure 18-2. If so, go back to work.

6. **Quit Disk Utility by choosing Disk Utility⇨Quit Disk Utility or by pressing ⌘+Q.**

7. **Reboot without holding the C key down.**

If First Aid finds damage that it can't fix, a commercial disk-recovery tool, such as Alsoft's DiskWarrior, may be able to repair the damage. And even if First Aid gave you a clean bill of health, you may want to run DiskWarrior anyway just to have a second opinion. Make sure that you're running a current version because older versions were not Mac OS X compatible.

If everything checks out with First Aid, try to boot from your hard drive again. If you still get the flashing question mark, proceed to the next section to try a little dance called zapping the PRAM.

Step 2: Zapping the PRAM

Sometimes your parameter RAM (PRAM) becomes scrambled and needs to be reset. *PRAM*, a small piece of memory that's not erased or forgotten when you shut down, keeps track of things such as printer selection, sound level, and monitor settings.

Try zapping your PRAM if your Monitors System Preferences or Print Center forgets your settings when you shut down or restart.

To zap your PRAM, just restart your Mac and press ⌘+Option+P+R (that's four keys — good luck; it's okay to use your nose) until your Mac restarts itself. It's kind of like a hiccup. You see the flashing question mark for a minute or two while your Mac thinks about it; then the icon disappears, and your Mac chimes again and restarts. Most power users believe that you should zap it more than once, letting it chime two, three, or even four times before releasing the keys and allowing the start-up process to proceed.

One of the things that gets zapped with the PRAM is your chosen start-up disk. So use the Startup Disk System Preference pane to reselect your usual boot disk.

Zapping the PRAM returns some System Preferences to their default settings (but interestingly, not the date or time), so you may have to do some tweaking after zapping the PRAM.

Figure 18-1:
First Aid,
ready to
perform its
magic on
the disk
named OSX.

Figure 18-2:
First Aid
repaired the
disk and
gives it a
clean bill
of health.

Step 3: Reinstalling OS X

I present the procedure to reinstall the system software last in this section because it takes the longest. I detail this procedure at great length in the Appendix.

Read the Appendix and follow the instructions. If you're still unsuccessful after that point, go back to the following section.

Step 4: Take your Mac in for repair

If none of my suggestions work for you and you're still seeing the flashing question mark, you have big trouble.

You could have any one of the following problems:

- ✔ Your hard drive is dead.
- ✔ You have some other type of hardware failure.
- ✔ All your start-up discs and your system software CDs are defective (unlikely).

The bottom line: If you still see the flashing question mark after trying all the cures that I list in this chapter, you almost certainly need to have your Mac serviced by a qualified technician.

If You Crash at Startup

Startup crashes are another bad thing that can happen to your Mac. These crashes are more of a hassle to solve than flashing question mark problems but are rarely fatal.

You know that a *crash* has happened when you see a System Error dialog, a frozen cursor, a frozen screen, or any other disabling event. A *start-up crash* happens when your system shows a crash symptom any time between flicking the power key or switch (or restarting) and having full use of the Desktop.

A start-up crash could happen to you someday. I surely hope not. But if it does, the easiest way to fix it is to reinstall OS X from the CD. I detail this procedure at great length in the Appendix. Read the Appendix and follow the instructions. If you're still unsuccessful after that point, come back and reread the "Step 4: Take your Mac in for repair" section earlier in this chapter.

Part V
The Part of Tens

The 5th Wave · By Rich Tennant

"Get ready, Mona — here come the stats."

In this part . . .

These last chapters are a little different — they're kind of like long top-ten lists. Although I'd like for you to believe that I included them because I'm a big fan of Dave Letterman, the truth is that Wiley always includes The Part of Tens section in its *For Dummies* books. This book continues the tradition. And because Wiley pays me, I do these chapters how I'm asked. (Actually, it's kind of fun.)

First, I tell you how to speed up your Mac experience. I then move on to a subject near and dear to my heart — awesome things for your Mac that are worth spending money on. Stay tuned for a collection of great Mac-related Web sites and finish out this section with a discussion of cool OS X applications that you may need someday.

Chapter 19

Ten (Or So) Ways to Speed Up Your Mac Experience

This chapter is for speed demons only. At some time in their Mac life, most users have wished that their machine would work faster — even those of us with Power Macintosh G4s. I can't help you make your processor faster, but I do cover things in this chapter that can make your Mac at least seem faster, and most of these tips won't cost you a red cent.

Use Those Keyboard Shortcuts

Keyboard shortcuts (see Table 19-1 for a way-groovy list of the more useful ones) can make navigating your Mac a much faster experience compared to constantly using the mouse, offering these benefits:

✔ By using keyboard shortcuts, your hands stay focused on the keyboard, reducing the amount of time that you remove your hand from the keyboard to fiddle with the mouse.

✔ If you memorize keyboard shortcuts with your head, your fingers will memorize them, too.

✔ The more keyboard shortcuts that you use, the faster you can do what you're doing.

Trust me when I say that learning the keyboard shortcuts for commands that you use often will save you a ton of time and effort.

Make a list of keyboard shortcuts and tape it to your monitor or somewhere where you'll see it all the time when using your Mac. (Heck, make a photocopy of the upcoming table!)

Table 19-1	Great Keyboard Shortcuts	
Keyboard Shortcut	*What It's Called*	*What It Does*
⌘+O	Open	Opens the selected item.
⌘+. (period)	Cancel	Cancels the current operation in many programs, including the Finder. Also the keyboard shortcut for the Cancel button in most dialogs.
⌘+P	Print	Brings up a dialog that enables you to print the active window's contents. (See Chapter 12 for info on printing.)
⌘+X	Cut	Cuts whatever you select and places it on the Clipboard. (I cover the Edit menu and the Clipboard in Chapter 6.)
⌘+C	Copy	Copies whatever you select and places it on the Clipboard.
⌘+V	Paste	Pastes the contents of the Clipboard at the spot where your cursor is.
⌘+F	Find	Brings up Find window in the Finder; brings up a Find dialog in most programs.
⌘+A	Select All	Selects the entire contents of the active window in many programs, including the Finder.
⌘+Z	Undo	Undoes the last thing you did in many programs, including the Finder.
⌘+Shift+?	Help	Brings up the Mac Help window in the Finder; usually the shortcut to summon Help in other programs.

Keyboard Shortcut	*What It's Called*	*What It Does*
⌘+H	Hide	(Usually) Hides the current application. Use the Application menu (the one that reads *Finder* when you're in the Finder) to Show All applications again. Some applications, such as BBEdit and Illustrator, have long used ⌘+H for something else and hiding the application would really confuse their longtime users, so they don't use this shortcut.
⌘+Q	Quit	Perhaps the most useful keyboard shortcut of all — quits the current application (but not the Finder because the Finder is always running).
⌘+Shift+Q	Log Out	Logs the current user out; the login window appears onscreen until a user logs in.
⌘+Delete	Move to Trash	Moves the selected item to Trash.
⌘+Shift+Delete	Empty Trash	Empties the Trash.

Learn to Type Better

One way to make your Mac seem faster is to make your fingers move faster. The quicker you finish a task, the quicker you're on to something else. Keyboard shortcuts are nifty tools, and improving your typing speed and accuracy *will* save you time. Plus, you'll get stuff done faster if you're not always looking down at the keyboard or up at the screen when you type.

You'll also find that as your typing skills improve, you spend less time correcting errors or editing your work.

The speed and accuracy that you gain has an added bonus: When you're a decent touch typist, you fingers will fly even faster when you use those nifty keyboard shortcuts (I list a gaggle of these earlier in the chapter in Table 19-1).

Resolution: It's Not Just for New Year's Anymore

Another setting that you can change to potentially improve your Mac's performance is the resolution of your monitor. Most modern monitors and video cards (or onboard video circuitry, depending upon your Mac model) are capable of displaying multiple resolutions on your monitor. You change your monitor's display resolution in the same place where you choose the number of colors you want: the Display tab of the Monitors pane of System Preferences. Click your resolution choice from the Resolutions list, which is located on the left side of this tab.

In Displays System Preferences, check the Show Displays in Menu Bar box to change resolutions and color depth without opening System Preferences. You can then select your resolution or color depth from the Displays menu that appears near the right end of your menu bar, as shown in Figure 19-1.

Here's the deal on display resolution: The smaller the numbers that you use for your monitor's resolution, the faster your screen refreshes. For a computer monitor, *resolution* is expressed as a dimension-type set of numbers (*number* x *number*). The first number is the number of pixels (color dots) that run horizontally, and the second number is the number of lines running vertically. Fewer pixels refresh faster. Therefore, a resolution of *640* x 480 updates itself faster than a resolution of *832* x 624; *832* x 624 updates faster than *1,024* x 768; and so forth.

Figure 19-1: Use the handy Displays menu to switch resolutions right from the menu bar.

Sun 02:42:55
640 x 480
800 x 500
800 x 512
800 x 600
1024 x 640
1024 x 768
1280 x 820
1280 x 1024
✓ 1600 x 1024
256 Colors
Thousands
✓ Millions
Open Displays...

This isn't true if you have an LCD (flat-panel) monitor or a PowerBook. In that case, the native resolution is usually faster. Which is the native resolution? Depends upon the monitor. For the Apple Studio Display 15-inch and most PowerBooks, it's 1,024 x 768. If you have a different flat screen, check out the documentation to see what the vendor recommends.

On the other hand, the speed difference between resolutions these days is relatively minimal. In fact, I can almost never tell the difference between one and the other. Furthermore, because you can see more onscreen at higher resolutions, a higher resolution reduces the amount of scrolling that you have to do and lets you have more open windows on the screen. Therefore, you could say that higher resolutions can speed up your Mac as well.

The bottom line is this: Choose a resolution based on your preference rather than which one you think might be faster. That said, if your Mac seems slow at a resolution setting of 1,600 x 1200, try a lower resolution and see whether it feels faster. Although you can use Mac OS X at resolutions of less than 1024 x 768, Apple has really designed the OS X windows and dialogs on the assumption that your resolution will be at least 1024 x 768.

A Mac with a View — and Preferences, Too

The type of icon display and the Desktop background that you choose affect how quickly your screen updates in the Finder. You can set and change these choices in the View Options windows. From the Finder, choose View⇨Show View Options (or use the keyboard shortcut ⌘+J).

The View Options window, like our old friend the contextual menu, is . . . well . . . contextual. Depending on what's active when you choose it from the View menu, you see one of three similar versions shown in Figure 19-2: folders in Icon view or the Desktop (left), folders in List view (middle), and folders in Column view (right).

The All Windows and This Window Only radio buttons in the View Options window display identical options. You choose the All Windows radio button to set the default appearance for all your Finder windows, and you choose the This Window Only radio button to set up just the current window. These buttons only appear for Icon and List view windows; Column windows are one-size-fits-all.

Figure 19-2:
Your
choices in
the View
Options
windows for
Icon view,
List view,
and Column
view.

Calculated moves

I recommend that you deactivate Calculate All Sizes (that is, deselect, or clear, its check box). If you activate it, the Finder calculates the size of every folder of every open window in List view and displays that number in the Size column. At least to me, the screen feels as if it redraws faster with this feature turned off. This feature is offered only for windows using the List view.

The Finder is kind of smart about the Calculate All Sizes option. If you try to do anything in the Finder while folder sizes are calculating — when you make a menu selection, open an icon, or move a window, for example — the Finder interrupts the calculation so that you can complete your task before it resumes calculating. So, in theory, you should never notice a delay when Calculate All Sizes is selected.

Try the Calculate All Sizes option both on and off. I don't know about you, but I find any noticeable delay unacceptable, and I notice a delay when this option is turned on, even on very fast Macs. Maybe this feature is just annoying and not actually slowing things down, but I can't stand having it on. If you want to know how big a folder is, just click it and choose File➪Get Info (or use the ⌘+I keyboard shortcut).

Getting ahead-er and other stuff

The Show Columns check boxes in the View Options window for List view — Date Modified, Date Created, Size, Kind, Version, and Comments — have a slight impact on screen update speed when you open a Finder window in List view. The Finder has to draw everything that you select here: With fewer items checked, the Finder updates windows faster.

The effect of these items on screen updating is pretty small, so your choice should be made based on what information you want to see in Finder windows, not on whether choosing them slows down your Mac. Play around with these options if you like, but unless your Mac is very slow, you probably won't notice much (or any) difference between on and off.

Get a New, Faster Model or Upgrade Yours

Apple keeps putting out faster and faster Macs at lower and lower prices. From time to time, Apple and other vendors offer reasonably priced upgrades that can transform your older, slower Mac into a speedy new one.

Check out the latest iMacs and eMacs — they're usually an excellent value. Or, if you crave portability, iBooks and PowerBooks are rocking good computers. Or consider a used Mac that's faster than yours. The big-time honcho of auction Web sites, eBay (www.ebay.com), has hundreds of used Macs up for auction at any given time. Shopping on eBay might just get you a better Mac at an outstanding price. Give it a try!

Get a G4 Accelerator

An *accelerator* is a card that replaces the processor (CPU) in your Mac with a faster one. Even if you have a G4 in your Mac already, you might be able to upgrade to a faster one.

But before you plunk down the cash for an upgrade, be sure that it's compatible with Mac OS X. Some upgrades only work with older versions of Mac OS, and those won't help you.

Visit www.macworld.com for information on the various upgrade options available and how they compare with each other. Upgrades start at a few hundred dollars and go up to more than a thousand clams. The older your Mac, the more bang you'll get for your G4 upgrade buck.

Get an Accelerated Graphics Card

An *accelerated graphics card* is designed to speed up one thing: the screen update rate. Accelerated graphics cards blast pixels onto your screen at amazing speeds. They're extremely popular with graphic arts professionals who would otherwise suffer slower screen redraws when working with 24-bit graphics. Most of them are also awesome for playing 3-D games. And because OS X's Quartz Extreme imaging architecture hands off part of its load to the processor on an accelerated graphics card, it might even make other tasks faster because it does some of the work that your Mac's main processor (CPU) used to do.

You can use a graphics accelerator only if your Mac has a slot for it; that's where you install one. Currently, you'll need a PowerMac G4 to use a graphics accelerator with OS X.

Visit www.macworld.com for information on the various graphics cards available and how they compare with each other. Cards start at around a hundred dollars and go up from there. And remember, the older your Mac, the more of a performance boost you'll see for your graphics card upgrade buck.

Get a New Hard Drive

Depending on how old your Mac is, a faster hard drive could provide a substantial speedup. If you have a relatively new Mac — any Mac with a G4 processor — the internal hard drive that came with it is pretty fast already. Unless you also need more storage space, a new hard drive may not be the best way to spend your bucks. On the other hand, if you have an older G3 model, a faster (and larger) hard drive could be just the ticket.

Fire Up Your Mac with FireWire

If you really crave speed, get a FireWire hard drive — all Macs released since February 2001 include at least one FireWire port.

FireWire, the state-of-the-art in connecting devices that need fast transfer speeds, is used to connect devices that require high-speed communication with your Mac, such as hard drives, CD burners, scanners, and camcorders.

In other words, FireWire is the fastest, easiest way to add storage to Macs that include it. Hard drives that connect via the Universal Serial Bus (USB) port work fine if you don't have FireWire, but they're as slow as molasses by comparison (USB runs at about 3 percent of the speed of FireWire). So if you have the need for speed, be sure you opt for a FireWire hard drive and not a USB model. You just plug it in and start using it. There's nothing to it!

Chapter 20

Ten (Or So) Ways to Make Your Mac Better by Throwing Money at It

In This Chapter

▶ Paying to make your Mac faster

▶ Paying to make your Mac life easier

▶ Drooling over some Mac toys

•••

*T*his is one of my favorite chapters. As you've probably figured out by now, I love souping up my Macs. I live to find ways of working smarter, saving time, and saving hand motion, and reveling in tweaking my Mac OS X machines. So it gives me great pleasure to share in this chapter my personal top ten things that you can buy for your Mac to tweak it and make it faster, easier to use, and (I hope) more fun.

The items listed in this chapter are things I have, use every day, love dearly, and would (and probably will!) buy again.

RAM

RAM, or *random access memory,* is your computer's primary working memory. The more you have, the smoother your Mac runs — period. If you have anything less than 256MB in your Mac, you'll like your Mac *a lot* better if you upgrade to 256MB or more. If you like to do a few things at once, more megabytes of RAM will make you a happier camper. (For what it's worth, RAM has never been cheaper than it is today — it's worth every penny.)

Back-up Software

The only two kinds of Mac users are those who have lost data and those who are going to. If your work means anything to you, get something that helps automate the task of backing up your files. Retrospect or Retrospect Express, both from Dantz Development (www.dantz.com), are the names to trust. And please, please read Chapter 17, which is titled, appropriately, "Back Up Now or Regret It Later." It may well be the most important chapter in this book.

A Better Monitor (Or a Second One)

If you have a tiny monitor, get a bigger one. With a larger monitor, you spend less time scrolling and rearranging windows and more of your time getting actual work done — which is a good thing, right? For example, one of my setups includes two monitors: a 15-inch Apple LCD (a flat-panel, much like a PowerBook monitor for your desktop computer) and a 24-inch NEC. It's an awesome setup — one that I highly recommend. With two monitors, you can have the menu bar and Finder windows on the first monitor, and document(s) that you're working on displayed on the second monitor. Or, when using a program like Photoshop (which has lots of floating palettes), you can put the palettes on one monitor and a document that you're working on can be displayed on the big one. And so on.

Flat-panel LCD displays, such as the Apple Studio Display, have come down dramatically in price over the past year. In my humble opinion, LCD displays are brighter and easier on the eyes than traditional CRT (glass picture tube) monitors. Apple must agree because they no longer sell CRTs other than the ones built into eMacs. If you can afford one, that's what you really want. Alas, owners of most iMacs, as well as most iBook owners, are out of luck on this tip — it's not possible to add a second monitor to these models. If you've got a later iMac that includes a video port, go ahead and get a bigger monitor.

A Fast Internet Connection

High-bandwidth connections (that is, fast Internet access) just *rock*. By adding a high-speed Internet connection, such as digital subscriber line (DSL) or cable modem, your capacity to communicate electronically will increase tenfold. With this add-on, you can join an online service, surf the Internet, e-mail your friends, and much, much more, at speeds ten or more times faster than a 56 Kbps-speed modem. Web pages that once took minutes to load appear onscreen almost instantly. If you can afford cable/DSL (around $45-$50/month in most places) and are in an area where you can get cable modem or DSL (not all places can yet), it's worth every penny.

Additional Hard/Removable/ Optical Drive (s)

Apple stopped including floppy disk drives with new Macs a couple of years ago. So now the only ways that you can load new files (programs, documents, games, or whatever) onto your Mac are by copying files from some other kind of removable media (like a Zip disk or a CD or DVD, see Chapter 9), or by downloading from the Internet.

If you want to back up your Mac or hand your buddy a disk with files on it, you'll need some kind of removable media drive. Zip and SuperDisk are the most popular magnetic media, but they are quickly losing popularity for being too small to be useful (around 200MB maximum per disk). On the other hand, there are millions of both types of drive in use today, making it a good choice if you plan to swap data with anyone who has this type of device.

Perhaps the best choice these days is a CD-R (recordable CD-ROM) drive or CD-RW (with unlimited writing capabilities) drive so that you can make your own CDs that contain files, music, or both! Both kinds of drives let you *burn* CDs (CD-RWs just let you burn 'em again and again). The new Apple SuperDrives even let you burn DVDs and these hold 4.7GB each. If you don't already have a burner, it's worth considering.

If you have a relatively new Mac, you may have a built-in Zip, CD-RW, or SuperDrive drive. If you do (or if you get an external one), for goodness' sake — use it to back up your stuff!

Games

Gaming on the Mac has never been better, and the game developers are getting better and better at coaxing even more performance out of OS X.

Some of the games I *love* include *The Sims* (and all the add-ons), *Links Championship Edition,* and every pinball game LittleWing has ever created. Try one — you'll be amazed at how far computer gaming has come.

Multimedia Titles

Many great games, references, and educational titles come on CD-ROM or DVD-ROM these days. You'll love 'em, and so will your kids. Your Mac is more than a computer — it's a full-blown multimedia player. Enjoy it.

Some Big Honking Speakers with a Subwoofer

Face it: Most Macs have crummy speakers (or worse, only one crummy speaker). With a decent set of speakers, games are more fun, music sounds like music instead of AM radio, and the voiceovers in your multimedia titles suddenly become intelligible. If you're into sound, you'll enjoy your Mac much more if you add a set of window-rattling speakers, preferably one with a massive subwoofer to provide that booming bass that sound lovers crave. So crank it up! I'm partial to Monsoon speakers by Songistics, but any good speakers kick the stuffing out of the speakers in any Mac.

If you have a DVD-ROM drive, a killer set of speakers makes watching movies on your Mac a zillion times better.

A New Mouse and/or Keyboard

If you're still using that hockey-puck mouse that came with your iMac, G3, or G4, do yourself a favor and beat it to death with a hammer. Then buy a real mouse. You'll be so much happier if you upgrade to a mouse that's easier to move around and maybe even has two or more buttons or a scroll wheel. You'll be amazed at how much easier it is to work with a mouse that fits your hand. OS X knows about multi-button mice and scroll wheels. With a two-button mouse, you no longer have to hold down the Control key while clicking to display a contextual menu — just click with the right-hand button.

Also, consider ditching that silly Chiclet keyboard if you're stuck with one (you know, those curved, tiny-keyed annoyances that first came with iMacs and that Apple continued to foist on users for many years). Third-party Mac keyboards on the market today are also a huge improvement over what probably came with your Mac and the new Apple Pro keyboard is an excellent product.

I'm partial to so-called ergonomic keyboards, which I find more comfortable for prolonged writing sessions. I also think I type faster with this kind of keyboard. My current axe is a Microsoft Natural Keyboard Pro. Even though it's a Windows keyboard and the modifier keys are mislabeled (the Command key says Alt and the Option key has a Windows logo on it), Microsoft offers excellent Mac drivers for OS X. Although this particular model has been discontinued, sadly, Microsoft offers other ergonomic keyboards in the Natural line of products. Shop around to find one that works for you.

Look into the clear Apple Pro keyboard and Pro Mouse if they didn't come with your Mac. They're pretty cool.

Chapter 21

Ten (Or So) Great Web Sites for Mac Freaks

A s much as I would love to think that this book tells you everything that you need to know about using your Mac, I know better. You have a lot more to discover about using your Mac, and new tools and products come out almost daily.

The best way to gather more information than you could ever possibly soak up about all things Macintosh is to hop onto the Web. There you'll find news, freeware and shareware software to download, troubleshooting sites, tons of news and information about your new favorite OS, and lots of places to shop. So make sure that you read Chapter 11 to get set up for the Internet because this chapter is all about finding cool stuff on the Web to help you use your Mac better while having lots of fun.

The sites in this chapter are the best, most chock-full-o'-stuff places on the Web for Mac users. By the time you finish checking out these ten Web sites, you'll know so much about your Mac and Mac OS X that you'll feel like your brain is in danger of exploding. On the other hand, you may just be a whole lot smarter. Happy surfing!

MacFixIt

www.macfixit.com

Frequent *Macworld* contributor and consultant Ted Landau put together an excellent troubleshooting site to help users solve common problems and keep current on compatibility issues with new system software and third-party products.

Alas, Ted has taken a less active role in the site of late, and there is now a surcharge to search the archives. This site isn't as useful as it once was, but it's still worth knowing and may, for some, be worth paying for.

VersionTracker.com

www.versiontracker.com

For free or shareware stuff, try VersionTracker. It's one of the best sites to search for software — for any version of Mac OS — by keyword. This treasure trove of software and updates is worth visiting even if you aren't looking for anything in particular. So check it out and download some games or something. I love this site.

MacInTouch

www.macintouch.com

For the latest in Mac news, updated every single day, check out MacInTouch.com. Authored by longtime *MacWeek* columnist Ric Ford and his staff of news hounds, this site keeps you on the bleeding-edge of Mac news, including software updates, virus alerts, and Apple happenings. I consider this a site that's essential to keeping up with Mac OS X.

MacMinute

www.macminute.com

Here's another great source of up-to-the-minute Macintosh news. It's a great site, updated many times a day with lots of useful stories, links, and other Mac info.

Apple Knowledge Base

http://kbase.info.apple.com/

Do you have a technical question about any version of Mac OS or any Apple product — including OS X? March your question right over to the Knowledge Base, Apple's searchable archives of tech notes, software update information, and documentation. The Knowledge Base is especially useful if you need info about your old Mac because Apple archives all its info here. Choose from a preset list of topics or products and type a keyword to research. You're rewarded with a list of helpful documents. Click any one of these (they're all links) to take you right to the info you seek. The site even has tools that can help narrow your search.

The Mac OS X Home Page

www.apple.com/macosx/

Part of Apple's main Web site, this section is all about Mac OS X, its cool features, how to get the most from it, what applications are available for it, and so on. Check in here to see what Apple has cooking.

ramseeker

www.macseek.com

One of the best ways to make your Mac better is to buy more random access memory (RAM). *RAM* is the readily available memory that your computer uses; the more you have, the smoother programs run. Although Mac OS X can run on a Mac with only 64MB of RAM, officially it requires 128MB and works even better and faster with more than that. As cheap as RAM is, the price that you pay for it can vary quite a lot. The best way I know to get the lowdown on RAM prices is ramseeker, which organizes memory prices by Mac type.

Outpost.com

www.outpost.com

Recently taken over by the great electronics retailer, Fry's, Outpost.com is all about buying stuff — and what big kid doesn't love his toys? Here you can find lots and lots and lots of Mac products, including Apple CPUs, memory, drives, printers, scanners, and other miscellaneous accessories. You'll love the prices, as well as the massive selection of Mac and non-Mac electronics products.

EveryMac.com

www.everymac.com

The author of this site claims that it is "the complete guide of every Macintosh, Mac Compatible, and upgrade card in the world." You can't argue with that. Become a member and sign up for forums. Check out the Forums and Q & A sections, too, for your Mac-related questions.

Inside Mac Games

www.imgmagazine.com

This is the best of the Mac gaming sites on the Web (at least in my humble opinion). Order CDs of game demos, download shareware, check out game preview movies, or shop for editors and emulators. Find forum camaraderie and troubleshoot gaming problems, too.

dealmac

www.dealmac.com

Shopping for Mac stuff? Go to dealmac ("Because cheap Mac stuff rocks," this site boasts) first to find out about sale prices, rebates, and other bargain opportunities on upgrades, software, peripherals, and more.

Chapter 22

Ten Mac OS X Apps That You Might Need Someday

Dig around the Mac OS X Applications folder or take a gander at the System Preferences application's main window, and you'll run across some programs and preferences that you won't use every day but are still kind of cool.

In this chapter, I tell you what some of these items do and whether you're likely to get much from them. Unfortunately, because of space limitations, I didn't talk much about any of them elsewhere in this book. And I can't really explain how to use each of these potentially useful goodies in much detail here. Instead, my objective is to briefly describe each one and then provide some insights on whether you need it or not.

Almost everything that I mention in this chapter includes a Mac OS Help feature. Use it to discover more about how these goodies work. Just search Mac OS Help for the item that you're interested in, and you'll get an eyeful.

Web Sharing

Web Sharing enables others to share documents on your computer through the Web. You can set up a Web site just by adding HyperText Markup Language (HTML) pages and images to the Sites folder in your home folder, and then activating Web Sharing in the Sharing pane of System Preferences.

Web Sharing works only while your Mac is connected to the Internet or an internal network. In other words, if you use a modem and connect to the Internet by dialing up, this application won't be a lot of use to you because your server (your Mac) will only be on the Internet when you've dialed up and made a modem connection. When you're not connected, your server won't be available except to other computers on your local network. That's not to say that Web Sharing can't be used this way, but you'll have to tell remote users when they'll be able to find it — and then make sure you dial up and make a connection at that time. Another downside to this method is that almost without exception, dial-up users will have a different IP address every time they connect, so you would have to tell folks your new address every time.

Furthermore, even if you keep your modem connected to the Internet 24 hours a day with a Digital Subscriber Line (DSL) or cable modem connection, using this feature could violate your agreement with your Internet Service Provider (ISP) because some ISPs prohibit you from running a Web site. And, most cable and DSL connections use dynamic IP address assignment through Dynamic Host Configuration Protocol (DHCP), which means that your IP address will change from time to time.

On the other hand, some ISPs don't care. Check with yours if you're concerned.

I do use this feature occasionally, but because I don't use it 24/7, I never bothered to check with my ISP. Do me a favor and don't rat me out.

FTP Access

File Transfer Protocol (FTP) is kind of like Web Sharing: It allows folks on the Internet to have access to files on your Mac. The difference is that FTP access is specifically designed to let you make files available for download, and Web Sharing is designed to let people view Web pages.

When you activate FTP by selecting the Allow FTP Access check box in the Sharing pane of System Preferences, users on the Internet have the same access to the contents of your Mac that they would if they were using file sharing. (See Chapter 16 for more on file sharing.) People who don't have accounts on your Mac can access Public folders and Drop Boxes — or any folder to which you grant everyone access, as I describe in Chapter 16.

Internet users can connect to your Mac with any FTP client application.

An *FTP client* is a program that offers FTP features — uploading files, downloading files, and so on. Better FTP clients can also do stuff like rename and delete remote files. On the Mac, Interarchy (which I discuss in the upcoming pages), Transmit, and Fetch are probably the best known FTP clients. Another Mac client that you may find easy to use is RBrowser or its freeware sibling, RBrowserLite. You can also find FTP clients for Windows, Linux, and most other operating systems (but because I use Macs, I don't know the names of the good ones).

Most Internet browsers can serve as FTP clients, as well as browsers (although they're mostly good only for downloading, and not much use for uploading, deleting, renaming, and other useful functions).

Interarchy is a great Mac FTP client, one that also performs many other Internet-related tasks you might someday need. For example, you can use it to search the Internet to find the files that you want, provide a wealth of information about your Internet connection, help manage remote servers, and remotely control your Macintosh across the Internet. Interarchy is shareware; you can read more about it or download a copy to play with at `http://groups.yahoo.com/group/interarchy/`. Its Web site is `www.interarchy.com`.

Applet Launcher

The *Applet Launcher* is an application that you can use to work with Apple's version of Java. *Java* is a programming language (or a platform, depending on who you ask) that's most frequently used in Web pages that you view on the Internet. Stand-alone Java programs, called *applets*, are available as well.

To calibrate or not to calibrate?

One thing you might want to try, even if you never plan to use ColorSync, is to calibrate your monitor. This process adjusts the red, green, blue, and white levels, and could make what you see on your screen look better than it does now.

To calibrate your monitor, follow these steps:

1. **Open the Displays System Preferences pane.**

2. **Click the Color tab and then write down the Display Profile that your Mac is currently using (it's in the list above the Calibrate button).**

3. **Click the Calibrate button.**

   The Display Calibrator Assistant appears.

4. **Follow the simple onscreen instructions to calibrate your monitor and create a custom display profile.**

5. **(Optional) When you get to the last screen in the Display Calibrator Assistant, you can either give your new profile a name and save it by clicking the Create button, or you can click the Cancel button to revert to the way your display was before you adjusted the calibration.**

If you click the Create button and then decide that you don't like the results of your calibration, just click the Display Profile that you wrote down in Step 2 from the list, and your monitor will go back the way it was before you calibrated it.

With Applet Launcher, you can run programs written in Java on your Mac, with no Web browser required. Mac OS X and Internet Explorer (the browser that comes with Mac OS X) also support Java within Web pages. So you have a choice — run stand-alone applets with Applet Launcher, or have your browser do the work of loading and launching Java programs that are part of a Web page. A nice variety of example applets are available via the Applets menu within Applet Launcher.

You'll find Applet Launcher in the Java folder within the Utilities folder (in your Applications folder).

ColorSync

ColorSync helps ensure color accuracy when scanning, printing, and working with color images. This package includes ColorSync software as well as pre-made ColorSync profiles for a variety of monitors, scanners, and printers.

A *ColorSync profile* is a set of instructions for a monitor, scanner, or printer, which tells the device how to deal with colors (and white) so that the device's output is consistent with other devices output (as determined by the ColorSync profiles of other devices). In theory, if two devices have ColorSync profiles, their output (on screen, on a printed page, or in a scanned image) should match perfectly. Put another way, the red (or green or blue or white or any other color) that you see onscreen should be exactly the same shade as the red that you see on a printed page or in a scanned image.

From the ColorSync pane in System Preferences, pick a profile or check to see that the profile ColorSync is using is the right one for your display, input, output, or proof device.

If you're not a graphics artist working with color files and calibrating monitors and printers to achieve accurate color matching, you probably don't need ColorSync (unless you've gotten hooked on iPhoto and want your printed inkjet color pictures to match up correctly).

Image Capture

Image Capture is a nifty little application that you use to download images from a digital camera to your Mac or from a variety of scanners. You'll find it in your Application folder. You can use it with many kinds of digital cameras and a number of different scanner models, so if you have more than one, you may be able to avoid having to install an application for each.

Unfortunately, Image Capture doesn't work with every digital camera. For example, Image Capture did not recognize my relatively new Olympus digital camera. To find out whether Image Capture works with your digital camera, plug the camera into one of your Mac's USB ports and open Image Capture. If the Camera menu at the top of the window reads No devices found, you're out of luck. The same steps apply to your scanner, except that you'll be checking the Scanner menu.

Image Capture can automate some parts of the image downloading process. For example, you can set it up to download all images from the camera into a pre-selected folder or to open automatically when you connect your camera to your Mac.

You may not want to use Image Capture if you prefer the program that came with your digital camera (the program that you use to import pictures from the camera) or iPhoto. On the other hand, you may have to use Image Capture if that program hasn't been upgraded to support Mac OS X and doesn't run under Classic (some programs just don't work with Classic). Because this is true of most scanner software at this time, Image Capture could be your best bet.

If Image Capture doesn't support your scanner, a shareware program for Mac OS X called VueScan from Hamrick Software (www.hamrick.com) supports scanning images with many different scanners, including ones that don't work with Image Capture. Its $40 price tag is a small price to pay if your scanner is going to otherwise just collect dust.

Finally, if the program that came with your camera doesn't run under Classic and Image Capture doesn't work with your camera, you'll have to reboot with OS 9 to run the program. (For more info on running Classic and OS X, and rebooting under OS 9.2.1, read through Chapter 14.)

Text-to-Speech

Use Text-to-Speech to convert onscreen text into spoken words from your Mac. This application is pretty much unchanged from earlier versions of Mac OS. With a whole slew of voices to choose from, you can have Text-to-Speech read dialog boxes, or even documents, aloud.

Sometimes hearing is better than reading. For example, I sometimes use Text-to-Speech to read a column or page to me before I submit it. If something doesn't sound right, I give it a final polish before sending it off to my editor.

You can activate this feature in the Speech System Preferences pane. Click the Spoken User Interface tab to check it out.

Text-to-Speech is kind of cool (the talking alerts are fun), but having dialog boxes actually produce spoken text becomes annoying real fast for most folks. But check it out! You might like it and find times when you want your Mac to read to you.

Speech Recognition

Speech Recognition enables your Mac to recognize and respond to human speech. With this feature, you can issue verbal commands such as, "Get my mail!" to your Mac and have it actually get your mail. You can also create AppleScripts and then trigger them by voice.

An *AppleScript* is a series of commands, using the AppleScript language, that tells the computer (and some applications) what to do.

You create AppleScripts with the Script Editor program, which you'll find in the AppleScript folder in the Applications folder.

You'll need a microphone (some Macs have them built-in) to use Speech Recognition. And you'll only be able to talk to your Mac when using applications that support Speech Recognition.

You'll find the Speech Recognition tab to the Default Voice tab's left in the Speech pane of System Preferences.

This application is clever and kind of fun, but it's also slow and requires a microphone. And I've never been able to get Speech Recognition to work well enough to continue using it beyond a few hours at best. Still, it's kind of neat (and it's a freebie), and I've heard many users profess their love for it. So you might want to check it out.

NetInfo Manager

NetInfo is a hierarchical database that contains much of the configuration information needed to manage what goes on behind the scenes of Mac OS X. NetInfo knows all your settings, who has an account on your Mac, what network addresses you're using, and lots, lots more. With NetInfo Manager, you can view and edit some of this information. Although it has a Mac interface, the database info displayed there will be pretty much incomprehensible to most folks.

NetInfo is a central location for a lot of important information. With NetInfo Manager, a savvy Mac user can do cool things that can't be done with the Network or Sharing System Preferences panes. But most average users won't want to play here. One suggestion: If you're at all curious about the internals of the UNIX operating system on which Mac OS X is based, start by learning a bit about NetInfo before you dive into the hard-core UNIX stuff (see the next section).

UNIX Tools: Terminal, Console, and Process Viewer

Mac OS X is based on the UNIX operating system, although its UNIX underpinnings are mostly hidden. While most Mac users are grateful to be able to ignore UNIX, if you know UNIX (or think you might like to), you'll find that you can do a lot of very geeky things with the UNIX tools included in Mac OS X.

You'll find all three programs in the Utilities folder within your Applications folder.

UNIX is not for the inexperienced or faint of heart. Before you even begin experimenting with it, you should get yourself a good UNIX primer and learn the ropes. And as usual, be very careful. Mucking around in the Mac OS X UNIX files gives you access to lots of stuff that isn't ordinarily available to you, which can very quickly lead to major problems if you're not absolutely sure what you're doing. If you want more info on UNIX, check out *Unix Bible,* 2nd Edition by Yves Lepage and Paul Iarrera (published by Hungry Minds, Inc.).

Terminal

Basically, *UNIX* is a command-line operating system. Instead of clicking buttons and dragging icons around the Desktop, you type commands (not in English, by the way) at a command line. To do this in Mac OS X, you use a program called Terminal, which you'll find in the Utilities folder in the Applications folder.

Terminal is nothing more than a single window with a line (or many lines) of very geeky-looking text — there are no menus or buttons to make your life easier. So Terminal is mostly useless unless you speak a decent amount of UNIX.

Console

Console is another UNIX tool that's used to show you technical messages from Mac OS X — in UNIX-speak, of course. It shows what UNIX processes are running, what devices are in use, and so on. Think of it as a UNIX troubleshooting and status-checking tool. Unfortunately, like Terminal, Console's only window is a wall of super-geeky-looking text — still no menus or buttons to make your life easier. Like Terminal, Console is mostly useless unless you speak a decent amount of UNIX.

Process Viewer

Process Viewer might be more useful for seeing what's going on under the hood than Console because it has a Mac interface (or at least it has some menus), a Find text field, and columns that you can sort. Think of it as another UNIX troubleshooting and status-checking tool.

Part VI
Appendix

The 5th Wave   By Rich Tennant

@RICHTENNANT

"I tell you, it looks like Danny, it sounds like Danny, but it's _NOT_ Danny!! I think the MAC has created an alias of Danny! You can see it in his eyes - little wrist watch icons!"

In this part . . .

*L*ast but certainly not least, I cover installing/
reinstalling Mac OS X in this Appendix. The whole
process has become quite easy with this version of the
System software, but if you have to install OS X yourself,
it would behoove you to read this helpful Appendix first.

Appendix

Installing Mac OS X (Only if You Have To)

In This Chapter

▶ Installing (or reinstalling) Mac OS X

▶ Setting up OS X with Setup Assistant

▶ Running OS X and OS 9 on the same Mac

*Y*ou'll probably never need this Appendix. Some of you will get Mac OS X pre-installed on a new Mac, and others will have installed it long before buying this book. And so, I expect that few of you will have to refer to this Appendix to install OS X on your Mac for the very first time.

But (and there's always a but, isn't there?), someday something unexpected might happen to your Mac. You could have a hard drive crash or a problem starting up from your hard drive, or maybe you'll see the flashing-question-mark icon when booting — all meaning that you'll need to *reinstall* OS X. And so, I expect some of you (and I hope not many) will have to refer to this Appendix for instructions on reinstalling OS X.

A Mac OS X reinstallation is a drastic final step. Be sure that you've tried all the stuff in Chapter 18 before even thinking about reinstalling OS X. If nothing else fixes your Mac, reinstalling Mac OS X could well be your final option before invasive surgery (that is, trundling your Mac to a repair shop). I save this solution for here at the very end of the book because it's the biggest hassle, and you don't want to reinstall OS X if something easier can correct the problem. So if you have to do a reinstallation, realize that this is more or less your last hope.

In this Appendix, you'll discover all you need to know to install or reinstall OS X, if you should have to. I say reinstalling is a hassle because although you won't lose the contents of your Home folder or stuff in your Documents folder (unless something goes horribly wrong or you have to reformat your hard disk), you could lose some System Preferences, which means that you'll need to reconfigure those panes manually after you reinstall. It's not the end of the world, but it can be inconvenient. That said, reinstalling OS X usually corrects all but the most horrifying and malignant of problems. And the process is relatively painless, as you'll soon see.

I'll stay with you through it all; be brave.

How to Install (or Reinstall) Mac OS X

In theory, you should only have to install OS X once. And in a perfect world, that would be the case. But you may find occasions when you have to install/reinstall it, such as

- ✔ If you get a new Mac that didn't come with Mac OS X pre-installed
- ✔ If you have a catastrophic hard drive crash that requires you to initialize (format) your boot drive
- ✔ If any essential Mac OS X files become damaged, corrupted, or are deleted or renamed

The following instructions do double duty: They're what you do to install OS X for the first time on a Mac, and they're also what you do if something happens to the copy of OS X that you boot your Mac from. That is, the process for installing or reinstalling OS X is exactly the same.

If you've backed up your entire hard drive, you might prefer to reinstall from your back-up disk or tape rather than reinstalling OS X from the Install Mac OS X CD. That way, you'll be certain that everything is just the way you left it, which is something you can't be sure of if you reinstall from the Install Mac OS X CD.

Here's how to install (or reinstall) OS X, step by step:

1. **Boot from your Install Mac OS X CD Disc 1 by inserting the CD into your machine's CD-ROM or DVD drive and then restarting your Mac while holding down the C key.**

   When Mac OS X has finished booting your Mac, the Install program launches automatically. Here is where you begin the process of installing or reinstalling Mac OS X.

2. **Unless you want to use a language other than English for the main language of Mac OS X, click the Continue button in the first screen you see; if you do want to use another language, select the language by clicking its name, and then click the Continue button.**

3. **Read the Important Information screen and then click the Continue button.**

4. **Read the Software License Agreement and then click the Continue button.**

A sheet drops down querying whether you agree to the terms of the license agreement. If you don't, you can't go any further, so I advise you to go ahead and click the Agree button.

If you're currently using any version of Mac OS except version 9.2.2, you might next see a dialog with the warning that you can't run Classic applications unless you have Mac OS 9.2.2 or a later version installed. You can't install Mac OS 9.2.2 right now (you're installing OS X!), but you can click OK and install it later. (Mac OS X, version 10.2 Jaguar does not come with a Mac OS 9.2.2 Install CD, so you're on your own here.) If you have Mac OS 9.2.2 installed, you won't see this dialog.

5. **Choose the disk that you want to install or reinstall Mac OS X on by clicking its icon once in the Select a Destination screen.**

At the bottom of the Select a Destination screen is the Options button, which offers three mutually exclusive choices:

    a. Upgrade Mac OS X: Choose this option to upgrade an earlier version of OS X installed on the disk that you choose in Step 5 above. Your Home and other files are left undisturbed; after the upgrade, things will be (more or less) as they were before, except that you'll be running the latest version of OS X.

    b. Archive and Install: Choose this option to move all the System components from your existing OS X installation into a folder named Previous System and then install a fresh new copy of OS X. The Previous System folder cannot be used to boot but it does contain any and all files that were in any of the OS X folders before you upgraded.

    If you select this option, a check box for a second option — Preserve Users and Network Settings — becomes available. Mark it if you want to import all the existing users of this Mac, their Home folders, and their network settings — but still archive all the old System stuff into the Previous System folder.

    If you choose this option, you skip the Setup Assistant discussed later in this Appendix.

    c. Erase and Install: Choose this option if you want to completely erase the disk that you selected in Step 5, starting completely from scratch.

    If you choose the Erase and Install option, the disk that you selected in Step 5 will be erased, and all your files will be deleted immediately! You should only choose this option if you've backed up all your documents and applications. In most cases, erasing the start-up disk is not necessary.

    If you select this option, the Format Disk As pop-up menu becomes available. Your choices are Mac OS Extended (the one you want) or Unix File System (the one you don't want).

Unix File System is not a good choice for most OS X users. Suffice it to say that 99.9 percent of you should absolutely and positively avoid Unix File System like the plague (and the other tenth of one percent know who they are and why they need a UFS disk.) 'Nuff said.

After you make your selection in this window, click OK to return to the Select a Destination screen and then click Continue.

Now you have the choice to perform an easy install or a customized install. The Easy Install copies all of Mac OS X onto your chosen hard drive (as you choose in Step 5); the Custom Install (click the Customize button at the bottom of the screen) enables you choose to install only the items that you want to install.

In almost all cases, Easy Install is the right way to go, and that's what I assume that you'll choose for the rest of these steps because you're either doing a complete install or reinstall of your operating system.

6. **To begin the installation, click the Install button.**

   The install process takes 10 to 20 minutes, so now might be a good time to take a coffee break. When the install process finishes, your Mac will ask you to insert OS X Install Disk 2. When it's done installing, your Mac will restart itself, and you can begin using Mac OS X . . . hopefully, trouble-free.

   After your Mac reboots, the Setup Assistant appears.

7. **Work your way through all of the Setup Assistant screens (you have to before you can begin working in OS X), which I show you how to do in the next section.**

Getting Set Up with Setup Assistant

Assuming that your installation (or reinstallation) process goes well and your Mac restarts itself, the next thing you should see (and hear) is a short, colorful movie that ends by transforming into the first Setup Assistant screen, fetchingly named Welcome.

To tiptoe through the Setup Assistant, follow these steps:

1. **When the Welcome screen appears, choose your country from the list by clicking it once, and then click the Continue button.**

   If your country doesn't appear in the list, select the Show All check box, which will cause a bunch of additional countries to appear in this list. Choose yours by clicking it and then click the Continue button.

   The Personalize Settings screen appears.

2. **Choose a keyboard layout from the list by clicking it once; then click the Continue button.**

If you're an American or want to use an American keyboard setup, click the U.S. listing. If you prefer a different country's keyboard layout, select the Show All check box, and a bunch of additional countries (as well as a pair of Dvorak keyboard layouts) appears in the list. Choose the one you prefer by clicking it and then click the Continue button.

The Registration Information screen appears.

3. Fill out the fields (name, address, phone number, and so on) and then click the Continue button.

If you're interested in what Apple will and will not do with this information, click the Privacy button on this screen and read the Privacy Policy.

The A Few More Questions screen appears.

4. Complete the form and then click the Continue button.

The Thank You screen appears.

5. Click the Continue button.

The Create Your Account screen appears.

6. Fill in the Name, Short Name, Password, Verify, and Password Hint fields and then click the Continue button.

This first account that you create will automatically have administrator privileges for this Mac.

Each of these fields has an explanation beneath it.

You can't click the Continue button until you've filled in all five fields.

The Get Internet Ready screen appears.

7. Select from two radio buttons — I'll Use My Existing Internet Service; or I'm Not Ready to Connect to the Internet — and then click the Continue button.

If you choose to use your existing Internet service, you'll see another series of screens in which you provide specific information about how you connect to the Internet, your IP address (if you have one), what kind of connection you have, and so on. If you don't know one (or more) of the items in this series of screens, don't worry. Just leave them blank and keep clicking the Continue button. Later, after the Setup Assistant finishes and you're up and running with OS X, you can ask your ISP (Internet Service Provider) about any empty fields, and then put in that information in the appropriate place (the Network and/or Internet System Preference panes).

8. When the next screen appears, click the Continue button.

The assistant will quit and in a few moments, the Mac OS X Desktop will appear. That's it. You're done.

For the very last time, don't forget that Macs sold after January 1, 2003 will not be able to boot into Mac OS 9 at all. Classic will be the only option for running OS 9 software on Macs made in 2003 and beyond.

Two ways to run two systems

If you're planning on using Classic applications at all, I need to tell you a little about how Mac OS X and Classic (Mac OS 9.2.2) coexist on the same computer. (If you'd rather just learn how to use Classic, you can skip this section and read Chapter 14 instead.)

Both Mac OS 9.2.2 and OS X can either be installed on the same volume — usually the single hard drive in your Mac — or on separate volumes. If they're installed on a single volume, as they would be if you got your Mac with Mac OS X pre-installed, the files that make up Mac OS 9.2.2 are buried within the complicated hierarchy of Mac OS X components. You probably won't have much to do with them, other than customizing some preferences. If you've used any version of Mac OS 9 (9.0.1, 9.0.4, or even 9.1), you won't find the familiar System Folder or be able to work with its files in the way that you're used to.

In some cases, Mac OS 9.2.2 and Mac OS X are installed on separate volumes on your Mac.

Volumes can be individual hard drives, or they can be partitions of a single hard drive. A *partition* looks and behaves like a hard drive, but it's actually just a section of the disk that is completely separate from the rest of the drive. In this arrangement, Mac OS X and Mac OS 9.2.2 each have their own partitions on the same hard drive. That means that you can install and customize a Mac OS 9.2.2 drive without affecting Mac OS X. They behave as if they were completely separate drives. When you launch Classic while running Mac OS X, Mac OS 9.2.2 launches from the other partition, and you have access to its System Folder, just as you would on a Mac with Mac OS 9.1 as the primary operating system.

If you're installing Mac OS X from scratch and you're comfortable with concepts such as drive partitioning and the like, I recommend that you install Mac OS 9.2.2 on two partitions or hard drives. In other words, install 9.2.2 on both partitions and then install OS X on one of them. Let the copy of OS 9.2.2 on the same disk (or partition) as OS X be the one that you use for Classic. Use the other copy of OS 9.2.2 to boot from when you need to run Classic apps or use Classic extensions/control panels that aren't supported by Classic (such as DVD Player, CD Audio Player, some CD burning software, full functionality for iTunes, and so on). You'll have more flexibility when using Mac OS 9.2.2 if you follow this advice, and you'll be able to troubleshoot both operating systems more easily if you keep them on separate drives. You'll also find that Classic starts up faster because it won't have all the extra control panels and extensions to load. You might also find it more convenient to store all your Classic applications on the partition or drive with OS 9.2.2 only rather on the OS X drive or partition. That's how I have the Mac used for writing this book arranged (check the screen shots).

If you have multiple partitions or drives — each of which has a copy of Mac OS 9.2.2 — you can choose which copy to use when launching Classic. Make this choice in the Classic pane of System Preferences. (Read more about this in Chapter 14.)

In addition to running Classic applications under OS X, you can choose to boot from Mac OS 9.2.2 any time you like. After you've installed OS X, you can switch between it and OS 9.2.2 quickly and easily. (Read about this process in detail at the end of Chapter 14.)

If you've got two copies of OS 9.2.2, boot from the one that's *not* on the same drive or partition as OS X.

Index

FOR DUMMIES®

A world of resources to help you grow

TRAVEL

0-7645-5453-0

0-7645-5438-7

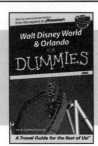

0-7645-5444-1

EDUCATION & TEST PREPARATION

0-7645-5194-9

0-7645-5325-9

0-7645-5249-X

HEALTH, SELF-HELP & SPIRITUALITY

0-7645-5154-X

0-7645-5302-X

0-7645-5418-2

FOR DUMMIES®

Helping you expand your horizons and realize your potenti

GRAPHICS & WEB SITE DEVELOPMENT

0-7645-1651-5

0-7645-1643-4

0-7645-0895-4

Also available:

Adobe Acrobat 5 PDF For Dummies
(0-7645-1652-3)

ASP.NET For Dummies
(0-7645-0866-0)

ColdFusion MX for Dummies
(0-7645-1672-8)

Dreamweaver MX For Dummies
(0-7645-1630-2)

FrontPage 2002 For Dummies
(0-7645-0821-0)

HTML 4 For Dummies
(0-7645-0723-0)

Illustrator 10 For Dum
(0-7645-3636-2)

PowerPoint 2002 For Dummies
(0-7645-0817-2)

Web Design For Dumm
(0-7645-0823-7)

PROGRAMMING & DATABASES

0-7645-0746-X

0-7645-1626-4

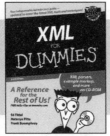

0-7645-1657-4

Also available:

Access 2002 For Dummies
(0-7645-0818-0)

Beginning Programming For Dummies
(0-7645-0835-0)

Crystal Reports 9 For Dummies
(0-7645-1641-8)

Java & XML For Dummies
(0-7645-1658-2)

Java 2 For Dummies
(0-7645-0765-6)

JavaScript For Dummi
(0-7645-0633-1)

Oracle9i For Dummies
(0-7645-0880-6)

Perl For Dummies
(0-7645-0776-1)

PHP and MySQL For Dummies
(0-7645-1650-7)

SQL For Dummies
(0-7645-0737-0)

Visual Basic .NET For Dummies
(0-7645-0867-9)

LINUX, NETWORKING & CERTIFICATION

0-7645-1545-4

0-7645-1760-0

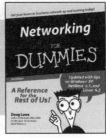

0-7645-0772-9

Also available:

A+ Certification For Dummies
(0-7645-0812-1)

CCNP All-in-One Certification For Dummies
(0-7645-1648-5)

Cisco Networking For Dummies
(0-7645-1668-X)

CISSP For Dummies
(0-7645-1670-1)

CIW Foundations For Dummies
(0-7645-1635-3)

Firewalls For Dummie
(0-7645-0884-9)

Home Networking Fo Dummies
(0-7645-0857-1)

Red Hat Linux All-in-C Desk Reference For D
(0-7645-2442-9)

UNIX For Dummies
(0-7645-0419-3)

Available wherever books are sold.
Go to www.dummies.com or call 1-877-762-2974 to order direct